ESSAYS ON SOCIAL REFORM MOVEMENTS

HISTORY AND CULTURE SERIES

ESSAYS ON SOCIAL REFORM MOVEMENTS

Edited by
Dr. Raj Kumar

DISCOVERY PUBLISHING HOUSE
NEW DELHI-110002

First Published – 2004

Reprinted – 2025

ISBN: 978-81-7141-792-6

Essays on Social Reform Movements

Published by:

DISCOVERY PUBLISHING HOUSE

4383/4B, Ansari Road, Darya Ganj

New Delhi-110 002 (India)

Phone: +91-11-23279245; 23253475; 43596065

Mobile: +91 9811179893 / +91 9871656464

E-mail: discoverybooksindia@gmail.com

orderdphbooks@gmail.com

namitwasan9@gmail.com

web: www.discoverypublishinggroup.com

Printed at:

Infinity Imaging Systems

Delhi (INDIA)

PREFACE

Encounter with the western culture and ideas influenced Indian societies, resulting in a number of social reform movements. These reform movements played an important role in shaping modern India.

Aim of this exercise is to make available to our readers writings and speeches of the leaders of those reform movements. We have also included bibliographical survey of the social reform movement in India which will enable our readers to carry out further research on the subject.

We take this opportunity to record our indebtness to authorities on the subject whose works we have included in attempting to prepare this book.

Professors S. Gopal, Ravinder Kumar, P.S. Gupta, A.R. Kulkarni, Sumit Sarkar, Rajat Ray, Sudhir Chandra, Karuna Karan, M.N. Das, N.S. Bose, P.N. Chopra, V.N. Dutta, B. Sheikh Ali and M.G.S. Narayanan have always been kind and helpful.

Librarians and staff members of ICHR, ICSSR, USI, IIC, and Supreme Court have been kind and helpful. I record my thanks to them.

My publisher and his staff members, ofcourse, deserves patronage of my readers.

Dr. Raj Kumar

CONTENTS

1
Introduction

Social reform movements played significant role in shaping modern India. We shall try to examine their political impact and study how these movements have acted and interacted on one another. There are two aspects to their political impact: one connected with the part these apparently religious organisations played in active politics and the other their ideological legacy.

THE THEOSOPHICAL SOCIETY

Very often charges were made against religious reform associations like the Theosophical Society and the Arya Samaj that they meddled with politics. A member of the Theosophical Society in an open letter to Sir S. Subramania Iyer, one of the prominent leaders of the society, stated that the Theosophical Society and the headquarters at Adyar represented an engine of great capacity, a means of propaganda of great power, but this engine had been used, and improperly used, for political propaganda. He narrated how, in his opinion, Annie Besant had used the society and its organs to promote her political ends. The authorities of the society did not accept the charge. They were, however, proud to say that the work of the Theosophical Society had contributed to the general awakening in India and that its members, in their individual capacity, had a tremendous part to play in the political life of the country. Writing on the work of the Theosophical Society in India, Annie Besant stated: 'To begin: the first Industrial Exhibition was held in Bombay at an early convention of the Theosophical Society, on the initiative of Colonel Olcott. Until the nation knew what it could produce, it was not possible to revive the national prosperity... The National Congress was founded by English and Indian theosophists, working hand-in-hand. The first meeting which suggested it was held at a convention of the Theosophical Society at Adyar; it was under the shelter of the banner of theosophy, when Mr. Hume and other Indian theosophists were present that the National Congress took birth.'[1] As many other claims to the source of inspiration for the foundation of the Congress this one is also a partial truth, but it indicates the theosophists' attitude towards the national awakening in the country.

The political role of the Theosophical Society was not confined to increasing the national pride which deepened the political awakening in the country, but extended to the widening of the gulf between the Hindus and the Muslims in the religious and social fields and consequently in the political field. As we noted, in spite of its claims to universality, the theosophists in India became fervent champions of ancient Indian religions like Hinduism and Buddhism. They also gradually developed an exclusive attitude. This alone would have antagonised the Muslims. But the theosophists went a step further. Annie Besant claimed: 'We began with the teaching of the unity, with the revival of religion. We passed on to the educational phase, and are now striving in a small measure indeed, but still effectively, to change the lines of national eudcation.'[2] But the national education, as conceived by theosophists, was on narrow lines. A.N. Hydari, a prominent Muslim, commenting on their sectarian educational institutions, stated: 'Mrs. Besant's Hindu College at Benares is the latest exemplification of this tendency, and while not for a moment blind to the necessity of providing for the special wants of any particular community, I deprecate the establishment of separate institutions from which members of other communities are excluded. The Aligarh College insists upon no such exclusion of the Hindus, and it would have been well if the Benares College had followed the like liberal policy.'[3]

THE ARYA SAMAJ

The Arya Samaj also was suspected of active participation in politics. According to Lajpat Rai, the founder of the Samaj held this view: 'Foreign government, perfectly free from religious prejudices, impartial towards all the natives and foreigners—kind, beneficient and just though it may be—can never render the people perfectly happy.'[4] He stated this as a maxim. In *Aryabhivinaya* as well as in his writings elsewhere he has stated:

> 'Let foreigners not rule our country,
> May we not lose our independence.'[5]

Dayananda Saraswati was clearly of the view that "good government is no substitute for self-government.' However, as Lajpat Rai himself an Arya Samajist and a political leader of eminence writes: 'There is, of course, no doubts whatever that the Samaj doctrine has a patriotic side... The Arya doctrine and the Arya education alike sing the glories of ancient India, and by so doing arouse the national pride of its disciples, who are made to feel that their country's history is not a tale of continuous humiliation. Patriotism and politics are not synonymous, but the arousing of an interest in national affairs is a natural result of arousing national pride. Moreover, the type of men to whom the Arya doctrine appeals is also the type of man to whom politics appeal, viz., the educated man who desires his country's progress, not ultra-conservative with the ultra-conservatism of the East, but to a greater or lesser extent, *rerum novarum cupidus et capax.* It is not, therefore, surprising that there are politicians among the Arya Samaj. But it is impossible to deduce from this that the Arya Samaj, as a whole, is a political body.' But the government was not satisfied with this explanation. During the extremists' agitation of 1907-1910 they carefully watched the activities of the Samaj: 'Some Aryas in government service were dismissed for the simple reason that they were members, or active members, of the Samaj...At one place the officer commanding a brigade issued an order to the effect that "all ranks" were "forbidden to attend the meetings of the Samaj or any other political body." In some districts a census of the Aryas was taken, and their names were entered in police registers as suspects.[6] Many of the critics of the Arya Samaj, both official and non-official, alleged that the Arya Samaj was a political body, particularly after the deportation of Lajpat Rai, when many Arya Samajists condemned the government's action and extended their sympathies to the deported leader.

This was cited as evidence to show that the Arya Samaj was a political body. Arthur Grey in his opening speech on the Patiala Sedition Case, on January 6, 1910 remarked: 'He (Swami Dayananda) points out that not only is the religion (Christianity) abominable in itself but those who practise it and profess to practise it are the rulers over India and who are in the habit of showing partiality to the followers of that religion and are in the habit of judging unjustly between the natives of this country and their own country...On page 186 (*Satyartha Prakash*) there is a whole chapter on the manner in which a country should be governed and the kind of people who should govern it... On page 187, he says: "Let no man abide by the law laid down by men altogether ignorant of the Vedas..." Again on page 188 he says: "If it is necessary a man should use his influence and the whole of his power to destroy a sovereign who does not happen to be acquainted with the intricacies of the Vedas".[7] In the same speech he asked later: '...is there no significance in the fact that in the last anniversary of the Arya Samaj appeared an appeal calling for funds to defend the alleged seditionists and the name of Lajpat Rai as their political leader?'[8] To this and other similar charges, the authors of the book *The Arya Samaj and its Detractors,* published in 1919, have tried to give a documented reply. They quote with approval the following comment made by E.P. Maclagan in the Punjab Census Report for 1891: 'The Arya faith is put forward as a revival, it takes us back to the time when the Aryan race in its prime ruled the north of India...Throughout its speculations and its doctrines, religious and social, the Samaj has always been at pains to show that the faith it promulgates owes nothing to English influence and English modes of thought, and the politicians of the Samaj have at times been tempted to carry the same principle into the realm of politics. The fact that the Aryas are mainly recruited from one class, and that the Samaj possesses a very complete organisation of its own, laid it open to the charge of supporting as a body the proclivities of a large section of its members; but the Samaj as such is not a political but a purely religious body.'[9]

During the Viceroyalty of Lord Hardinge, the government seemed to have come to the conclusion that there was no substantial reason to suspect that the Arya Samaj was in any sense a subversive organisation. Many Arya Samajists, no doubt, continued to take part actively in the political movements, while many other Arya Samajists cooperated with the government in various fields. To sum up: the charge that the Arya Samaj, as an organisation, was committed to political movements of an anti-government nature, was baseless; but the total effect of its propaganda in relation to the raising of national pride was conducive to the strengthening of a political movement aimed at the liberation of the Indian people from a foreign government.

There was, however, another field in which the work of the Arya Samaj did have an indirect political repercussion. Its broad Hindu revivalist character would have antagonised the Muslims, who were themselves undergoing a revivalist experience. When it began to conduct the campaign of *Shuddhi* to recover the Hindu converts of Islam into their former religion, the conflict between the two communities came out in the open. The Muslim reaction to it took an aggressive form; some Muslims started a new movement, called 'Tabligh', to counteract the evil effects of *Shuddhi* and launched a vast propaganda to push on Islam by all kinds of means. Then tension created by this situation, when combined with many factors, led to riots, disturbances, murders, abduction of women and minors. The hostility between the Arya Samajists and the Muslims did not stop with these events. Later, when the Muslim League began to champion the cause of Pakistan, its leaders very often pointed out to what they considered to be the anti-Muslim activities of the Arya Samaj. The circulation of the book of the Arya Samaj's founder, *Satyartha Prakash,* was resented by the Muslims. The Arya Samajists, in turn, were also suspicious of the Indian Muslims' attitude towards pan-Islamism and other political questions. Thus this political aspect of the Arya Samaj became a constant factor in the political scene during the Indian national movement, at least, in the Punjab.

RAMAKRISHNA MISSION AND SWAMI VIVEKANANDA

Another religious movement accused of direct participation in the political movement is the Ramakrishna Mission founded by Swami Vivekananda. Here again there is no evidence to establish that the Mission was directly involved in political activities. But there is no doubt that the Swami's utterances had a political significance. One of the Swami's disciples, who played a prominent part in the terrorist political movement in Bengal, writes in one of his books: *Vivekananda the Socialist* was written at the request of the writer's young comrades of the youth movement that was in full swing in Bengal in 1928-29, to guide them in their work. As Swamiji's sayings were the sources of inspiration to the young revolutionaries of Bengal and outside during the days between 1901-1916, so Swamiji's utterances and exhortations to the youth of India to work for the masses and to uplift them may guide the youthful workers in the labour and peasant field.[10] There are enough known facts to confirm that the Swami's sayings did inspire the young revolutionaries during 1901-1916. During police raids on their houses books of Swami Vivekananda were frequently found. The Executive Committee of the revolutionary society, that was established in Calcutta in 1902, had among its five members, Sister Nivedita, a European lady who was a disciple of Swami Vivekananda.

Raja Rao and Iqbal Singh have described Vivekananda as 'a fighter more than a thinker, possessing a practical rather than a mystical mind'. Vivekananda was the voice of new militant nationalism, whose peculiar manifestation in India, a country of spiritual traditions, was to be religious.'[11] His utterances fully confirm this. The Swami once said: 'For the next fifty years this alone shall be our key-note—this, our great Mother India. Let all other vain gods disappear for that time from our minds. This is the only God that is awake, our own race, everywhere His hands, everywhere His feet, everywhere His ears. He covers everything. All other gods are sleeping. What vain god shall we go after and yet cannot worship the God that we see all around us, the *Virat*?'[12] On another occasion he said: "I am a socialist not because I think it is a perfect system, but half a loaf is better than no bread."[13]

Quotations of this type can easily be multiplied to show that Swami Vivekananda was very much interested in raising the political status of India and improving the conditions of the people. But unlike the other Hindu religious movements, which had a revivalist character, the Ramakrishna Mission did not breed an exclusive attitude and consequently did not antagonise the Muslims. For one thing, its members did not proselytise like the Arya Samaj. The Ramakrishna Mission through its work did not also reach as large a number of people as the Arya Samaj did with its varied activities. The former, in its early stages, was mainly confined to the highly educated people in the cities and it devoted much attention to the lofty philosophical questions which had a universal appeal. Unlike the Arya Samaj its influence was not locally confined to two or three provinces (states) in India, but was national. Its intellectual influence went even beyond the borders of India as was evident from the successful functioning of Ramakrishna Missions in many other countries.

THE MUSLIM RELIGIOUS MOVEMENTS

The political significance of the religious revivalism among the Indian Muslims was different from that of the Hindu religious revivalism. As members of a minority community, who looked to the record of Muslims outside India to discover past glory and to get inspiration, the Indian Muslims, under the influence of the revivalist trend, were not keen to promote solidarity among all the Indians as one nation or as one political entity. On the other hand, at least in the religious and social field, they were emphasising their separateness. There was one difference between their separateness and the separateness preached by Sir Syed Ahmed and those who belonged to the Aligarh school. While the latter wanted the Muslims to keep away from the political and other movements directed against the West in general and the British Government in particular, the former was firmly opposed to the aggressive attacks on Islam by the Christian missionaries and to the acknowledgement of Western civilisation as superior to the indigenous civilisation of Asia, and particularly to the Arab-Islamic civilisation. This formal rejection of the West was common to both the Hindu and Muslim revivalists. When after the Great War the Khilafat agitation was organised, the Indian Muslim could easily join the Indian National Movement directed against the British Government in India. This was an occasion when the Hindu and Muslim revivalists found a common enemy and fought as allies in a common struggle. Thus for a temporary period the religious revivalists among the Indian Muslims strengthened national solidarity.

THE TOTAL EFFECT OF THE RELIGIOUS MOVEMENTS

Although the different religious reform movements made different impacts on the Indian mind, occasional attempts were made by many writers and leaders to establish that they were in essence inspired by the same motives and the ultimate aim of all of them was the same. A typical analysis is one made by Lajpat Rai: 'I will begin by examining into the respective programmes of reformers and the revivalists and see if there are any vital and real differences which justify so much contemptuous talk of each other. On both sides, I believe that the social reform programme begins, and very rightly too, with the question of early marriage. I confess I am unaware of any radical difference between the views of the reformers and the revivalists on the point.... From the question of child-marriage we may proceed to the great evil of the present divisions and sub-divisions of caste. Mrs. Besant and her school have already pronounced against the sub-divisions in the main castes. Her defence of the original Hindu conception of four castes principally coincides with the view of the Arya Samajists in the matter and practically knocks the present caste system on the head, though in theory only. In practice neither the Arya Samajists nor the reformers can go further than denunciation. All of them agree that a beginning should be made with the sub-divisions.... From castes let us proceed to the question of foreign travel, and here again we find a practical unanimity.... Then let us take the great question of female education. I know of no sensible man in the country, not to speak of the revivalists only, who is a man of culture and education, who is opposed to it. The school of Mrs. Besant, the Arya Samajists and the reformers are all pledged to it.... Similarly we do not think there is much difference of opinion at least so far as practical measures feasible at present are concerned, on the necessity of raising the social status and bettering the conditions of low castes.... We think we have almost exhausted the list of prominent subjects comprised in the list of reforms advocated by the social reformers, having reserved one important matter to be discussed last, *viz.*, the question of widow marriage. On this question there exists undoubtedly real difference of opinion between the so-called reformers and the so-called revivalists. We grant that the question is a very important one; but still we are not prepared to admit that a difference on this single question justifies all that bitterness which characterises the writings of these two classes about one another.[14] This analysis is correct as far as it goes. But it does not go far enough in assessing the implications of the two approaches. As Lajpat Rai himself says: "The real significance of these words—'reform' and 'revival'—if any, seems to be in the authority or authorities from which the reformers and revivalists respectively seek their inspiration for guidance in matters social. The former are bent on relying more upon reason and the experience of European society, while the latter are disposed to primarily look at their *shastras* and the past history, and the traditions of their people and the ancient institutions of the land which were in vogue when the nation was in the zenith of its glory."[15] This is not a difference to be brushed aside as a minor one. Both in regard to the degree of success achieved by each one of these movements and in regard to the intellectual legacy of each one of them to modern India, the difference in approach between the reformers and the revivalists was of utmost importance.

Historically speaking, the reformers came first. The West has changed the axis of Indian culture as it had moved so far. This has been done, among other ways, by the creation of a new 'class', the 'middle class', who differ from the industrial bourgeoisie by being 'non-productive' and from the earlier Indian bourgeoisie, by being 'non-commercial'. They belong to the limited number of liberal professions thrown open to the English educated Indians by the British Government. The complaint of these gentlemen against the British rule was chiefly centred in the limited opportunities for higher government services and in trade and commerce. Industry was at the periphery. As days passed, the nature of the foreign rule was divulged and its economic implication was slowly realised. But there was hardly a leader of note then who abjured the West in blind reaction. In fact, the new middle class, which was essentially the creation of political and administrative exigencies, accepted the Western values as symptoms of progress. These values were rationality with its corollary of science, democracy of parliamentary type, and a special type of liberal individualism which the British had thrown up in their own country. It must be said to the credit of the new middle class that these values were assiduously learned.... The mixture of idealism and empiricism which characterised British thought of the nineteenth century led to the spirit of reformism. Most of the new elite were social and political reformers.[16] But they had one difficulty in performing their functions in India. They were socially and psychologically distant from those who did not know English and who constituted 90 per cent of the population.

Explaining the decline of the Brahmo Samaj, Bipin Chandra Pal, himself a Brahmo Samajist, wrote: "When in 1879 I left the university and went to Cuttack, the Brahmo Samaj was still a great intellectual and moral force in the country. Middle-19th century rationalism and individualism of European culture were still the dominating ideas in the life and evolution of modern Bengal. But the conflict of political interests between the new generation of English-educated Indians and the British officialdom in the country, and the more fundamental cultural conflict between European modernism and Indian medievalism soon provoked a new revolt against this foreign domination in the wake of which followed a new national self-consciousness which, in the first flush of its newly-found pride of race and culture, commenced to repudiate whatever was foreign, irrespective of the intrinsic reason and value of it, and set up a new defence even of these social institutions and religious and spiritual tendencies that had previously been openly repudiated as false and harmful."[17]

This was how Lajpat Rai, an Arya Samajist, viewed the same development: 'The voice of the Brahmo Samaj was a mere wail in the wilderness. The Brahmo leaders' chief weapon was rationalism, which could appeal but to a few. Even in the case of these few, the Brahmo Samaj at that time was considered to be a kind of reformed or refined Christianity, resembling more the unitarian church than the monotheism of the Vedas or the

Vedicism of Rammohun Roy. Whatever little Hinduism it contained in its original form gradually dropped off, as the leadership passed into hands which had grown strong on English food and English thought.... The Sadharan Brahmo Samaj was a protest against Keshab's interpretation of Christianity.... Torn by internal dissensions of this character, the Brahmo Samaj had ceased to be an effective shield for the protection of Hindu theism from the assaults of Christians when Swami Dayananda completed his education with Virjananda about 1860."[18]

There was another weakness from which Brahmo Samajists and other reformers suffered. Owing to the social pressure, many of them found it difficult to act in accordance with the principles they advocated. An eloquent speaker in Social Reform Conferences conducting the purification ceremonies in orthodox fashion after a foreign travel or arranging his young daughter's marriage even when she was a child, was not altogether a rare event. Keshab Chandra Sen himself yielding to this tendency and trying to justify it on the basis of his 'revelations' was only a spectacular example. An Indian scholar described the situation thus: "The fact of the matter was this; although brilliant individual scientists worked against odds and made their genius felt, the seizure of whole people by the scientific spirit, if not the whole people, at least, of the English educated community, remained a different story, independent of the number of Nobel laureates and Fellows of the Royal Society. And it was this story that was not permitted to unfold itself by the executive of interests completely uninterested in the spread of scientific attitude among the people, nay, antagonistic to it. That such hostility was not uncommon in Europe is an irrelevant consideration. There, the needs of industrial progress partly countered the hostility. Here, scientific attitude would sharpen the critical attitude towards the ruling powers—literary education had been bad enough: it would mean industrialisation—not a safe state of affairs; it would mean social revolution—where then would the devout common man, the loyal Rajahs, Knights, Rai Bahadurs and Khan Bahadurs go? So, naturally, the immediate effect of the incidence of the West upon India as colonial economy was against scientific attitude and its permeation. The side-effect was the wonderful spectacle of science graduates being the repositories of all the worst prejudices that priestcraft had ever concocted. It is extraordinary how they discovered the latest scientific discoveries in the ancient texts, how they defended the indefensible social systems in the name of Western science, how they Indianised Western science."[19] This view insofar as it suggests a conscious action on the part of the executive of the vested interests is an exaggeration; but it is a correct picture of the weak position of the scientific spirit among the educated Indians in India in the nineteenth century. It is also true that this weakness was inherent in the situation arising from the political and economic backwardness of this country.

The slow political progress in 'British India' and the existence of irresponsible, and very often autocratic, political systems in Indian states under the princely order was not conducive to the promotion of the scientific spirit among the people; nor was the slow pace of economic development, particularly in the industrial field. In other words, liberalism in India in the nineteenth century had no solid foundations in a middle class and capitalist class arising from rapid industrialisation; it had only its spokesmen arising from a professional class created by Western education. There was, naturally, a gap between the theory and practice of a large number of Indian social and religious reformers in the nineteenth century. However, it cannot be denied that by putting forward high ideals before the public they did advance the progress towards democracy to a limited extent. This had its own healthy repercussions in the political field also. It is true that in that field, the first advance was made only in the spread of ideas; but this itself was of great significance in a country which, at least in its immediate past, had been devoid of such ideas.

To sum up, the political significance of the activities of the religious and social reformers was that they widened the horizon of the Indian mind in the realm of ideas. As institutions, the Brahmo Samaj, the Prarthana Samaj or the Social Conference did not have a major role to play in the political field. This was true also of the early phase of the Aligarh school, the character of which changed later.

The situation was different in regard to the revivalist organisations. They made their impact on the political field both in the realm of ideas and as organised movements. We have already noted the factors which contributed to revivalism and the reaction against reforms. As Bipin Chandra Pal stated: 'The revival of medievalism in the Brahmo Samaj itself was certainly by no means the least powerful of these. In 1876, or there about, Colonel Olcott and Madame Blavatsky landed at Bombay with a new message and a new mission. And the Theosophical Society which they founded was perhaps the most powerful of the forces that brought in this movement of Hindu religious revival and social reaction. This society told our people that instead of having any reason to be ashamed of their past or of the legacies left to them by it, they have every reason to feel justly proud of it all, because their ancient seers and saints had been the spokesmen of the highest truths and their old books, so woefully misunderstood today, had been the repositories of the highest human illumination and wisdom.... This new message, coming from the representatives of the most advanced culture and civilisation the world has yet known, at once raised us in our own estimation and created self-confidence in us.'[20] Vivekananda's visit to the United States and the reports of his 'success' at the Parliament of Religions and elsewhere also had the same effect. Commenting on the impression he made at the conference, Marie Burke said: 'Perhaps the tangible result of the Congress was the feeling it aroused in regard to foreign missions. The impertinence of sending half-educated theological students to instruct the wise and erudite Orientals was never brought home to an English-speaking audience more forcefully.'[21] Another factor was the work of the Western Orientals. When the results of their researches and translations of ancient Sanskrit books were published, the Western educated Indian became increasingly proud of his past. When Indian scholars like Dayananda Saraswati gave his interpretation of the ancient religious texts, which was to some extent in line with modern thinking, and rejected the sanctity of many other books, a section of intelligentsia found it less difficult to accept them. Then there was the growing conflict between the foreign rulers and the educated Indians owing to the new features in the national and international situations and the developments in British economy. All these developments helped the revivalist tendencies. On an ideological level, the initial effect of these revivalist movements was to give rise to national sentiments and help political awakening in the country.

These revivalist forces, when once they were set in motion eventually took the form of counter-reformation. As D.P. Mukerji says, 'It was, of course, on the ideological plane. The educated were being weaned away from the Indian inheritance and it was necessary to stop the rot. Naturally, the Hindu reaction carried some of the absurdities of the occasion for the reaction. In this period, more claims were made for Hindu philosophy and Hindu customs than even the Rishis dared. Western science was contemptuously referred to in the lectures in the halls of theosophy.'[22] This was naturally a step backward from the attempts of the earlier leaders to spread the scientific spirit, though, perhaps, only theoretically.

In a country like India, where the population was mainly divided into Hindus and Muslims and where the former constituted a predominant majority, this religious revivalism had other repercussions. A scholar on *Modern Indian Culture* notes the anti-democratic and theocratic trends in these movements. 'A deeper reaction than that of the Babus and the scholars came in the wake of religious revival. It was more than a reaction, it was almost a revulsion.... The late Bhoodeb Chandra defended the Hindu social system in the first sociological treatise on Indian society written by an Indian; and Raj Narain, the beef-eater of earlier days, lectured on the 'superiority of Hinduism over all other forms of faith' under the auspices of the National Society. Raj Narain inspired Naba Gopal Mitra in founding the *Hindu Mela* and a national paper, but could not make him favour a democratic form of government. The 'National Naba Gopal' thought that India was destined to be religious and that dictatorial rule was most suited to India. Bhoodeb, the first Indian Inspector of Schools, did not care much for representative government and the like and remained an orthodox gentleman of some charm. Another well-known writer of this school, Akshay Chandra Sircar, went so far as to say (1874) that Islam was the real difficulty in the national unity of India and India was not a nation.... Whatever the Hindu defenders of Bankim may say, his novels do not show many traces of affection for the Muslim.'[23] The same author discovers even the seeds of Pakistan in these Hindu revivalist movements: "If the radicals were middle class in their moorings, and completely indifferent, if not hostile, to the Muslims and to the masses, it was difficult for others to realise that they too were sons of the soil, equal to the Hindus in their common subjection and impartial poverty. Such radicalism could be boiled down to the protection of Hinduism, the education of India to the hand of the Hindus, that of the Hindus with the middle classes who would not remain clerks and deputy collectors in the subordinate services but would go higher and higher until they reached the ante-rooms of the Belvedere. This legacy of Hindu resurgence and middle-class domination became the mortmain of the Congress. It was invested in nationalism; and the interest is Pakistan. The mischief started in Bengal and has lasted longest in Bengal.'[24] This is an over-simplification of a highly complex issue, but there is no doubt that the Hindu revivalism of the nineteenth and early twentieth centuries, as well as the Muslim revivalist movement of this period, had a lot to do with the later Muslim separatist movements.

To sum up, the political impact of the revivalist movements on an ideological level was to give self-confidence to the rising nationalism, but it bred religious obscurantism and narrow sectarianism.

A very remarkable feature of modern Indian history is that some political movements ran almost parallel to some religious movements. There was the early phase of the Indian National Congress, led by the 'moderates' who owed allegiance to Western political ideas, which was comparable to the Brahmo Samaj and the Prarthana Samaj which wanted the reconstruction of Indian society on modern and Western lines. This was followed by the 'extremist' political agitation of the early nineteen-hundreds, which apparently stood for the rejection of Western ideas and embodied in itself a certain degree of Hindu revivalism: this had its counterpart, in the religious movements like the Arya Samaj and the Ramakrishna Mission which partake of these characteristics. Then, again, while the two former movements, though an advance in the realm of ideas, did not influence a large number of people because they had a narrow social base; the latter, with its large support, while became very effective in fulfilling their limited tasks of social reconstruction and political regeneration. This was another interesting aspect of these apparently revivalist movements: in practice, though not in theory, they were more democratic than the so-called reform movements, because they had roots in the native soil.

These were the contradictions inherent in the Indian situation at the beginning of the twentieth century; to be very effective as a reform movement in the religious and social fields, its leaders had to take into account the traditions and even the prejudices of the people and make concessions to them. This meant turning back from some of the highly advanced views of the times. It also resulted in working within the framework of organisations with direct appeal to members of one faith. The superstructure of these ideas and institutions thus created did not vanish from the scene when their progressive functions were fulfilled: on the other hand, they lingered on for a long time and considerably influenced the later intellectual and political movements of the country.

These contradictions would have been solved only by an economic expansion which would have led to the emergence of a new social class, with solid foundations in the country. Representatives of such a class would have become effective spokesmen of rationalism and enlightenment. Not only did this development not take place; but even in the limited fields of politics and administration, the educated people were not given many opportunities under Birtish rule. In a country like India where large and well-organised minority owed allegiance to a religion different from that of the majority, and where the rulers pursued the policy of 'divide and rule', the competition among large numbers of people for a few administrative posts and seats in the legislatures took a communal turn. And combined with many other developments, this led to a situation in which religion could play a prominent part in the political developments of the country.

REFERENCES

1. Annie Besant, *The Birth of New India* (Madras, 1917), pp. 358-9.
2. *Ibid.*, p. 388.
3. C.Y. Chintamani, *Indian Social Reforms* (Madras, 1901), Part I, pp. 367-8.
4. Lajpat Rai, *Arya Samaj* (London, 1915), p. 176.
5. Dayananda Saraswati: *Aryabhivinaya* (Lahore, Samvat 1994), p. 214.
6. Lajpat Rai, p. 193.
7. Munshi Ram and Rama Deva, *The Arya Samaj and its Detractors* (Dayanandabad, 1919), appendix 9.
8. *Ibid.*, p. 12.
9. *Ibid.*, n.8, p. 19.
10. Bhupendranath Datta, *Swami Vivekananda, Patriot-Prophet* (Calcutta, 1954), p. 1.
11. Raja Rao and Iqbal Singh, ed., *Changing India* (London, 1939), p. 106.
12. *The Complete Works of Swami Vivekananda*, Vol. III (Almora, 1946), pp. 300-1.
13. Swami Vivekananda, *Letters of Swami Vivekananda* (Almora, 1940).
14. Lajpat Rai, *Lala Lajpat Rai: The Man and His Word* (Madras, 1907), pp. 118-21.
15. *Ibid.*, p. 148.
16. D.P. Mukherji, *Diversities* (New Delhi, 1958), p. 244.
17. Bipin Chandra Pal, *Memories of My Life and Times in the Days of My Youth* (Calcutta, 1932), p. 424.
18. Lajpat Rai, *The Arya Samaj* (London, 1951), pp. 240-2.
19. D.P. Mukherji, n. 18, p. 176.
20. Bipin Chandra Pal, n. 19, pp. 424-5.
21. Marie Louise Burke, *Swami Vivekananda in America* (Calcutta, 1958), p. 85.
22. D.P. Mukerji, *Modern Indian Culture* (Bombay, 1948), p. 27.
23. *Ibid.*, pp. 93-4.
24. *Ibid.*, pp. 94-5.

2

Why Social Reforms?*

About sixty years ago, none among us had any idea of the reform of our society and a conference such as this was out of the question. But since that time we have come in closer contact with Western civilization chiefly through the means of English education; and that has led us to take interest in the concerns of Indian society in general and consider its good to be our good, and has evoked in us feelings of justice and passion for the various classes that compose our society. If then you are animated by these sentiments, the task before us today will present no difficulties. For the end aimed at by the propositions that will be laid before you is justice and fair play to all classes of persons, the alleviation of their sufferings and the removal of obstacles in the free development of our individual activities.

And first, a good many of the proposals have reference to the condition of the female portion of our society. Gentlemen, one-half of the intellectual, moral, and spiritual resources of our country is being wasted. If our women were educated, as they ought to be, they would be a powerful instrument for advancing the general condition of our country. They will bring up every new generation in a manner to perform its duty efficiently and will shed the influence of the benign virtues peculiar to them on men and, so to say, humanise them. All the means of educating women, therefore, that have been indicated in the propositions, you will, I feel sure, approve of. You will see that

* Address at the Ninth Social Conference.

the opening of high schools is one of them. That necessarily implies that the study of English language and literature is considered to be beneficial to our women. Though there has been some difference of opinion as regards this point, still I believe, the necessity of such education has been recognised by the majority. But I think it still remains an open question whether our ideal for the education of women ought to be the same as that for the education of men—whether after they finish their high school education, they ought to be made to go through the whole university course up to the M.A. degree. If bitter complaints have recently been urged as to the great pressure which our university education imposes upon our men, such stronger grounds there are for fear as regards women, whose constitution is more delicate and certain incidents in whose life and whose domestic duties tax them so heavily. Perhaps after finishing a high school education, if further progress is desired, there should be a selection of such subjects as are more calculated to develop the peculiar aptitudes of womanly nature. The other points concerning our daughters and our sisters have reference to the unjust and cruel sufferings to which our present social usages subject them, and which no man in whom the sentiments of justice and compassion are developed can find it in his heart to tolerate even for a moment. The misery of our widows has been the subject of frequent remark; I will, therefore, not detain you long by a full exposition of it. I will only make a general observation that society which allows men to marry any number of times even up to the age of sixty, while it sternly forbids even girls of seven or eight to have another husband after one is dead—which gives liberty to a man of fifty or sixty to marry a girl of eleven or twelve, which has no word of condemnation for the man who marries another wife within fifteen days after the death of the first, is a society which sets very little value upon the life of a female human being, and places woman on the same level with cattle and is thus in an unsound condition disqualifying it for a successful competition with societies with a more healthy constitution. Often times the marriage of a girl under certain circumstances proves her death-warrant. This matter has within the last few years forced itself powerfully upon my observation. A young man of thirty or thirty-five loses his first wife; straightaway he proceeds to marry another, who is a girl of ten or twelve. That girl dies by the time she reaches the age of twenty; another takes her place, immediately after; she too dies similarly; then comes a third who meets with the same fate; and a fourth is married by the preserving man and is eventually left a widow before she is out of her teens. A great many such cases have occurred within the last few years and amongst our educated men. The medical men, whom I have consulted, say that the results are due to the marriages being ill-assorted, *i.e.,* to the great inequality between the age of the girl and the strong and vigorous man. I do not know how else to characterise these cases except as cases of human sacrifice. Surely, if the men who have married girls successively in this manner are educated men, their refined sentiments and feelings ought to make them spare poor innocent girls and marry grown-up women—widows, if unmarried ones are not to be had. Gentlemen, this case of ill-assorted marriage deserves greater condemnation at our hands than the other, which is the only one that seems to be contemplated in one of the resolutions to be brought forward, and in which an old man of even fifty or sixty marries a girl of ten or twelve.

I will next call your attention to those points in the resolutions which concern the institution of castes. And first of all allow me to observe that a very great revolution has been effected in this matter by the mere fact that we are governed by a people amongst whom the sense of equal justice for all classes of people has received a high development. A Shudra at the present day is not more heavily punished than a Brahmin for the same crime. Manu, Yajnavalkya and others have been set aside in this respect, and the privileges, which in the eye of the criminal law, men of the highest caste enjoyed, have been taken away from them. I remember about forty-five years ago when a Brahmin was hanged for committing a murder at Ratnagiri, it created a stir among the people, since such a punishment for a Brahmin was opposed to all past traditions of the country. But, of course, the change did not provoke active hostility and has been acquiesced in on all sides. Similarly a Shudra's tongue is not now cut off for repeating the letters of the Vedas. On the contrary, if a teacher in a government school refuses to teach the sacred *mantras* to a Shudra, he is apt to be dismissed from service. In our schools and colleges we have to teach Sanskrit literature including the Vedas to all castes and classes. But it is very much to be regretted that the treasure of knowledge which has thus been thrown open to all, is not availed of by the lower castes to the extent to which they should. This is to be accounted for in a great measure by the fact of the old traditional feeling not having gone out—education is not what the Shudra thinks of first, nor endeavours made by others to induce him to educate himself and smoothen his path to a university degree. Similarly, the railways have been effecting a silent revolution. A holy Brahmin does not scruple to sit in a third class carriage by the side of a Mahar, whose very shadow is an abomination on ordinary occasions.

The Hars and Mangs on this side of the country and the Pariahs, on the other, who form the lowest classes, have been entirely neglected. They are the out-castes of Hindu society, and have been from the remotest times in a very degraded condition. The reference made to this fact by a Mahar Haridas in his prefatory remarks, while performing a Kirtana at my house a few years ago, was very touching. He said, "the Vedas and Shastras have cast us aside, but the Santas or saints of the middle ages have had compassion on us." And be it said to the credit of the Santas of Maharashtra headed by the Brahmin Eknath and to the Santas of other provinces that they had compassion for the out-castes of Hindu society, and admitted their claims to religious instruction and a better treatment. If then in those olden days these pious men, with their hearts elevated by faith and devotion, admitted the lowest Shudra to religious communion and instruction, shall we, upon whom a greater variety of influences has been operating, refuse to exert ourselves for bringing enlightenment in the dense darkness in which his mind is shrouded? And I believe from the opportunities I have had of observation that the despised Mahar possesses a good deal of natural intelligence and is capable of being highly educated. So that to continue to keep him in ignorance is to deprive the country of an appreciable amount of intellectual resources. And generally, allow me to observe that the rigid system of castes which prevails among us will ever act as a heavy drag on our race towards a brighter future. To tie men down to certain occupations, even when they have no aptitude for them, renders those men less useful to the country. When all men belonging to a certain caste must follow certain occupations only, the field is over-stocked and poverty is the result. You can get a Brahmin schoolmaster for five or six rupees a month, but a good carpenter or stonemason cannot be had unless you pay from twenty to twenty-five rupees per mensem. And unless perfect freedom is allowed to men in this respect, and each allowed to make the best possible use of his own powers, the country cannot economically advance. Special privileges enjoyed by certain castes must keep the members of others in a disadvantageous position in the rivalry and competition of life. In order that a nation as a whole may put forth all its power, it is necessary that there should be no special privileges and special restrictions. Again the principle of caste has throughout our history operated in such a way that each caste has now come to form a separate community with distinct usages, even as to the kind of food that is eaten and the manner in which it is cooked. And there is no social inter-communication between them of a nature to bind them together into one whole. Hence instead of there being a feeling of sympathy between different castes, there is often a feeling of antipathy. As long as this state of things lasts, I shall feel greatly obliged to any one who will explain to me how it is possible to form a united Hindu nation. If, therefore, we feel at all concerned as regards the future of our country in the great struggle that is going on in the world, something must be immediately done to induce a feeling of unity among these distinct communities and convert active antipathy into active sympathy.

And I will here make bold to assert that the chronic poverty of the agricultural classes and the depredations of the proverbial *Saukar* or money-lender constitute a great social evil. The government has been endeavouring to do a good deal by means of mere special legislation; but that does not seem to have remedied the evil and the money-lender continues to charge interest from 18 to 25 per cent on loans raised on the security of lands, and two or four pice per rupee per month, *i.e.* 37½ or 75 per cent on smaller sums lent for shorter periods; and there are also enhancements of interest, when the money is not paid at the stipulated time. In this manner, the poor peasant is ever a prey to the rapacity of the money-lender and is never allowed to raise his head. This is a political as well as a social question. The government has been on several occasions urged to establish agricultural banks, but it has not yet seen the wisdom of doing so, and we, too, whose countrymen the agriculturists are, have not shown particular solicitude to remedy the evil by establishing banks of our own. I do not think any special banking institution with elaborate machinery, such as has been recently proposed, is wanted. An ordinary bank with agencies at the district towns and sub-agencies for circles with a radius of about ten miles will, I think, fully answer the purpose. Money should be lent on the security of land at an interest from 9 to 12 per cent payable about the same time as the land revenue. Sympathetic, though firm, treatment should be accorded to the peasants and the agents employed should not be unscrupulous men exacting prerequisites for themselves. But I will not trespass on the province of the man of business, and whatever be the scheme that may be considered suitable and whatever its details, this I feel certain about, that shrewd men ought not to be allowed to prey upon the ignorance and entire helplessness of the agricultural classes and perpetuate their wretched condition.

Then there are other points in the resolutions, the aim of which is to remove positive obstacles to our healthy development. The early marriage of boys and girls is of this nature, since its effect is to undermine the strength of both and bring forth a progeny of weak children. The growth of the parents themselves, intellectual as well as physical, is stunted: and in a course of evolution our race must become incapable of that energy and stillness of application, which are so necessary under the conditions brought into existence by the rivalry and competition of races. The prohibition of travel in foreign countries I would put under the same head, since it acts as an obstacle to the free expansion of our energies and capacities.

These are the principal points aimed at by the social reformer. You will see that what is necessary in order that these reforms may come into practice is that there should spring up in our hearts a sense of justice, a keen sympathy for the sufferings of others and a love for one's own country and race, and an anxiety for their future well-being. If the feelings have been awakened in us with any degree of intensity, they cannot fail to realise themselves in some sort of action, and I believe that the contrary holds true that when no action follows, the feelings are either not awakened at all, or if really awakened, are very weak. It is this fact and also the general conservatism of our nature as well as the fear of excommunication that hold us back and we devise a number of excuses for our inaction. Sometimes we are disposed to leave the whole matter to the action of time, thinking that all we desire will come into practice just as the rigidity of caste rules is being gradually lessened by railway travelling and such other circumstances. But time is not a force, it is simply a conception of the mind to connect events together and cannot work any changes. If, therefore, any changes have come on in the course of time, they must be brought about by the force in the human heart that leads to action. As a matter of fact, such changes are often very extensive and important. For instance, the practice of early marriage of girls, and of female infanticide and Kulinism have come into existence in comparatively recent times. But if you examine their origin, you will find that the first owes its introduction probably to the circumstances that when the girls grew up, they went wrong in some cases. In order to prevent such a result, they were tied down to a husband before they were of an age to go wrong. To avoid sin was, of course, a laudable object, but the desire was not under the guidance of reason. Consequently the many evil effects of early marriages were over-looked, and the attainment of that one object was exclusively attended to. If, however, the desire to prevent the evil had been under the guidance of reason, other modes would have been devised for effecting it than the one actually chosen. Similarly, the practice of female infanticide and of Kulinism must in the beginning have arisen from family pride. One's daughter should not be married into a family possessing no importance or distinction. To marry her into a high family requires a heavy expenditure of money, which the father cannot afford, and in the case of Kulinism such a family is not available. Hence rather than suffer the disgrace of allying himself with a low family, he allowed his daughter to be destroyed, and in the other case to be married to one who had innumerable wives already. Here again you will see that the motive of action was not under the guidance of the higher feelings of love and tenderness for a human being and especially for one's own child. Thus then what time brings about is very often not under the guidance of reason or the higher feelings of our nature, and consequently very often degradation is the result and not elevation. It will, therefore, not do to leave reform to time or the slow and unconscious operation of causes. It must be effected from a conscious intention, and the motive force should be, as above remarked, a sense of justice, a keen sympathy and an anxiety for the future of one's own country. Unable to appreciate the feelings of the true reformer, we often accuse him of being hasty in desiring to do everything at once—we sometimes say that if he had adopted a particular way, the reform he desires would have long come into practice. Comments such as these I always suspect, especially when they come from a man who has done little or nothing practical. I am, however, not an advocate of headlong action. The motive force of reform should be powerful in our hearts, but they must be tempered in a manner not to lead us to cut ourselves from a vital connection with the past. We should not adopt the procedure of the French Revolution, but imitate the mode of action of English people, whose pupils we are. They have realised as great changes as the French Revolution sought to effect, but in a manner which connects them with the past history of the country. It will not be impossible to devise such a mode of action. One who has returned from foreign travels should live like an ordinary Hindu. A remarried widow should conduct herself just like an ordinary Hindu lady. And even as regards caste, we should behave towards each other in ordinary matters as if no such distinction existed between us; while as to eating together and intermarriage, they must come in by and by especially when the sharp distinctions as to usages and customs between the several castes are obliterated by a closer intercommunication than that which exists at the present day. But the great danger of delayed reform is that in a short time the feeling which dictated it becomes cool, and the necessity for it is entirely forgotten. To prevent this result it is essential that the motive springs of reform should always be kept alive in our hearts. We should make an earnest effort never to lose sight of the goal we have to reach. But the modest proposal that will be laid before you as regards these two matters, *viz.*, inter-communication as regards eating and marriage-alliance between members of the sub-divisions of the same caste, involves no violent change whatever; consequently, there is, I believe, no excuse for delaying its realisation. Generally it may be observed that what we have to avoid is the formation of a separate caste cut of from all social intercourse with any of the existing Hindu castes—that is to say—we should avoid such complete isolation, as, for instance, conversion to Christianity leads to. And most of the reforms we advocate involve no break of continuity. Some of them will be welcomed by the orthodox people themselves, and as regards a great many others what we propose is merely to go back to the more healthy condition in which our society once existed. In ancient times girls were married after they had attained maturity, now they must be married before; widow-marriage was in practice, now it has entirely gone out; women were often highly educated and taught even music and dancing, now they are condemned to ignorance and denied any accomplishments. The castes were only four in number, now they are innumerable. Inter-dining among those castes was not prohibited, now the numberless castes that prevail cannot have inter-communication of that nature. Consistently with the maintenance of continuity in this manner, there ought to be, I think, as much action as possible. A strong public opinion must be created among the whole body of educated natives, condemning any departure from the programme of reform, while no mercy should be shown to one who does what even the orthodox disapprove, and at sixty marries a girl of ten or twelve, or another wife immediately after the death of the first. The exhibition of any caste partiality must also be severely condemned, as no religious rules require it. Unless we act in this manner, all our advocay of reform will sink into the merest sentimentality more demoralising in its effects than sturdy orthodoxy.

But even sentimental advocacy is an homage done to a right cause and consequently is better than stolid indifference or active hostility. This, however, is unfortunately the mental attitude of a great many educated natives in all parts of the country. In Bengal, as was pointed out by our friend the honourable Mr. Justice Ranade the other day, social reform is now confined to Brahmos. The great body of educated Bengalees, who are not Brahmos, are indifferent or hostile. The late Ishwar Chandra Vidyasagar, who inaugurated the reform about widow-marriage and first ransacked our *Smriti* literature to be able to make out that it was sanctioned by the *Shastra,* and worked for a life-time to make it popular, was in his latter days filled with despondency and expressed his conviction to visitors from this side of the country that Hindus as Hindus would never accept social reform. It is certainly a matter of the deepest regret that it should be confined to a religious body. We on this side have not come to this pass yet, though we have our full share of indifference and hostility. The aim of our reformers here has always been to reform our society—our nation. I am happy to find that our Madras friends agree with us in this respect. Reform through the agency of caste, which is attempted in some parts of the country, is very unsatisfactory. Very little can be effected in this way. The reduction of marriage expenses and measures of this nature only can be carried out by its means, and the great dangers of this method are that caste which has corroded the vitals of this country will be strengthened by it.

Thus then we should nurture in our hearts the great forces which bring about the reform of society, *viz,* truth, justice, and sympathy. Two of the greatest historians of England have told us that the moral law governs the affairs of the world; its observance alone ensures national prosperity. One of these I have quoted elsewhere, and will now ask your attention to the observations of the other. The strongest of the forces which are steadily bearing nations onward to improvement or decay are, according to Lecky, the moral ones. "Their permanent political well-being", he says, "is essentially the outcome of their moral state." The moral law seeks to purify private life and to effect social justice, and through these alone is the political well-being of a nation possible. And evolutionary science is beginning to teach us the same lesson. Competition and rivalry are the necessary conditions of progress towards a higher condition among men as well as among the lower creatures. This competition and this rivalry tend to establish the supremacy of the stronger individual over the weaker; his race propagates itself and that of the other disappears. It is this law that is leading or has led to the extinction of the aboriginal races in the presence of the stranger European races in America, Australia, New Zealand and other islands. This competition and rivalry need not assume the form of an actual war of extermination. It has been clearly ascertained that even in the midst of profound peace, the primitive races show a tendency to disappear. If this law were in operation in our country, our future must be very gloomy. But our climate will, I think, come to our rescue as it has been ascertained that the stronger races of Western Europe cannot, if settled here, exhibit the same energy and perseverance that they do in temperate regions. Colonisation of India by the European races is, therefore, an impracticability; but does not deliver us from the dangers of competition and rivalry with them. And again that law must be in operation among us to ensure our own progress. But to estimate its full effects we must understand the conditions under which it acts in the case of man. Man is a social animal, and the competition that comes into operation in his case is a competition between societies. The ancient history of the human race consists of war between such societies and the triumph of one and subjugation of another. This competition and rivalry between different societies is going on still, and in order that a society may carry on the contest to a successful issue, it is necessary that it should be so organised that the individuals composing it should not be borne down by artificial restrictions, but be able to put forth their best powers and capacities. The effect of this would be to place the individual in a more advantageous position to conduct the battle of life, and thus to render the society, of which he is a member, fitter for competition and rivalry with other societies. But it is the development of sympathetic or altruistic feelings only amongst the privileged classes and the society generally that can lead to the removal of the disabilities of others and the redress of their grievances. Without such feelings, internal dissensions and eventual degradation must be the results. And these feelings are now leading the English people to devise means for relieving the chronic poverty of the lower classes, to readjust the relations between labour and capital, and undertake a variety of schemes to relieve distress and misery. It is a patent fact acknowledged by all disinterested persons that the English people have developed the altruistic feelings in a higher degree than any other European nation, and, by the way, this constitutes the basis of our hopes in a better future for our country. Just as England had been endeavouring to remove the disabilities and sufferings of the lower classes of her population, so shall efforts not be wanting on her part to remove our disabilities and sufferings. But the law of social evolution cannot cease to operate; and in order that our society may be able to hold its own in the competition and rivalry with other societies, which is inevitable, we must abide by the conditions of that law. That law is thus stated by the latest writer on the subject, whose book has created a great stir: "That the moral law is the unchanging law of progress in human society, is the lesson which appears to be written over all things. No school of theology has ever sought to enforce this teaching with the directness and emphasis, with which it appears that evolutionary science will in the future be justified in doing. In the silent and strenuous rivalry in which every section of the race is of necessity continually engaged, permanent success appears to be invariably associated with certain ethical and moral conditions favourable to the maintenance of a high standard of social efficiency and with those conditions only." If then social efficiency and consequent success are what we desire in our contest with other races, we must, because the law is immutable, endeavour to realise those ethical and moral conditions. We must cultivate a sense of justice and a love and sympathy for others, relieve the poor widow of her sufferings, remove the disabilities of womankind and of the lower classes, and allow free play to the energies and capacities of all. And the necessity for our doing so becomes the more imperative from our political condition. If we ask England to remove our disabilities, we must as a necessary preliminary show that we are worthy of the favour by removing the disabilities of the oppressed classes of our society. Thus and thus alone will our country prosper. Every scheme for bettering our condition is destined to fail if it does not make provision for the growth of these sympathetic virtues and through them for the realisation of social reform. Let us then invigorate and elevate our souls by ever placing before our mind's eye the precept of the great Indian reformer of the sixth century before Christ, the Lion of the Sakya race, Goutama, the enlightened; 'Cultivate a mind boundless (as sympathy) for all beings as is that of the mother, who protects her only son by sacrificing her own life'; and with him proclaim from this social conference hall, 'May all living beings, feeble or strong, long, great, middle-sized or short, small or large, seen or unseen, living far or near, born or to be born, be happy!'

—R.G. Bhandarkar

3

Importance of Social Reform*

Once more we meet in this busy week of December, this time in your historical and holy city, to take stock of our year's achievements, to count our losses and gains, and to pledge ourselves to help each other in the unceasing struggle to better our condition. When from our distant provinces we start on these annual pilgrimages, we are often twitted for our pains by those who take credit to themselves for superior wisdom, and the question is often asked, what mad freak lays hold of so many earnest minds in the country, which leads them to pursue this mirage of national elevation, which recedes further from our grasp the more eagerly we run after it. This same irreverent doubt also weighs down upon some among our own body in our weak moments, and it seems to me very necessary, before we enter upon more serious work, to purify ourselves by the discipline of a rigorous course of self-examination for the struggle. Nothing strikes our critics, both European and Native, as more manifestly absurd than this our faith that these annual gatherings will prove helpful in attaining the objects we seek. Progress in the art of self-government, both in its national and individual bearings, it is urged by some of our native friends, can never be secured by these half-confused gatherings of races and creeds and interests, and the jumble of tongues, and the tame imitation of methods not our own. Our European critics

* During the Sixth Social Conferenee at Allahabad a public meeting was held on the 25th December, 1892. Mr. M.G. Ranade delivered this address.

are more wise in their generation, and some of the wisest among them have demonstrated to their own satisfaction that all Oriental races have had their day, and that nothing is now left to them but to vegetate and die, and make way for their betters. Political elevation and social emancipation, religious or spiritual enlightenment—these gifts have not been, and will never be, according to their philosophers, vouchsafed anymore to the Indian races. If these black forebodings were really inspired prophecies, our outlook would be dark indeed. Happily for us these prophecies are not true, and what is more, it is in our power to falsify them. History does not countenance them, and the teachings of science are not in their favour. No earnest prayer, no self-denying aspiration, no sincere battling with falsehood and ignorance, can ever under God's Providence end in failure. The methods may have to be changed, but the struggle is ever the same, and none need despair. It is not the gains that you make outside of you, it is not what you have but what you yourselves become, that makes or mars a man's or a nation's destiny. Particular reforms may be out of our reach, or may not be for our advantage; but the earnest desire for reform and sincere efforts of self-sacrifice directed towards their attainment cannot but elevate us above our weakness, and strengthen our strong points, and plant the banner of union in hearts torn with centuries of strife and disunion. This is the moral interest of the struggle, and those who cannot appreciate this invaluable privilege of fighting in the ranks in such a struggle are—what shall I call them—superior persons living in a paradise of their own. If indeed history and science both declared against us, we might find it necessary to pause. But the history of this great country is but a fairy tale, if it has not illustrated how much invasion from abroad has tended to serve as a discipline of the chosen race, and led to the gradual development of the nation to a higher ideal if not of actual facts, at least of potential capabilities. The nation has never been depressed beyond hope of recovery, but after a temporary submerging under the floods of foreign influences, has reared up its head—absorbing all that is best in the alien civilisation and polity and religions. The testimony of science paints in the same direction. If the environments determine the growth, a change in the environments must bring about a change in the political and social organism. There is thus no cause for despair if we only remember one great lesson of history and science, namely, that no development of the body politic is possible unless the new heat animates all our powers and gives life and warmth to all our activities.

When we meet at these annual gatherings to seek our political elevation, we must not lose sight of the fact that our social emancipation should go along with it, if we desire to be an individual consistent whole, with a just balance of power in all our movements. In other words, the social evolution must take place side by side, if it should not precede the political growth that we desire to achieve. What is it, some of you will ask, that you require of us to do in this work of internal freedom? I would reply, the evolution that we should seek is a change from constraint to freedom—constraint imposed by our own weaker nature over the freedom of our higher powers. It is a change from credulity to faith, from credulity which behoves without grounds to faith which builds itself upon a firm foundation. Our station in life, our duties and our limits of action are certainly fixed for most of us by circumstances over which we have no control; but there is still a large margin left for freedom of action. We voluntarily contract that margin, and bind ourselves by fetters, and glory in them as the Mahomedan fakir in Bombay, who thinks himself specially favoured because he bears heavy iron chains. The change which we should all seek is thus a change from constraint to freedom, from credulity to faith, from status to contract, from authority to reason, from unorganised to organised life, from bigotry to toleration, from blind fatalism to a sense of human dignity. This is what I understand by social evolution, both for individuals and societies in this country. Even if we accept the evolution view to be correct, it should not be forgotten that the environments which surround us have changed, and are not the same that they were a hundred years ago. Peace and order reign throughout the land instead of the old disturbances which made the preservation of life one's chief care. Instead of our country being a sealed book, we are now a part of the community of nations, feeling joy and sorrow in their prosperity of distress. In our own country distance and local barriers which so long separated us, have been removed and we are made more mobile and coherent than we ever were before. These are only physical changes. More important still is the discipline, afforded us by the example and teaching of the most gifted and free nation in the world, whose rule guarantees to us a long continuance of these favourable conditions. The reign of law is supreme. Human skill and human sympathies are busy at work to correct all our failings, and it cannot well be that all this should have happened as a mere accident in human story. The European philosophers themselves admit that wholesale migration and infusion of new blood can alone revive the old effete Oriental races. I contend that the changed order of things described above are the new environments in which, without change of place, we have been forced to migrate, they infuse new blood into our veins and they bring down from heaven the spiritual fire which has strength enough to purge us of our grosser selves, if we only will do our duty. On their own theory, therefore, there is no cause for the despair which European thinkers feel. The process of growth is always slow, where it has to be a sure growth. The best natures naturally want to shorten this long process in their desire to achieve the work of a century in a decade. This temptation has to be resisted, and in this respect the teachings of the evolution doctrine have great force, because they teach that growth is structural and organic and must take slow effect in all parts of the organism, and cannot neglect any and favour the rest. There are those amongst us who think that in this connection the work of the reformer is confined only to a brave resolve to break with the past and do what our individual reason suggests as proper and fit. The power of long-formed habits and tendencies is, however, ignored in this view of the matter. "The true reformer has not to write upon a clean slate. His work is more often to complete the half-written sentence. He has to produce the ideal out of the actual, and by the help of the actual." We have one continuous stream of life flowing past us, and "we must accept as valid the acts which are noted in the past, and on the principles of the past", and seek to turn the stream with a gentle bend here and a gentle bend there to fructify the land; we cannot afford to dam it up altogether or force it into a new channel. It is this circumstance which constitutes the moral interest of the struggle, and the advice so frequently given—that we have only to shake our bonds free and they will fall off themselves—is one which matured and larger experience seldom supports. We cannot break with the past altogether; with our past we should not break altogether, for it is a rich inheritance and we have no reason to be ashamed of it. The society to which we belong has shown wonderful elasticity in the past, and there is no reason for apprehending that it has ceased to be tractable. Patient and persistent action is required. While respecting the past, we must seek to correct the parasitical growths that have encrusted it and sucked the life out of it. This is, at least, the spirit in which the societies and associations which are represented at the social Conference seek to work. They seek no change for its own sake or because it is fashionable elsewhere. They seek their inspiration in the best traditions of our own past, and adjust the relations of the past with the present in a spirit of mutual forbearance. The *Shastras* they revere, but they respect the spirit more than the letter of the old law. The road is difficult and beset with dangers, but as it is the only sure road, there is no choice. Looked at in this spirit, we may now review the work of the past year, and although, as in the political sphere of our activity, we have both gained and lost ground, there is, on the whole, no cause for thinking that we have wasted our opportunities during the year that is about to close. Being in touch with friends in all parts of the country, I can speak with some authority, and I am glad to testify to the fact that it cannot be laid at the door of the different local associations that they have been idle all the year round. In the Bengal Presidency an agitation initiated by Kumar Bonoy Krishna Bahadur, and supported by such men as Sir Romesh Chandra Mitra and Pandit Mahesh Chandra and Babu Surendra Nath Bannerji, has been carried on in the matter of removing hindrances in the way of the free admission of men who go to foreign countries. *Vyavasthas* numerously signed by Pundits and others have advanced the solution of that question to a sensible extent. In the N.W. Provinces and Oudh, the Kayastha associations and their conference have done a great deal for that community in the way of checking intemperance and extravagance, and promoting education. In the Punjab, the healthy activity of the local Arya Samajas has given to that body a position of great usefulness in the education and training of the community of the country. Two re-marriages, one in high life and the other in consonance with the old practices, have taken place with apparent approval of many orthodox leaders. Lower down in Rajputana the Walterkrit Rajputra Sabha has developed its organisation and enforced its rules with greater success than before, and the movement is now spreading among other classes of the community. The leading Native States are lending their support to the cause of reform officially. In Guzerath in our own Presidency, His Highness the Maharajah Gaikwar has been appealed to for help by the Mahajans of thirty leading sub-castes to help them in raising the limit of marriageable age and checking extravagance. In the British territory in the same province, the Kunbi population has been similarly profiting by the operation of the rules framed under the Infanticide Acts. In the rest of the Presidency, the Marwadi Jains at Nasik and the Kayastha Prabhus have held conferences for the promotion of reform in their own community. In Bombay a re-marriage was celebrated the other day which was also an inter-marriage. In Poona owing to local distractions much has not been done, but the Poona Association has received several more pledges, and some of the highest families in the city have arranged mutual marriage alliances, the actual celebration of marriage being postponed till the girls arrive at puberty. Even the local distraction had a higher moral interest than what people, looking superficially, would be prepared to admit. As the question is, however, still undecided, it would be premature to prophesy the final results. But there are evident signs that the struggle has commenced in earnest and it will end in a compromise creditable to both the parties. In Mysore, His Highness the Maharajah's government is prepared to undertake legislation in respect of marriage reform, and has been good enough to show His Highness's appreciation of the work of the conference by deputing a learned Shastri of his court to help us in our deliberations. In Malabar the proposed legislation of marriage among Nairs has made some progress. In the Madras Presidency, three re-marriages took place, one of them being an inter-marriage. A new association of earnest workers has also been formed there, which represents the young Madras party, and promises the happiest results. Two of our most prominent workers undertook missionary tours in the Punjab, in the Central Provinces and in the Berars, at great self-sacrifice. In the Central Provinces a Native Christian was taken back into his caste by the leading pandits of Jubbalpore. Taking things as they are, this is not, I hope, a very unsatisfactory account of the year's work, and it shows that the conscience of the country is touched in all great centres, and with better organisation, greater courage of conviction and more faith in Providence, we may hope that this process of social regeneration or evolution, if you like so to call it, will continue to grow in strength and in power. To help that growth by bringing all workers together once a year to exchange views and sympathies is the object with which we meet here. Last time the people of Allahabad gladly welcomed our efforts and we feel quite sure of a similar welcome on this occasion.

—M.G. Ranade

4

The Principles of Social Reforms*

The decadence of a community does not necessarily mean its decadence in numbers. So far as numbers go, thanks to the custom of early and compulsory marriage, we have undergone no decay at all. The contract of a more vigorous and manly race has proved fatal to many an aboriginal race in the world. The ancient Peruvians, the Aztecs and the Caribs were exterminated by the more hardy races of Europe; and in Australia, in Africa and in America the aboriginal races are meeting with the same fate. But in the ceaseless vicissitudes of our history in the past, we have preserved our identity; and not only have we preserved our identity but have even preserved some of the more marked features of our distinct civilization. We have certainly multiplied in numbers. The innate vitality of the race has enabled it to resist the fate that overtook some ancient races and are overtaking the Pacific islanders, the Maoris, and the Negroes in Africa and America. Still, the degeneration is perceptible along many a vein in the national character. We have preserved many of the softer and more passive elements of character—but have degenerated in the rougher, the more active, and the more manly elements. We are the same patient, peace-loving, orderly, industrious, simple and spiritual people that we were centuries ago. We preserve the same tenderness to animal life, the same sense of family obligations, the same regard for personal purity, the same metaphysical cast of mind. But patriotism, love of enterprise, co-

* Address at the Madras Hindu Social Reform Association.

operative faculty, adventure, energy, aspiration, devotion to duty and such like qualities, we have lost, if we ever possessed them. In fact, as the author of *Social Evolution* would put it, we have lost the qualities which contribute to 'social efficiency'.

Speaking of the prosperity of nations and the causes of it Mr. Lecky says: "Its foundation is laid in pure domestic life, in commercial integrity, in a high standard of moral worth and of public spirit, in simple habits, in courage, uprightness and a certain soundness and moderation of judgement, which springs quite as much from character as from intellect. If you would form a wise judgement of the future of a nation, observe carefully whether these qualities are increasing or decaying. Observe specially what qualities count for most in pubic life. Is character becoming of greater or less importance? And the men who obtain the highest posts in the nation, men of whom in private life and irrespective of party, competent judges speak with genuine respect? Are they of sincere convictions, consistent lives, indisputable integrity?.... It is by observing this moral current that you can best cast the horoscope of a nation." It is this moral current which, according as it is clear, healthy and vigorous, or the reverse, determines the position of a nation in the world. The happiness of man, under modern conditions, depends far more upon what may be called his social qualities—qualities, that is to say, which enable him to act in co-operation with a large number of men—then upon his qualities as an isolated individual! The individual will no doubt continue to wield influence on his neighbours, but the progress of the community no longer depends to the same extent as it did in ancient times, on the towering genius of an individual, be he a ruler, a statesman or a general. It depends on the collective activity of a large number moving together at a time. The power of organization is, therefore, so important in these days as a factor of progress. It is these qualities that contribute to social efficiency that really constitutes in modern times the superiority or inferiority of race. Says Mr. Benjamin Kidd: "Nor even of the possession of high intellectual capacity can science give up any warrant for speaking of one race as superior to another. The evolution which man is undergoing is over and above everything else, a social evolution. There is, therefore, but one absolute test of superiority. It is only the race possessing in the highest degree the qualities contributing to social efficiency that can be recognized as having any claim to superiority. But these qualities are not as a rule of the brilliant order, nor such as strike the imagination. Occupying a high place amongst them are such characteristics as strength and energy of character, humanity, probity and integrity, and simpleminded devotion to conceptions of duty in such circumstances as may arise."

THE CLUE TO REFORM ACTIVITY

It is this test as to the condition of a nation that should supply the clue to true reform activity. Whatever institution, custom, belief, or notion retards the development of this social efficiency, should be modified or discouraged, and others more subservient to this end should be gradually evolved. If we consider the programme of our work having regard to this test, we will see its importance and its wisdom. A baby-born race and a race whose children are brought up by illiterate mothers cannot develop much of the qualities which I have alluded to. We search in vain in such a race for the qualities of courage, of enterprise, of adventure, and of a fearless facing of responsibilities instead of shirking them or flying away from them. Nor can a people who treat their women as if they were intended for no higher duties than the personal service of their husbands and who heartlessly consign their unfortunate widows to a lot of perpetual privations, show much of chivalry, generosity, sympathy with the weak, self-sacrifice, and dignity of family life. Nor, again, is it possible that a people divided as the Hindus are into castes with all the narrow feelings and antipathies that they nurse, learn qualities so essentially social as patriotism, fellow-feeling, a sense of the equality of all men, and sacrifice for others. "Caste is the greatest monster we have to kill," said Dr. Bhandarkar speaking in this city three years ago, and indeed it is. More than all other evils of our social system, it has contributed to the crushing of the high moral feeling, of the ethical nature of the Hindu, and of that divine instinct—the sense of man's duty to man, irrespective of birth or rank. Take again the foolish custom of looking upon foreign travel as a violation of religious duty. I do not know that any conceivable state of Hindu society in the past could have furnished reasons for the necessity of such prohibition. But there can be no doubt that this self-inflicted isolation was the cause of serious deterioration in the character of the people. They became ignorant and conceited, and while they lost one strong incentive to sustained advancement in the arts of civilisation which a free intercourse with foreign countries should have supplied, they lost all knowledge of the outside world, believed that their own country and their own people constituted God's universe, flattered themselves that everything worth knowing they already knew, and that human race could not advance further than the stage they had themselves reached. It is no longer possible for the people of India to remain in this state of isolation. They will have new blood infused into them by a free intercourse with the active races of other parts of the world. This silly prohibition is so opposed to the needs of modern times that an increasing number of Hindus, disregarding this prohibition, visit foreign countries for purposes of education and commerce. The well-known terrors of excommunication are no longer able to stop the flowing tide bursting through this old and time-worn barrier. No healthy social progress is possible without every facility being provided for foreign travel. Fancy what the condition of England would be if a prohibition were placed on her best men leaving their native country! What—will even Japan be under such prohibition? The conclusion is, therefore, obvious that the social customs and prejudices which we are engaged in combating are inimical to the growth of those qualities that I have alluded to as constituting important factors in 'social efficiency.'

OUR DIFFICULTIES ARE SPECIAL AND MORE FORMIDABLE

We are fully sensible of the stupendous difficulties besetting endeavours to sweep away abuses centuries old, to change customs that are interwoven into the very life of the people, and to adapt ancient institutions to modern requirements. These difficulties are special in this country and are more formidable than elsewhere. Because the changes we desire and we strive to bring about are not like the gradual, natural and organic transformation of an existing institution to suit a fresh want. In Western countries social changes mean more or less improvements on existing bases; the spirit of the nation, of the institutions and of the ends desired remains the same through successive developments. Each new step marks the continued evolution of society, helped and directed by the forces it spontaneously develops. But in India, we have more or less to pour new wines into old bottles. The ideals of thinking Hindus in these days are not those that moved our ancestors, of whose conceptions of human well-being, the institutions, customs, etc., that we have inherited are the embodiment. Our modern ideals are more or less derived from the experience of Western countries and the forces that make them living and keep them in operation are also more or less foreign. We want to become a nation like Western nations; we want to be healthy like them; active, enterprising, free and moral like them; and our aspirations, it may be safely said, have comparatively little in common with those law-givers and reformers of old whom we hold answerable for the social features confronting us at the present moment. Many of these features are hostile to these aspirations. Still, we cannot pull down the Hindu social edifice as the tower of the Connemara Library was pulled down the other day, and erect another to suit exactly our new purposes. The process involves a good deal of destructive work, however slowly and cautiously effected. It must be a good deal more than mere adaptation. What process of adaptation, for instance, can make the joint family system, degradation of women, and caste, suit modern ends? They must be adapted and adapted until they cease to exist. Changes must be more abrupt, the transition more violent, the old and the new more dissimilar in this country than has been the experience in more fortunate countries.

THE PENALTY SHOULD BE PAID

The Hindu community should pay the penalty of its past neglect. For centuries it has been away from the path of true progress. The peculiar social system of the Hindus worked well enough so long as they were an independent and self-contained community. But it had within itself seeds of decay, because it was not a self-working system adapting itself to fresh environments as they arose. It was not designed to promote solidarity and a uniform progress of the whole. The spiritual aspiration that dominated the thoughts and the whole altruistic activity of the higher classes was antagonistic to all material interests and obscured the paramount need of strengthening the social organization in view of security from external danger as well as of internal well-being. The high level of material prosperity which the nation was able to reach on account of favourable physical conditions, soon resulted in effeminacy of character—a result which came about all the more easily by the aversion of the people to material advantages naturally induced by their spiritual ideals. Buddhism went to strengthen this aversion, and by admitting all castes into its spiritual fold, extended it to the whole population. The military defence of the country against external dangers was of course neglected, our ancestors being evidently under the belief that outside India there were no people capable of invading her and established a foreign rule subversive of their own religion and civilization. Arts and industries were despised, no social status being accorded to the classes following them. Women were deposed from the position which they had previously occupied, and came to be looked upon as mere instruments of men's pleasure. All education which was not spiritual or ecclesiastical was ruled mischievous. The nation became effeminate, priest-ridden, disorganized, stagnant and utterly unfit for self-defence. When once the tide of foreign invasion began to flow into the country, the degradation was complete and during nearly a thousand years, the best efforts of its most valiant champions, such as they were, were directed towards keeping the nation up somehow, preserving the prized inheritance of old, in religion, literature and traditions, and towards feeding the people with a hope of a better time, in a future cycle of the world's evolution. During this long period, no original achievement in any sphere of human activity, not even in the intellectual sphere, can be traced to the Hindus. While we were thus in a stagnant condition, other nations of the world made wonderful progress, and some of them in particular, who were steeped in barbarism at a time when the Hindus were in the pinnacle of glory, have become masters of the world including our own dear motherland. The world has been progressing rapidly, while we were in a trance, and now being roused once more into consciousness by the quickening contact of the West, we find ourselves amidst strange surroundings, which threaten our fresh born consciousness with extinction if we do not accept and assimilate them. The civilization we have managed to preserve through a series of unparalleled vicissitudes is antiquated and unsuited to modern conditions, and however reluctant we may be to tear ourselves from the past and however difficult the process may be, we must recognise it to be inevitable. We can only do our best to make the transition from the old order to the new as smooth as possible, although, as I have said, it cannot be as smooth as it can be in other countries.

CASTE AS THE BASIS OF THE SOCIAL SYSTEM MUST BE CHANGED

The Hindu society is founded on caste, which by its extreme conservatism, by its jealousy of foreigners and by its careful preservation of the purity of blood, has preserved the identity of the nation in spite of the large infusion of foreign elements in its composition. We recognise the service that this institution has done to the people in the past. But conditions have changed and caste too will have to change its spirit if not its form. The caste basis of society is essentially one of inequality as determined by certain artificial significance of birth and of barriers arbitrarily created to limit the sphere of human faculties. Whatever meaning there might have been in this inequality and restriction in the original conception, it can have no rational meaning whatever in these days. Modern world will not acknowledge special claims of individuals to special means of spiritual salvation. The Pariah as well as the Brahmin will be allowed to seek his own means of salvation. Any application of coercion will only end in the individual community coerced seeking relief by entering other social systems where greater liberty is promised. Nor is there in our country in these days any temporal authority, as there was in former times, to apply coercion to enforce obedience to a social polity, at once irrational and degrading according to prevailing conceptions. If equality then must be conceded to all classes in spiritual concerns, it must be conceded in matters temporal too. We can no longer lay down arbitrarily that certain occupations are open to a certain caste and others to other castes. Each person's aptitude and opportunity are the only determining factors in the choice of occupation. The great principle of social relation in these days is a perfect equality of footing to all. The history of the modern world is mostly the history of the struggle against a monopoly of power and prestige in certain classes; the privileged classes having been deprived of their privileges, the masses are emancipated and elevated, bringing together all members of the community on a footing of equality and removing all obstacles placed by society or the state before individuals in the rivalry of life. Thanks to the *Pax Britannica,* the tyranny of caste is being broken down, and theoretically at all events the Pariah and the Brahmin can compete together in life with equal freedom. No Indian is now handicapped for the accident of his birth.

Caste, as the basis of society, and custom, as the regulating force of its activity, are not a healthy combination. It is wonderful how amongst us custom has usurped the place of reason, sentiment, and religion itself, as a standard of right and wrong. In our social relations it is recognised as a dominant motive of action. In every society custom is, no doubt, more or less powerful. In the name of fashion, of pubic opinion or of social convention, it plays the tyrant. The Englishman is a slave of it in certain spheres of action as the Hindu; but the Hindu is a more craven slave than any other civilised race. The difference is one of degree, but in this world all differences between right and wrong, good and bad, or between opposites of any kind, are ultimately of degree. At all events they are practically so. When, therefore, a conservative Hindu justifies or defends the intolerable tyranny of custom by referring to a similar state in other countries, his reasoning is specious. Nobody says English society or any other society is perfect, and reformers there too are irritated at the obstruction of custom. It is indeed entitled to regard in certain comparatively unimportant spheres of conduct. In dress, in forms of civility, in mere ceremonies, and in conventions generally, the sway of custom is innocuous. Beyond these limits that sway should not be allowed to trespass. On the other hand, when its influence intrudes into relations, when underlie the elevation and refinement of human nature and when it obstructs the healthy play of sentiment or the application of reason, it becomes mischievous. I shall illustrate what I mean. The Hindus have their own dress, their own forms of courtesy, their own domestic and social ceremonies. Whether these are altered or whether they remain the same matters little. The power of custom in these and kindred matters is tolerable. But when it claims control over actions concerning the health and happiness of individuals and of the well-being of the community as a whole, it transcends its limits and should be checked. In the great question of the re-marriage of widows, for instance, our people admit the hardship of life-long widowhood and they also admit the scriptural sanction for re-marriage. They admit too the expediency, from a worldly point of view, of reform. Parents are not callous to the claims of their widowed child on their affection; the widow's suffering, her privation, her disfigurement and her unhappy lot generally, often break their heart. Instances of parents who take their unfortunate child's lot so much to heart that they themselves vow life-long abstinence, are not unknown. They feel that the young widow might be misled, and after their own lives, she will be utterly helpless. Yet, all these considerations, pressing so strongly in favour of the one step that will make themselves and their child happy, are set aside, merely because custom is opposed to it. Religion is not against it, morality is not against it, nor expediency, nor even the general feeling of the caste. But custom overrides all, and holds both reason and sentiment captive. Similarly in regard to marriage, it is custom that limits the field of choice to the caste to which the boy or the girl may belong. The Shastras recognize only four castes, but these four have now become forty thousand, a caste, in some instances, consisting of but a few families. Yet the alliance must be formed within the limits of that caste, and the result is marriage at an excessively tender age and at a ruinous cost. These two evils would be greatly avoided if marital relations were allowed within a wider field. As a fact, however, a Hindu parent will rather marry his young daughter to an invalid, to a very old man, to a man without any means of livelihood, than marry her to a boy of a different caste whatever may be his recommendations. Many a young girl and many a young boy are made unhappy all their life in consequence of this restriction. Yet the only justification of this restriction is custom. There is nothing else prohibiting alliance within a wider area than a single caste. Again, ask our countrymen the reason for the restrictions on the liberty of our women. Ask them why the woman should not move about as freely as the man, why she should not go about with a pair of shoes and an umbrella, why she should not drive out with her husband, why she should not extend her knowledge and refine her manners by mixing in society, why she should not, in fact, do so many other things, which, without offending the orthodox sense of propriety, she might do to understand better the world and human nature and make herself more intelligent and more self-reliant. The reason they will give is custom. The less advanced the state of society is, the more extensive and more powerful is the sway of this tyrant. In a primitive state, custom not only regulates social conduct but controls industry also. It fixes the wages, it limits the market, and determines generally the relation between capital and labour. Modern conditions have almost taken away this latter power from custom, but they have been powerless to depose it as a ruling moral force.

CASTE SHOULD BE REPLACED BY EQUALITY AND CUSTOM BY REASON AND SYMPATHY

Caste, then, as the basis of social status should be replaced by equality of footing to all, and custom as a motive of action should be replaced by reason and sympathy. I have already said that so far as the state can help in the establishment of this equality of footing, it is secure to all classes of people. But there are a thousand corners and turns into which the influence of the State does not penetrate and where social dealings are subject to the caprice of public opinion and individual feeling. In the eye of the law, the Pariah and the Brahmin are, no doubt, on a footing of equality, but the law cannot reach the trifles as well as the important transactions of life, and it is quite open to the landlord, the moneylender and the high caste man, to oppress the Pariah in countless ways. Caste breeds pride and selfishness, and the man of the higher caste thinks it his privilege to despise the man of the lower caste. Every endeavour should be made to break down this spirit, although the less essential and the more extraneous forms of caste may linger. The position of custom being taken by reason and sympathy, or rather by sympathy tempered by reason, our social relations will be less stereotyped, and more in accord with the fresh knowledge and experience we acquire every day in consequence of a freer and quicker intercourse among the communities of the world. Sympathy, the first impulse to action, while its form in practical effect is determined by reason. Then the incongruity we perceive, in the light of modern knowledge, between the ideal and the existing state, will press on us with greater force until the desired transition from the old and less rational, to the new and the more rational order, takes place. Mr. Lecky well observes: "As impartial examination of great transitions of opinion will show that they have usually been effected not by the force of direct arguments, not by such reasons as those which are alleged by controversialists and recorded in creeds, but by a sense of the incongruity or discordance of the old doctrines with other parts of our knowledge." It is the duty of all interested in our social well-being to bring home to the popular mind with an ever-increasing pressure this sense of incongruity, which will then raise a general revolt against the sovereignty of the ruling twins—caste and custom.

ELEVATION OF WOMEN

If the victory of the social feeling over self-love is the key to the regeneration of social existence, if a moral transformation must precede and real advance, and if a pressing sense of incongruity must bring on transition, then this victory, this transformation and this pressure should be manifest in the family before they can assert themselves outside. The claim of woman to a higher status should be recognised. It is self-love, narrow sympathy, and a low standard of conduct that constitute the cause of the subordination of woman to man. The Hindu conception of society, though fairly cognizant of the respect due to woman, does not provide for the growth of her status into equality with man. Even in Europe the equality of the two sexes is a modern idea, though there is a far nearer approach to it there than in this country. Our joint family system is not favourable to that undisputed sovereignty which she has a right to wield in the home, and even the freedom which is hers theoretically is considerably curtailed. There is no doubt that in ancient and medieval periods the Hindu woman enjoyed both at home and outside a higher status and greater freedom than she does at present. The deterioration is chiefly the result of the backward notions which our Mahomedan rulers brought with them, and to the decay of the Hindu character itself. The Mahomedan rule has to answer for many faults in our social arrangements at present, and among them the selfish and ungenerous view taken of the rights of the other sex is not the least deplorable. Buddhism too contributed materially, I believe, to this result. I do not propose to go here into a historical enquiry of the causes of the present degraded condition of our women, but I may observe that in the more sympathetic and rational views we, Social Reformers, hold on the position of women, we mostly reproduce, to suit modern ideals, the conception of our forefathers. We hold that the true test of civilization is the position of women, and the incongruity between our pretensions outside our home and our practice within it, should gradually lead to a greater harmony between our two lives.

THE HINDU WOMAN WILL LOSE MUCH TO HER DOMESTICITY

Much as the family is the sphere where the virtues of womanhood have their chief scope, there is no reason why woman any more than man should be dead to all the interests of the world at large. From the experience of European countries it is evident that there is almost an unlimited scope for the benevolent exercise of the peculiar charm and grace with which feminine nature is endowed. What women do in the Western countries as teachers, nurses, and generally as ministering angels to the poor and suffering, through a hundred means and organizations, that the Indian women too can do. As the civilization of our country breaks away from its old moorings and proceeds along Western lines, the Hindu woman will cease to be confined, in her interests as well as movements, within the walls of the home, but will live outside as well as within the house. Imagine what influence the joint family system has on the position of women. It is the feelings and ties that this system generates that procure to the woman some male guardian in all her conditions and stages of life. But if this joint family system declines—which it must as a result of non-agricultural occupations becoming more common—she will have to depend on herself and lose her extraneous support to the increasing extent. She will of necessity learn self-reliance and will be driven to support herself. In proportion as this happens she will lose her domesticity. Towards the same result will tend the influence of Western training which is opposed to the seclusion of woman, so that we may predict a serious and radical change in her future position.

HINDU WOMEN SHOULD BE AWAKENED TO THE WIDER INTEREST OF THEIR COUNTRY

I entirely agree with Mrs. Benson, the lady to whose sympathy and active interest in our social questions we are so deeply indebted, in her opinion that the Indian as well as English women want to be "awakened to an intelligent interest in the social problems concerning them and their children, and to the wider interests of their country." This is a high ideal, and in order that the Hindu woman may perform the part which it should assign to her, she should be armed with the necessary education. How do you expect ignorant mothers to know their duties to their children, realize their awful responsibility not only for the good breeding of their children, but also, through their children for the well-being of the country at large, and to perform these duties satisfactorily? Recently, a medical authority pointed out that because Indian mothers do not know how to feed their infants, a little more than one-half of all the infants born survive to enter on a second year of life. Herself miserably ill-fed and hurried into the solemn responsibilities of maternity while yet a child, the mother had not to feed her baby the food which nature provides in her; and resorting without knowledge to methods of artificial feeding, she kills the child out of her very tenderness! How in a hundred other ways the ignorance of the child-mother renders her unfit to discharge her solemn duties and to bring up children morally and physically healthy, you are all as aware as myself. Outside the home, there are a hundred ways in which an educated woman can serve her country. The great work of the education of her sex will alone occupy thousands, and what can be more honourable or patriotic than the work of emancipating them from their condition of ignorance which attenuates their faculties and dims their charm? As nurses and physicians, and as inspirers, if not leaders, of every movement aiming at the increase of human happiness or the alleviation of human suffering, they can most worthily fulfil their nature. The ignorance and degradation to which women are subjected by the tyranny of man involve an incalculable waste of beneficent human force which God could not have intended to be so wasted.

WOMEN SHOULD RECEIVE THE HIGHEST AND MOST LIBERAL EDUCATION POSSIBLE

In order that woman may rise to the full sublimity of her nature, it is obviously absurd to train her in an elementary and in a thoroughly inefficient and milk-and-water system of education, which is all that we have in our country and which many people think is quite enough. My own opinion is that their education should be as high, as scientific and as invigorating as the education of men. We recently heard of a high authority saying that female education should proceed in this country on conservative national lines. What these conservative national lines are, it is difficult to say. But it is obvious that in this great question—as in most others—regard should be had more to the requirements of the future than to the facts of the past. You do not expect the educated Hindus of the future to be the same as his educator ancestor of the medieval times was. As the India of the twentieth century will not be the same as the India of Asoka's or Vikramaditya's time, and as the social conditions and the responsibilities of the citizen will differ from those which were known in the times past, so the training and culture of our future generations will have to differ from those of our ancestors. The educated Hindu woman, any more than the educated Hindu man, cannot possibly adhere to the so-called conservative national lines. The calls on her energy, her sense of duty, and her social virtues will necessarily differ and her education should be liberal and invigorating enough to enable her to meet the changed conditions. Nor is the stress which timid people lay on national continuity so necessary. There is no fear, in these days, of Robespierres of social revolution. There can be no sanguinary convulsions or forcible sweeping away of old institutions such as characterised social transitions in times past. Persuasion and not force is the instrument of change, and though entirely new ideals and thoughts and convictions may come to prevail, the actual transition must be the slow process of peaceful persuasion by example as well as by precept. This transition may be quicker or slower according to the besetting conditions, but it can be no other than peaceful.

THE PARAMOUNT OBJECT TO DEVELOP SOCIAL QUALITIES

Let me go back to my central idea which I want you to keep before your mind while you listen to me, the idea, that is, that social efficiency or social feeling or altruism, as opposed to self-love or egotism, is the true test of the progress of a community. If this standard is to determine the education of Indian women, you will understand how the kind of education advocated in some quarters falls grievously short of the level that has to be reached. I say nothing against the desire—with which I most cordially sympathise—to preserve and not to weaken by a wrong training in schools the peculiar graces of Hindu feminine nature. But I must say that excessive stress on this is apt to become mere cant. These graces, as well as the qualities that are not reckoned graces, are the result, so far as they do not arise from the physical and climatic condition of the country, of the habits and activities of life. A well-born Hindu woman, for instance, will not walk briskly in the street, will not laugh or talk aloud, and will not show off her dress or ornaments. These qualities of modesty impart to our women a peculiar charm. But it is quite possible that altered conditions of life may modify these and other peculiarities, as a similar modification is already taking place in the case of our educated men. The modesty which marked the bearing and demeanour of the late Sir T. Muthusamy Iyer and for which he used to get a good deal of praise, is not the most prominent trait in the character of the younger generation, and in the other attributes too which used to be associated with Hindu character, a quiet and perceptible change is taking place; and for that reason we do not mean to demand a change in the education system and a reversion to the system which trained the mind and formed the character of our ancestors. Similarly, the education of our daughters should not be determined by these comparatively subordinate considerations. The paramount object is to develop social qualities, and whatever education will conduce to this end, that on the whole should be accepted as the best education. *Ramayanam, Mahabharatam* and *Srimad Bhagavatam* afford excellent training in a way, but they cannot be the mental nourishment which God and Nature have provided for the human race for all time and under all conditions. Fancy the education of the Teutonic race being placed altogether on the basis of the New Testament or the History of the Saints!

PATRIOTISM AS A PHASE OF SOCIAL FEELING

I have said that 'social efficiency' is the test of progress and that the community that has not developed a sufficient measure of altruism, social feeling or a preference of the common weal over selfish desires, lacks the vitality essential to sustain its progress. In a word, wherever a sense of national life is absent, there the fatal germs of decay are at work. No other illustration of this principle is wanted more than the history of our own race. Another illustration is furnished by the downfall of the Roman Empire—an empire whose rise and fall seem to be an endless reservoir from which illustrations for principles of social progress are drawn. The Roman Empire fell to pieces, says the author of *National Life and Character*, "not because its administrators were always inefficient, or its armies weak, or its finances and mechanical resources inferior to those of the nations which overpowered it, but because there was really no sense of national life in the community". The author adds: "Unless the general feeling in a people is to regard individual existence and fortunes as of no practical account in comparison with the existence and self-respect of the body politic, the disintegrating forces of time will always be stronger in the long run than any given organization." Not that there was no organisation which demanded and received the homage of the Hindus; but this organization was not the state or the community as a whole; but it was the caste; and the caste feeling together with the system of village communities confined the sympathy and activity of the people within extremely narrow limits. They never allowed a national feeling to grow. In fact, the very conception of a Nation, a State, a Commonwealth, was wanting.

EXAMPLE OF INDIVIDUALS

Thus, according as such our social institutions and customs as hinder the growth of what I have called (borrowing the expression from Mr. Benjamin Kidd—the author of *Social Evolution*), 'Social Efficiency'—in other words a spirit of altruism, social feeling, or a sense of national life, are modified or adapted, according as an equality of footing is made secure to all classes in the competition for life, according as the women of the country are educated and enjoy freedom of thought and movement, and according as the people are permeated with this sense of national life, social progress would be made under favourable conditions. But the ground may be cleared, the conditions may be favourable, the fulcrum and the lever may be sound and in their proper place, yet the momentum to lift the lever up may be wanting. And this momentum must come from the example of individuals—individuals such as moulded its destiny. Statesmen, poets, men of science, inventors of mechanical contrivances—all these no doubt contribute to progress, but they can help progress and turn its direction in its advance, but cannot impart the initial moving force, which comes from those great men who by the power of their lofty character and sublime deeds and the burning enthusiasm they impart to masses of men, sweep away abuse and falsehood, stamp out superstitions, open new paths and establish fresh ideals for the elevation and advancement of the human race.

But this initial moving force may come from humble individuals and operate within a limited sphere as well as from those rare geniuses or heroes whose spirit sweeps over a whole country or continent. As Mr. John Morley says, "what we see every day with increasing clearness is that not only the well-being of the many, but the chances of exceptional genius, moral or intellectual, in the gifted few, are highest in a society where the average interest, curiosity, capacity, are all highest." The humblest individual can, therefore, come to the help of the genius and can contribute to the gradual raising of the average standard of national sense in the community. The humblest of us can by diligently using our own minds and diligently seeking to extend our own opportunities to others, help to swell the common tide, on the force and the set of whose currents depends the prosperous voyaging of humanity.

THE STATE AND THE CHURCH

Two powerful agencies that have done a great deal to advance social well-being in other countries are not available to our cause in this country, namely the State and the Church. Here the State represents an alien power, which is not well-informed on Hindu social questions and which lacks that propelling force which the wielders of that power would come under if they were of the people, and if they shared directly in the consequences of our social evils and in the adverse feeling and sense of incongruity they create. Where the ruling power is in the hands of our countrymen such as it is in native principalities, you see how it has been possible to move in the direction of reform; and if only the British rulers of India would realize their responsibilities as Hindu statesmen do, and if they are less timid in facing orthodox opposition, a great accession of strength would accrue to forces of reform. In regard to the church also, we are at a great disadvantage. There is nothing amongst us corresponding to the great and powerful institution called the Church in Christian countries. Our forefathers never thought of giving to their religion the strength of an organised institution and I must say that the Hindu religion, in its present degradation and weakness, has paid a frightful penalty for this neglect. Our Mathadhipaties and priests are themselves corrupt and sunk in ignorance and superstition. If anything, they constitute a force hostile to rational and healthy reform. Fancy the great Sankarachari Swami of Sringeri, disregarding the secession of disciples from whom he derives his temporal affluence and spiritual status, placing himself at the head of the party of reform and while denouncing the evils grossly revolting to humanity and common sense, openly advocating the changes that a true insight into the present and future needs of the country and a genuine and enlightened patriotism demand; how easily, then, will the devoted band of reformers crush opposition and win victories! But this is not to be. Cannot the reformers instal Swami Vivekananda or some spiritual hero like him into a reformed Sankarachari as there was a second Pope for some time in Europe!

—*G. Subramania Iyer*

5

Traditions and Social Reform

To the reformers I will point out, I am greater reformer than anyone of them. They want to reform only little bits. I want root and branch reform. Where we differ is exactly in the method. Their's is the method of destruction, mine is that of construction. I do not believe in reform; I believe in growth. I do not dare to put myself in the position of God and dictate unto our society: "This way you shall move and not that way." I simply want to do my humble work, like the squirrel in the case of the building of Rama's bridge which was quite content to put on the bridge his little quota of sand dust. This is my position. This wonderful national machine has worked through ages; this wonderful river of national life is flowing before us. Who knows and dares say whether it is good and how it shall move? Thousands of circumstances are crowding around it, giving it a special impulse, making it dull at times and quicker at others. Who dares command its motion? Ours is only to work, as the Gita says and stand by contented. Feed it with the fuel it wants, but the growth is its own; none can dictate its growth to it. Evils there are plentiful in our society. So are there evils in every other society too. Here the earth is soaked sometimes with widow's tears; there in the West the air is poisoned with the breath of the sobs of the unmarried. Here poverty is the great bane of life; there the life-weariness of luxury is the great bane that is upon the race. Here men want to commit suicide because they have nothing to eat. Evil is everywhere, like rheumatism. Drive it from the foot, it goes to the head, drive it from there, it goes somewhere else. It is a question chasing it from place to place; that is all, Aye, children, to remedy evil in true way. Our philosophy teaches that evil and good are eternally conjoined, the obverse and the reverse of the same medal. Have one, you have to get the other: make one billow in the ocean, it must be at the cost of the same hollow somewhere. Nay, all life is evil No breath can be created without killing someone else, not a morsel of food can be eaten without depriving somebody of it. This is the law. This is philosophy. Therefore, the only thing we can do is to understand that all this work against evil is more subjective than objective. The work against evil is more educational than actual, however big men may talk. Aye, this is the first idea to be realised with respect to work against evil and this ought to make us calmer, this ought to take fanaticism out of our blood; and then the history of the world teaches us that wherever there have been fanatical reforms the only result was that they defeated their own ends. No greater upheaval for the establishment of right and liberty can be imagined than the war for the abolition of slavery in America. You all know about it. And what has been its result? The slaves are a hundred times worse today than they were before the abolition. Before the abolition these poor Negroes were the property of somebody, and, as properties, they had to be looked after so that they might not deteriorate. Today they are the property of nobody. Their lives are of no value: they are burnt alive on mere pretences. They are shot down; no law for their murderers, for they are niggars, they are not human beings, they are not even animals, and that is the effect of such a violent taking away of evil by law or by fanaticism. Such is the testimony of history against every fanatical movement, even for doing good. I have seen that. My own experience taught me that. Therefore, I cannot join any one of these condemning societies. Why condemn? There are evils in every society; everybody knows it: every child of today knows it: he can stand upon a platform and give us a harangue on the evils in Hindu society. Every uneducated foreigner who comes in globe-trotting, takes a vanishing railway view of India and lectures most learnedly on the awful evils in India. We admit it. Everybody can show what evil is, but he is the friend of mankind who finds a way out of the difficulty. Like the drowning boy who cried to the philosopher, when the philosopher was lecturing him: "Take me out of the water first," so our people cry: "We have had lectures enough, societies enough, papers enough, where is the man who lends us a hand to drag us out? Where is the man who loves us really? Where is the man that has sympathy with us?" Aye, that man is wanted. That is where I differ entirely from these reform movements. A hundred years they have been here. What good has been done excepting the creation of a most vituperative, a most condemnatory literature? Would to God it was not there! They have criticised, condemned, abused the orthodox until the orthodox have caught their tone and paid them in their own and the result is the creation of a literature in every vernacular which is the shame of the race, the shame of the country. Is this reform? Is this leading the nation to glory? Whose fault is this?

There is then, another great consideration. Here, in India, we have always been governed by kings; kings have made all our laws: now the kings are gone and there is none left to take their place. The government dares not; it has to fashion its ways according to the growth of public opinion. It takes time, quite a long time, to make a healthy, strong, public opinion which will solve its own problems and in the interim we shall have to wait. The whole problem of social reform, therefore, resolves itself into this: Where are those who want reform? Make them first. Where are the people? The tyranny of the minority is the worst tyranny that the world ever sees. A few men who think that certain things are evil will not make a nation move. Why does not the nation move? First educate the nation, create your legislative body and then the law will be forthcoming. First create the power, the sanction from which the law will spring. The kings are gone; where is the new sanction, the new power of the people? Bring it up. Therefore, even for social reform, the first duty is to educate the people and you have to wait till that time comes. Most of the reforms that have been agitated for during the last century have been ornamental. Everyone of these reforms only touches the first two castes, and no other. The question of widow marriage would not touch 70 per cent of the Indian women and all such questions only reach the higher classes of Indian people who are educated, mark you at the expense of the masses. Every effort of these classes has been spent in cleaning their own houses, making themselves nice and looking pretty before foreigners. That is no reformation. You must go down to the basis of the things, to the very roots. That is what I call radical reformation. Put the fire there and let it burn upwards and make an Indian nation. And the problem is not easy. It is a big and a vast problem before us. Be not in a hurry, and, mark my words, this problem has been known these several hundred years.

Today it is the fashion to talk of Buddhism and Buddhistic agnosticism, especially in the South. Little do they dream that this degradation which we have in our hands today has been left by Buddhism. This is the legacy which Buddhism left in our hands. You read in books written by men who had never studied the rise and fall of Buddhism that the spread of Buddhism was owing to the wonderful ethics and the wonderful personality of Gautama Buddha. I have every respect and veneration for Lord Buddha, but mark my words, the spread of Buddhism was less owing to the personality of the great preacher and more owing to the temples that were built, the idols that were erected and gorgeous ceremonies that were put before the nation. Thus Buddhism progressed. The little fireplace in the houses in which were poured the libations was not strong enough to hold its own against these gorgeous temples and ceremonies and later, on the whole, things degenerated. It became a mass of filth of which I cannot speak before this audience but those who want to know it may look into those big temples, full of sculptures, in Southern India and this is all the inheritance we have from the Buddhists. Then arose the great reformer, Sankaracharya and his followers and all these hundreds of years, since his rising to the present day, has been the slow bringing back of the Indian masses to the pristine purity of the Vedantic religion. These reformers knew well the evils which existed, yet they did not condemn. They did not say: "All that you have is wrong and you must throw it out." It could never be so. Today I read that my friend, Dr. Barrows, says that in 300 years Christianity overthrew the Roman and Greek religious influences. That is not the word of a man who has seen Europe, and Greece, and Rome. The influence of Roman and Greek religions is all there, even in Protestant countries, only with changed names, old gods coming in a new fashion. They change their names; the goddesses become Marys and the gods become saints and the ceremonials become new; even the old title of Pontifex Maximus is there. So these wholesale changes cannot be. They are not so easy and Sankaracharya knew it. So did Ramanuja. These changes cannot be. The only other way left to them was slowly to bring up the masses to the highest ideal of the existing religion. If they had sought to apply the other method they would have been hypocrites; for the very fundamental doctrine of their religion is evolution, the soul going up towards the highest goal, thorugh all these stages and phases; and all these stages and phases therefore are necessary and helpful and who dares condemn them?

It has become a trite saying and every man swallows it at the present time without questioning that idolatry is wrong. Aye, I once thought so and for the penalty of that I had to learn my lesson sitting at the feet of a man who got his everything from idols; I allude to Ramakrishna Parmahamsa. Hindus, if such Ramakrishna Paramahamsas are produced by idol worship, what will you have—the reformer's creed or any number of idols? I want an answer. Take a thousand idols more if you can. Produce Ramakrishna Paramahamsas through idol worship. God speed you! Produce such noble creatures by any means you have. And idolatry is condemned. Why? Nobody knows except that some hundreds of years ago some man of Jewish blood happened to condemn it, that is, he happened to condemn everybody else's idols except his own. If God is represented in any beautiful form or any symbolic form, said the Jew, it was awfully bad: it was sin. But if He was represented in the form of a chest, with two angels sitting on each side, and a cloud hanging over it, it was the Holy of Holies. If God comes in the form of a dove, it is the Holi of Holies, but if He comes in the form of a cow it is heathen superstition; condemn it. This is how the world goes. That is why the poet says: "What fools we mortals are!" That is why it is difficult to look through each other's eyes and that is the bane of humanity. That is the basis of hatred and jealousy, of quarrel and of fight.

Boys, moustached babies, who never went out of Madras, standing up and wanting to dictate laws to three hundred millions of people with thousands of traditions at their back! Are you not ashamed? Stand back from such blasphemy and learn first your lessons! Irreverent boys, simply because you can scrawl a few lines upon a paper and get some fool to publish it for you, you think you are the educators of the world, you think you are the public opinion of India! Is it so? Therefore, this I have to tell the social reformers of Madras, that I have the greatest respect and love for them. I love them for their great hearts and their love for their country, for the poor, for the oppressed. But what I would tell them with a brother's love is that their method is not right. It has been tried these hundred years and has failed. Let us try some new method and that is all. Did India want reformers ever? Do you read the history of India? Who was Ramanuja? Who was Sankara? Who was Nanak? Who was Chaitanya? Who was Kabir? Who was Dadu? Who were all these great preachers, one following the other, a galaxy of stars of the first magnitude? Did not he try all his life to admit even the Pariah to his community? Did he not try to admit even Mahomedans to his own fold? Did not Nanak confer with Hindus and Mahomedans and try to bring about a new state of things? They all tried and their work is going on. The difference is this. They had not the fanfaronade of the reformers of today; they had not the curses on their lips, the modern reformers have. Their lips pronounced only blessings. They never condemned. They said unto the people that the race must always grow. They looked back and they said: "O Hindus! What you have done is good, but my brother, let us do better." They did not say: "You have been wicked, now let us be good." They said: 'You have been good, but let us now be better.' That makes a whole world of difference. We must grow according to our natural growth. Vain it is to attempt the lines of action foreign societies have engrafted upon us. Impossible it is. Glory unto God that it is impossible, that we cannot be twisted and tortured into the shape of other nations. I do not condemn the institutions of other races; they are good for them, but not for us. What is meat for them may be poison for us. This is the first lesson to learn. With other sciences, other institutions and other traditions behind them, they have got their present systems. We with our traditions, with thousands years of karma behind us, naturally, we can only follow our own bent, run in our own grooves, and that we shall have to do.

—***Vivekananda***

6

Revival and Reform*

The reports of this year's work which have been received from nearly sixty associations, large and small, and which have been summarised up-to-date, complain that their work for the year has not been as successful as in the previous two years. And yet to those who can read between the lines, there are manifest signs which show that the work has been as earnestly pursued as ever. To instance a few cases: Under the head of female education, the Bethuen College of Calcutta, the Girls' High Schools at Poona and Ahmedabad, the Kanya Maha Vidyalaya at Jullundar, the Sing Sabha's Girls' School at Lahore, the Maharani's Girls School at Mysore, the Mahakali Pathshala organised by the Mataji Tapeswini Bai, a Maratha lady in Calcutta, and the Sylhet and Mymensingh Unions, all show a record of progress each in its own line of development. There is not a single reform association of any position in the country which has not lent its best efforts to raise the standard and popularise the system of female education. Many associations, sabhas and samajas maintain independent girls' schools of their own, and others have their home classes more or less actively employed in carrying on the work of the schools to educate the more advanced students. Others again have their lectures for ladies, and ladies' associations, such as at Ahmedabad, Bombay and Madras, started and maintained by the ladies themselves. Though the condition of female education is still very backward,

* Address at the Eleventh Social Conference.

and though the experiments that are now carried on, are on different lines; the signs are clearly visible that throughout India, the national awakening to the necessity of developing the moral and intellectual capacities and aptitudes of our sisters has found universal recognition.

As regards another sign of this liberal movement which seeks to do equal justice to the rights of the female as of the male sex, it is satisfactory to note that though the number of widow marriages this year has been smaller than that of the previous years, still all the provinces have taken part in the movement. The reports show that in all 25 widow-marriages were celebrated throughout India during the past year: Punjab 10, Bombay 6, Central Provinces 4, Madras 3, North-West Provinces and Bengal 1 each. The widow-marriages in the Central Provinces have been all brought about directly or indirectly by the persistent efforts of Rao Bahadur Kolhatkar, the president of this gathering. For the re-marriages in Punjab the credit is due to Dewan Santaram and his friends of the Widow Marriage Association there; and in regard to Bombay the same honour is due to Mr. Bhagwandas, the son of the late Madhavdas Raghunathdas in whose house two re-marriages were celebrated. The credit of the widow-marriages celebrated in Madras is due to Rao Bahadur Viresalingam Pantulu. There was thus not a single province in which friends of the cause did not manifest their active interest in it, which remark does not equally hold good for the previous years. The paucity in the total number was partly due to the calamities of the year being a Sinhast year. Another good sign of the times which may be noted is the fact that some of the castes, in which no re-marriages had been celebrated before, joined in the movement for the first time this year. It was also reported in the papers that the Maharajah of Nabha, in the Punjab, had exercised his influence in favour of bettering the condition of Hindu widows, and inducing influential Hindu gentlemen to support the widow-marriage movement. In the Chandraseniya Kayasth Prabhu caste of Bombay, a similar pronouncement was made by the leaders of the community in favour of re-marriage, and it was resolved to bring up the subject before the next Kayasth Prabhu Conference to be held at Baroda. Another satisfactory indication of the times is furnished by the fact reported from Gujerat, that the Audich Brahmin community at Damun made a similar pronouncement in favour of widow marriage in their caste. The Widows' Homes at Baranagar and Poona have also been successfully maintained notwithstanding pecuniary difficulties, and the number of widows attending the homes has slightly increased, thanks to the efforts of Mr. Sasipada Banerjee of Baranagar and Professor Karve of Poona.

As regards foreign travel, the year has had a good record to show. Several Saraswata gentlemen have returned from England, and though the Guru of the caste has refused admission to them, the reform party at Mangalore and in North Canara have succeeded is showing openly their sympathy with these men. Raja Nowlojee Rao Gujar, a scion of the princely house of Nagpur, returned from England, and was well received, and Messrs. Booti and Alonikar of Nagpur, Mr. Krishna Rao Bholanath of Amedabad, Professor Gokhale of Poona and Mr. Ketkar of Gwalior, have similarly, though not formally, been admitted by some of their caste people, and the opposition has not ventured to place any difficulties in their way. Two Bhatia gentlemen, for the first time in that community, left for England with the full support of their caste. In the Punjab, several young men in the Biradari castes, who had been to England, were admitted back without any opposition. Two young men from the Aurorbans caste went to England last year. The liberal section of the Cashmere Pundits' Sabha is strongly in favour of foreign travel. These instances show that slowly but surely in all parts of the country, the prejudice against foreign travel is on the wane, and that before long the orthodox community or the communities will learn to tolerate these departures from custom as an inevitable change.

In regard to the question of inter-marriage, the Bengal papers announced an inter-marriage in high life between two sub-divisions of the Kayastha community, which hitherto kept aloof. In the Punjab, there was a betrothal between two sub-castes of the Serin community. This was the first instance of an inter-marriage between these two sub-divisions. Many of the widow-marriages have also been instances of inter-marriage and for the first time last year two instances of inter-marriage between Madrasee and Bengalee gentlemen and ladies occurred.

The North-West Provinces reports show instances of similar fusion between sub-divisions of the Kayastha caste there, and in Gujerat there is a similar tendency manifest in some of the castes to amalgamate together.

As regards the postponement of infant marriages, the reports from all provinces show a decided tendency to increase the limits of marriageable ages of girls and boys. In the Punjab, the Aurorbans Sabha has passed a resolution that no girl belonging to the caste should be given in marriage unless she has completed her twelfth year. In the Madras Presidency, the opinion is gaining ground that the time has now come for applying to Government for legislation on the subject to fix at least the marriageable age for boys, if not for girls, and lay down a maximum limit of age for old persons who marry young girls, on the plan adopted by the Mysore Government. The Madras Provincial Social Conference and the Godavari District Conference expressly passed resolutions on this subject. The Hindu Social Reform Association at Madras has also appointed a committee to draw up a memorial with the same object. The Hon'ble Mr. Jambulingam Mudaliar is reported to be contemplating the introduction of a Bill into the local council there on this subject. There have also been individual instances in some parts of the country where grown-up girls have been married without experiencing any very bitter opposition from the caste.

Nearly all the Associations have been pledged to support the Purity movement, including the anti-nautch and temperance agitation and the work done during the year shows considerable progress under both these heads.

To turn next to another question in which the conference has been interesting itself for the past few years—the admission of converts from other faiths—some progress has been made during the year. The Shuddhi Sabha admitted nearly 200 Mahomedan converts this year. Hitherto the movement for the re-admission of converts to other faiths back into the Hindu society was chiefly confined to the Punjab. This year, however, there have been also instances of such conversions in Bengal, the North-West Provinces, and far away in Burmah, one of them being a convert Christian and the others Mahomedans. The Shuddhi Sabha of Lahore and the Arya Samaj there have deservedly taken the lead in this movement, and it will be a source of great strength to them that the movement has been taken up in the other provinces also. The Central Provinces reports for the year show that Mr. Shankar Shastri of Jubbulpore has published a pamphlet on the subject, and it is a strange coincidence that Professor Rajaram Shastri Bhagwat of Bombay read this year a paper before the branch of Asiatic Society there, showing how in old times the non-Aryan races were brought within the fold of the Aryan system.

As regards the reduction of extravagent expenses in marriage, a very important movement was started in Calcutta under the auspices of leading Kayastha gentlemen, including such men as Sir Romesh Chandra Mittra and the Hon'ble Mr. Chander Madhub Ghose, who met at Babu Ramanath Ghose's house; and passed several resolutions which are likely to be attended with good results. Nearly every one of the reports of the North-West Provinces contain details of the manner in which the Kayasthas, the Bhargavas, the Chaturvedis, the Vaishyas, the Jains and other castes have tried to lay down sliding scales of marriage expenditure, curtailing extravagance under many heads, abolishing nautch parties, fireworks, and other useless items. In the Punjab, the Aurorbans have very considerably reduced the extravagance in marriage expenses. On the Bombay side, the Bhatia Mandal and the Dasa Oswal Jains have successfully worked in the same direction. Even in far off Baroda, the Dasa Porwal Bania caste people have been moving in the matter. Following the example of the Rajputra Hitkarni Sabha, many non-Rajput castes in Rajputana and Malwa have laid down rules which are enforced by the same sanctions as those of principal Sabha.

As regards conference work generally, it may be noted that caste conferences are the order of the day in all parts of India. I have, on previous occasions, mentioned the gatherings annually held this week in several large towns in the North-Western Provinces of the Kayastha and the Vaishya community. This year was distinguished by the holding of the first Provincial Social

Conference in Madras, in which presidency also we have had two district conferences, one of the east coast in the Godavari District, and the other on the west coast at Mangalore. New associations are being formed under very favourable auspices in many parts of the country, notably in the Bombay and Madras Districts, to support the work of the conference, and to give effect to its resolutions.

Encouraged by the success which has attended the efforts of the Mysore Government and the Malabar Marriage Law passed in the Madras Council, two Bills of great social importance have been introduced, one in the Imperial Council, to bring under better control religious charities and endowments and another has been introduced in the Madras Council to remove all doubts in and codify the law in regard to what constitutes self-acquired property under the Hindu joint family system. Both these Bills have suggested subjects for discussion at the ensuing conference this year, and it is not, therefore, necessary for me to enlarge upon their importance. There is a third measure before the Viceroy's Council which, though it relates to a particular section of the Mahomedan community, has a wider bearing which interests us all. The Memon section of this community in Bombay were originally Hindu converts and though they embraced Mahomedanism, they retained their old Hindu customs in regard to inheritance and succession and these customs were recognised by our law courts. A majority of that community, however, now desire that in place of the Hindu customs, the Mahomedan Law should govern their succession to the property of deceased persons. The Government of India accordingly intend to pass a sort of a permissive measure, by which a member of this community may retain or abandon the old rules by a formal declaration of his choice, which choice, once made, will be final. The subject bristles with difficulties, but the permissive legislation, if it proves a success in actual operation, will furnish a precedent which may prove a considerable help to those who wish to have more liberal laws of inheritance and succession without change of religion.

Such, gentlemen, is the brief record of the principal social events of the year. Many ardent spirits amongst us will no doubt be very much dissatisfied with the poverty of this record. At the same time, we must bear in mind that hundreds and thousands—nay millions of our countrymen will regard this poor record as very revolutionary and condemn this as one of the unseen causes which has brought about physical and moral catastrophes upon the land by way of punishment for the sins of the reformers. These are two extreme sides of the question, and it is not for me to say to an audience like this on which side the balance of truth may be found. The *Arya Patrika* of the Punjab, which is a recognised organ of the Arya Samaj there, has in its words of advice to the conference expressed its view that we are radically in the wrong in seeking to reform the usages of our society without a change of religion, and it seriously suggests that we should, in the first instance, become members of their Samaj and this conversion will bring it all desired reforms. Many enthusiastic friends of the Brahmo Samaj entertain similar views and give us similar advice. All I can say to these welcome advisers is that they do not fully realise the situation and its difficulties. People have changed their religion and yet retain their social usages unchanged. The native Christians, for instance, especially the Roman Catholic section among them, and many sections of Mahomedans are instances in point. Besides, it has been well observed that even for a change of religion, it is too often necessary that the social surroundings must be liberalised in a way to help people to realise their own responsibilities and to strengthen them in their efforts. Lastly, these well-meaning advisers seem to forget that the work of reform cannot be put off indefinitely till the far more arduous and difficult work of religious conversion is accomplished. It may take centuries before the Arya or Brahmo Samaj establish their claims for general recognition. In the meanwhile what is to become of the social organisation? Slowly but surely, the progress of liberal ideas must be allowed to work its way in reforming our social customs, and the process cannot be stopped even though we may wish it. In the case of our society especially, the usages which at present prevail amongst us are admittedly not those which obtained in the most glorious periods of our history. On most of the points which are included in our programme, our own record of the past shows that there has been a decided change for the worse, and it is surely within the range of practical possibilities for us to hope that we may work our way back to a better state of things without stirring up the rancorous hostilities which religious differences have a tendency to create and foster. There is no earthly reason whatsoever why we should not co-operate with these religious organisations or why they should not rather co-operate with us in this work in which our interests are common; because the majority of our countrymen hold different views about religion from those which commend themselves to these Samajas. I am speaking these words with a full sense of my responsibility, for I am in my humble way a member of one, if not of both the Samajas, and I am a sincere searcher after religious truth in full sympathy with the Arya and Brahmo Samaj movements, and I hope, therefore, that these advisers of ours will take my reply in the same spirit and will not misunderstand me. Schismatic methods of propagation cannot be applied with effect to vast communities which are not within their narrow pale.

On the other side, some of our orthodox friends find fault with us, not because of the particular reforms we have in view, but on account of the methods we follow. While the new religious sects condemn us for being too orthodox, the extreme orthodox section denounce us for being too revolutionary in our methods. According to these last, our efforts should be directed to revive, and not to reform. I have many friends in this camp of extreme orthodoxy and their watchword is that revival, and not reform, should be our motto. They advocate a return to the old ways and appeal to the old authorities and the old sanction. Here also, as in the instance quoted above, people speak without realising the full significance of their own words. When we are asked to revive our institutions and customs, people seem to be very much at sea as to what it is they seem to revive. What particular period of our history is to be taken as the old? Whether the period of the *Vedas,* of the *Smritis* of the *Puranas* or the Mahomedan or modern Hindu times? Our usages have been changed from time to time by a low process of growth and in some cases of decay and corruption; and we cannot stop at a particular period without breaking the continuity of the whole. When my revivalist friend presses his argument upon me, he has to seek recourse in some subterfuge which really furnishes no reply to the question—what shall we revive? Shall we revive the old habits of our people when the most sacred of our caste indulged in all the abominations as we now understand them of animal food and drink which exhausted every section of our country's zoology and botany? The men and the gods of those old days ate and drank forbidden things to excess in a way no revivalist will now venture to recommend. Shall we revive the twelve forms of sons, or eight forms of marriage, which included capture, and recognised mixed and illegitimate intercourse? Shall we revive the Niyoga system of procreating sons on our brother's wives when widowed? Shall we revive the old liberties taken by the Rishis and by the wives of the Rishis with the marital tie? Shall we revive the hecatombs of animals sacrificed from year's end to year's end, and in which human beings were not spared as propitiatory offerings? Shall we revive the *Shakti* worship of the left hand with its indecencies and practical debaucheries? Shall we revive the *Sati* and infanticide customs, or the flinging of living men into the rivers, or over rocks, or hook swinging or the crushing beneath Jagannath car? Shall we revive the internecine wars of the Brahmins and Kshatriyas, or the cruel persecution and degradation of aboriginal population? Shall we revive the custom of many husbands to one wife or of many wives to one husband? Shall we require our Brahmins to cease to be landlords and gentlemen, and turn into beggars and dependants upon the king as in olden times? These instances will suffice to show that the plan of reviving the ancient usages and customs will not work our salvation, and is not practicable. If these usages were good and beneficial, why were they altered by our wise ancestors? If they were bad and injurious, how can any claim be put forward for their restoration after so many ages? Besides, it seems to be forgotten that in a living organism as society is, no revival is possible. The dead and the buried or burnt are dead buried, and burnt once for all, and the dead past cannot, therefore, be revived except by a reformation of the old materials into new organised beings. If revival is impossible, reformation is the only alternative open to sensible people; and now it may be asked what is the principle on which this reformation must be based? People have very hazy ideas on this subject. It seems to many that it is the outward form which has to be changed, and if this change can be made, they think that all the difficulties in our way will vanish. If we change our outward manners and customs, sit in a particular way or walk in a particular fashion, our work according to them is accomplished. I cannot but think that much of the prejudice against the reformers is due to this misunderstanding. It is not the outward form, but the inward form, the thought and the idea which determines the outward form, that has to be changed if real reformation is desired.

Now what have been the inward forms or ideas which have been hastening our decline during the past three thousand years? These ideas may be briefly set forth as isolation, submission to outward force or power more than to the voice of the inward conscience, perception of fictitious differences between man and man due to heredity and birth, passive acquiescence in evil or wrong-doing, and a general indifference to secular well-being, almost bordering upon fatalism. These have been the root ideas of our ancient social system. They have as their natural result led to the existing family arrangements where the woman is entirely subordinated to the man and the lower castes to the higher castes, to the length of depriving men of their natural respect for humanity. All the evils we seek to combat result from the prevalence of these ideas. They are mere corollaries to these axiomatic assumptions. They prevent some of our people from realising what they really are in all conscience, neither better nor worse than their fellows, and that whatever garb men may put on, they are the worse for assuming dignities and powers which do not in fact belong to them. As long as these ideas remain operative on our minds, we may change our outward forms and institutions and be none the better for change. These ideas have produced in the long course of ages their results on our character and we must judge their good or bad quality, as St. Paul, says, by the fruits they have borne. Now that these results have been disastrous, nobody disputes or doubts, and the lesson to be drawn for our guidance in the future from this fact is that the current of these ideas must be changed, and in the place of the old worship we paid to them, we must accustom ourselves and others to worship and revere new ideals. In place of isolation, we must cultivate the spirit of fraternity or elastic expansiveness. At present it is everybody's ambition to pride himself upon being a member of the smallest community that can be conceived, and the smaller the number of those with whom you can dine or marry or associate, the higher is your perfection and purity, the purest person is he who cooks his own food and does not allow the shadow of even his nearest friend to fall upon his cooked food. Every caste and every sect has thus a tendency to split itself into smaller castes and smaller sects in practical life. Even in philosophy and religion, it is a received maxim that knowledge is for the few and that salvation is only possible for the esoteric elect with whom only are the virtues of sanctity and wisdom and that for the rest of mankind they must be left to wander in the wilderness and grovel in superstition, and even vice, with only a colouring of so-called religion to make them respectable. Now all this must be changed. The new mould of thought on this head must be, as stated above, cast on the lines of fraternity, a capacity to expand outwards, and to make more cohesive inwards the bonds of fellowship. Increase the circle of your friends and associates, slowly and cautiously if you will, but the tendency must be towards a general recognition of the essential equality between man and man. It will beget sympathy and power. It will strengthen your own hands, by the sense that you have numbers with you, and not against you, or as you foolishly imagine, below you.

The next idea which lies at the root of our helplessness is the sense that we are always intended to remain children to be subject to outside control, and never to rise to the dignity of self-control by making our conscience and our reason the supreme, if not the sole, guide to our conduct. All past history has been a terrible witness to the havoc committed by this misconception. We are children, no doubt, but the children of God and not of man and the voice of God is the only voice which we are bound to listen. Of course, all of us cannot listen to this voice when we desire it; because from long neglect and dependence upon outside help, we have benumbed this faculty of science in us. With too many of us, a thing is true or false, righteous or sinful, simply because somebody in the past has said that it is so. Duties and obligations are duties and obligations, not because we feel them to be so, but because somebody reputed to be wise has laid it down that they are so. In small matters of manners and courtesies this outside dictation is not without its use. But when we abandon ourselves entirely to this helpless dependence on other wills, it is no wonder that we become helpless as children in all departments of life. Now the new idea which should take up the place of this helplessness and dependence is not the idea of a rebellious overthrow of all authority, but that of freedom responsible to the voice of God in us. Great and wise men in the past, as in the present, have a claim upon our regards, but they must not come between us and our God—the Divine principle enthroned in the heart of every one of us high or low. It is this sense of self-respect, or rather respect for the God in us, which has to be cultivated. It is a very tender plant which takes years and years to make it grow. But there is the capacity and the power, and we owe it as a duty to ourselves to undertake the task. Revere all human authority, pay your respects to all prophets and all revelations, but never let this reverence and respect come in the way of the dictates of conscience, the Divine command in us.

Similarly there is no doubt that man differs from man in natural capacities and aptitudes and that heredity and birth are factors of considerable importance in our development. But it is at the same time true that they are not the only factors that determine the whole course of our life for good or for evil, under a law of necessity. Heredity and birth explain many things, but this law of *Karma* does not explain all things! What is worse, it does not explain the mystery that makes man and woman what they really are, the reflection and the image of God. Our passions and our feelings, our pride and our ambition, lend strength to these agencies, and with their help the law of *Karma* completes our conquest, and in too many cases enforces our surrender. The new idea that should come in here is that this law of *Karma* can be controlled and set back by a properly trained will, when it is made subservient to a higher will than ours. This we see in our everyday life and necessity or the fates are, as our own texts tell us, faint obstacles in the way of our advancement, if we devote ourselves to the law of duty. I admit that this misconception is very hard to remove, perhaps the hardest of the old ideas. But removed it must be, if not in this life or generation, in many lives and generations, if we are ever to rise to our full stature.

The fourth old form or idea to which I will allude here is our acquiescence in wrong or evil-doing as an inevitable condition of human life, about which we need not be very particular. All human life is a vanity and a dream and we are not much concerned with it. This view of life is in fact atheism in its worst form. No man or woman really ceases to be animal who does not perceive or realise that wrong or evil-doing, impurity and vice, crime and misery and sin of all kinds is really our animal existence prolonged. It is the beast in us which blinds us to impurity and vice and makes them even attractive. There must be nautches in our temples, say our priests, because even the gods cannot do without these impure fairies. This is only a typical instance of our acquiescence in impurity. There must be drunkenness in the world, there must be poverty and wretchedness and tyranny, there must be fraud and force, there must be thieves and the law to punish them. No doubt these are facts, and there is no use of denying their existence, but in the name of all that is sacred and true, do not acquiesce in them, do not hug these evils to your bosom, and cherish them. Their contact is poisonous, not the less deadly because it does not kill, but it corrupts men. A healthy sense of the true dignity of our nature, and of man's high destiny, is the best corrective and antidote to this poison. I think I have said more than enough to suggest to your reflecting minds what it is that we have to reform. All admit that we have been deformed. We have lost our stature, we are bent in a hundred places, our eyes lust after forbidden things, our ears desire to hear scandals about our neighbours, our tongues lust to taste forbidden fruit, our hands itch for another man's property, our bowels are deranged with indigestible food. We cannot walk on our feet, but require stilts or crutcher. This is our present social policy, and now we want this deformity to be removed; and the only way to remove it is to place ourselves under the discipline of better ideas and forms such as those I have briefly touched above. Now this is the work of the reformer. Reforms in the matter of infant marriage and enforced widowhood, in the matter of temperance and purity, intermarriarge between castes, the elevation of the low castes, and the readmission of converts, and the regulation of our endowments and charities, are reforms only so far and no further, as they check the influence of the old ideas and promote the growth of the new tendencies. The Reformer has to infuse in himself the light and warmth of nature, and he can only do it by purifying and improving himself and his surroundings. He must have his family, village, tribe, and nation recast in other and new moulds, and that is the reason why Social Reform becomes our obligatory duty, and not a mere pastime which might be given up at pleasure. Revival is, as I have said, impossible; as impossible as mass-conversion into other faiths. But even if it were possible, its only use to us would be if the reforms elevated us and our surroundings, if they made us stronger, braver, truer men with all our faculties of endurance and work developed, with all our sympathies fully awakened and refined, and if with our heads and hearts acting in union with a purified and holy will, they made us feel the dignity of our being and the high destiny of our existence, taught us to love all, work with all, and feel for all. This is the reformer's true work, and this in my opinion is the reason why the conference meets from year to year, and sounds the harmonies in every ear which can listen to them with advantage.

—M.G. Ranade

7

A Plea for Judicial Reform*

Q. Have you observed the operation of the Judicial System in India?

A. I have long turned my attention towards the subject, and possess a general acquaintance with the operation of that system more particularly from personal experience in the Bengal Presidency, where I resided.

Q. Do you think that the system hitherto acted upon is calculated to secure justice?

A. The judicial system established in 1793, by Lord Cornwallis, was certainly well adapted to the situation of the country, and to the character of the people as well as of the government, had there been a sufficient number of qualified judges to discharge the judicial office, under a proper code of laws.

Q. Explain particularly in what points you consider the practical operation of the system defective.

A. In the want of sufficient number of judges and magistrates, in the want of adequate qualification in many of them to discharge the duty in foreign languages, and in the want of proper code of laws, by which they might be easily guided.

---

* The following is a report of Raja Rammohun Roy's evidence before the Select Committee of the House of Commons on the affairs of the East India Company.

Q. Can you explain what evils result from the want of a greater number of judges?

A. First, the courts being necessarily few in number in comparison to the vast territories under the British rule, many of the inhabitants are situated at so great a distance from them that the poorer classes are, in general, unable to go and seek redress for any injury, particularly those who may be oppressed by their wealthier neighbours, possessing great local influence. Secondly, the business of the courts is so heavy that causes often accumulate to such an extent that many are necessarily pending some years before they can be decided, an evil which is aggravated by subsequent appeals from one court to another, attended with further delay and increased expense. By this state of things wrong-doers are encouraged, and the innocent and oppressed in the same proportion discouraged, and often reduced to despair. Thirdly, such a mass of business transacted in foreign languages being too much for any one individual, even the ablest and best intentioned judge may be disheartened at seeing before him a file of causes which he can hardly hope to overtake; and he may therefore be thus induced to transfer a great part of the business to his native officers, who are not responsible and who are so meanly paid for their services and they may be expected to consult their own interests.

Q. Will you inform us what evils arise from the want of due qualification in the judges?

A. It is but justice to state that many of the judicial officers of the Company are men of the highest talents, as well as of strict integrity, and earnestly intent on doing justice. However, not being familiar with the laws of the people over whom they are called to administer justice by these laws, and the written-proceedings of the court, answers, replies, rejoinders, evidence taken, and documents produced, being all conducted in a language which is foreign to them, they must either rely greatly on the interpretation of their native officers, or be guided by their own surmises or conjectures. In one case, the cause will be decided by those who in point of rank and pay are meanly situated, and who are not responsible to the government or public for the accuracy of the decision founded on conjecture and must be very liable to error. Still, I am happy to observe that there are some judicial officers, though very few in number, whose judgement and knowledge of the native languages are such that in cases which do not involve much intricacy and legal subtlety, they are able to form a correct decision, independent of the natives around them.

Q. Can you point out what obstructions to the administration of justice are produced by the want of a better code of laws?

A. The regulations published from year to year by the local government since 1793, which serve as instructions to the courts, are so voluminous, complicated, and many instances, either too concise or too exuberant, that they are generally considered not a clear and easy guide; and the Hindu and Mohammedan laws administered in conjunction with the above regulations, being spread over a great number of different books of various and sometimes doubtful authority, the judges, as to law points, depend entirely on the interpretations of their native lawyers, whose conflicting legal opinions have introduced great perplexity into the administration of justice.

Q. Is there any other impediment to the fair administration of justice besides those you have stated?

A. The first obstacle to the administration of justice is that its administrators and the persons among whom it is administered have no common language. Secondly, that owing partly to this cause and also in a great measure to the difference of manners, etc., the communication between these two parties is very limited; in consequence of which the judges can, with the utmost difficulty, acquire an adequate knowledge of the real nature of the grievances of the persons seeking redress, or of the real character and validity of the evidence by which their claims are supported or opposed. Thirdly, that there is not the same relation between the native pleaders and the judge as between the British bar and the bench. Fourthly, the want of publicity owing to the absence of reports and of a public press, to take notice of the proceedings of the courts in the interior; consequently there is no superintendence of public opinion to watch whether the judges attend their courts once a day or once a week, or whether they attend to business six hours or one hour a day, or their mode of treating the parties, the witnesses, the native pleaders or law officers, and others attending the Courts—as well as the principles on which they conduct their proceedings and regulate their decisions; or whether in fact they investigate and decide the causes themselves, or leave the judicial business to their native officers and dependants. (In pointing out the importance of the fullest publicity being afforded to judicial proceedings by means of the press, I have no reference to the question of a free press, for the discussion of local politics, a point on which I do not mean to touch). Fifthly, the great prevalence of perjury, arising partly from the frequency with which oaths are administered in the courts, having taken from them the awe with which they were formerly regarded, partly from the judges being often unable to detect impositions in a foreign language, and to discriminate nicely the value of evidence amongst a people with whom they have in general so little communication; and partly from the evidence being frequently taken; not by the judge himself but by his native officers (*Omlah*), whose goodwill is often secured at hand by both parties, so that they may not endeavour to detect their false evidence by a strict examination. Under these circumstances the practice of perjury has grown so prevalent that the facts sworn to by the different parties in a suit are generally directly opposed to each other so that it has become almost impossible to ascertain the truth from their contradictory evidence. Sixthly, that the prevalence of perjury has again introduced the practice of forgery to such an extent as to render the administration of justice still more intricate and perplexing. Seventhly, the want of due publicity being given to the regulations which stand at present in a place of a code of laws. From their being very voluminous and expensive, the community generally have not the means of purchasing them; nor have they a sufficient opportunity of consulting or copying them in the judicial and revenue offices where they are kept. As these are usually at a distance from the populous parts of the town, only professional persons or parties engaged in suits or official business are in the habit of attending these offices. Eighthly and lastly, holding the proceedings in a language foreign to the judges, as well as to the parties and to the witnesses.

Q. In what language are the proceedings of the courts conducted?

A. They are generally conducted in Persian, in imitation of the former Mohammedan rulers, of which this was the court language.

Q. Are the judges, the parties, and the witnesses sufficiently well acquainted with that language to understand the proceedings readily?

A. I have already observed that it is foreign to all these parties. Some of the judges, and a very few among the parties, however, are conversant with that language.

Q. Would it be advantageous to substitute the English language in the courts, instead of the Persian?

A. The English language would have the advantage of being the vernacular language of the judges. With regard to the native inhabitants, it would no doubt, in the mean time, have the same disadvantage as the Persian; but its gradual introduction in the courts would still, notwithstanding, prove ultimately beneficial to them by promoting the study of English.

Q. What is your opinion of the general character and conduct of the judges in their official capacity as such?

A. I am happy to state that in my humble opinion the judicial branch of the service is at present almost pure; and there are among the judicial servants of the Company gentlemen of such distinguished talents, that from their natural abilities, even without the regular study of the law, they commit very few, if any, errors in the administration of justice. Others are not so well gifted, and must therefore rely more on the representations of their native officers, and being free from any local check on their public conduct, their regularity, attention to business, and other judicial habits, are not equal to the wishes of their employers, nor calculated to give general satisfaction.

Q. Do they borrow money to any extent from the natives?

A. Formerly they borrowed to a great extent; at present this practice is discouraged.

Q. Why are the natives prevailed upon to lend to the judges, and other civilians, money to such an extent?

A. Natives not having any hope of attaining direct consideration for the government by their merits or exertions, are sometimes induced to accommodate the civil servants with money, by the hope of securing their patronage for their friends and relatives, the judges and others having many situations directly or indirectly in their gift; sometimes by the hope of benefiting by their friendly disposition when the natives have estates under their jurisdiction; and sometimes to avoid incurring the hostility of the judge, who, by Regulation IX of 1807, is empowered not only to imprison, but inflict corporal punishment, by his own authority under certain legal pretences on any native, whatever his respectability may be.

Q. What is your opinion of the judicial character and conduct of the Hindu and Mohammedan lawyers attached to the courts?

A. Amongst the Mohammedan lawyers I have met with some honest men. The Hindu lawyers are in general not well spoken of, and they do not enjoy much of the confidence of the public.

Q. What is your opinion of the official character and conduct of the subordinate native judicial officers?

A. Considering the trifling salaries, which they enjoy, from 10, 20, 30 or 40 rupees to 100 rupees a month (the last being the allowance of the head native officer only), and the expenses they must incur, in supporting some respectability of appearance, besides maintaining their families (the keeping of a palanquin alone must cost the headman a sum of between 20 and 30 rupees per month), and considering also the extent of the power which they must possess, from their situations and duties as above explained, and the immense sums involved in the issues of causes pending in the courts, it is not to be expected that the native officers, having such trifling salaries, at least many of them, should not avail themselves sometimes of their official influence, to promote their own interests.

Q. What is your opinion of the professional character and conduct of the pleaders?

A. Many pleaders of the Sudder Dewanee Adawlut are men of the highest respectability and legal knowledge, as the judges are very select in their appointment, and treat them in a way which makes them feel that they have a character to support. Those of the Provincial Courts of Appeal are also generally respectable, and competent to the discharge of their duties. In the Zillah Courts some respectable pleaders may also be met with, but proper persons for that office are not always very carefully selected; and in general, I may observe, that the pleaders are held in a state of too much dependence by the judges, particularly in the inferior courts, which must incapacitate them from standing up firmly in support of the rules of the court.

Q. Do you think the natives of the country are qualified to discharge judicial functions of this nature; and from what class would you select the jurors?

A. They are assuredly qualified, as I observed before, and the jurors at present may be judiciously selected from retired pleaders (vakils) and retired judicial officers, from agents employed by private individuals to attend the court (Mukhtars) who are generally well qualified, and from the other intelligent and respectable inhabitants as above observed. To avoid any undue bias or partiality, both parties in a suit should have a right of objecting to any juryman, who can be shown to have an interest in the cause, or particular connection with either party.

Q. Do you think the natives are competent and eligible to all judicial situations, or to only subordinate ones?

A. As many of them, even under the present manifold disadvantages, already discharge all the judicial functions, even the most arduous, it will not be very difficult, I think, with proper management, to find qualified persons amongst the natives for any duty that may be assigned to them. Many, however, as in other countries, are only fit for subordinate situations.

Q. Does any inconvenience arise from making the revenue Commissioners also Judges of Circuit?

A. Such a union of offices is quite incompatible and injurious. The judge of Circuit discharges duties of the highest importance, being invested with the power of life and death, and imprisonment during life in chains, the infliction of corporal punishment, and the confiscation of property. He is, besides, charged with the preservation of peace and good order in several extensive districts; and it is morally impossible, therefore, that he can fulfil the expectations of government and the public, if his attention be at the same time engrossed and distracted by political commercial or revenue transactions. In criminal suits, moreover, he labours under a peculiar disadvantage, not being assisted by a Bar composed of persons of liberal education, or by a body of honest, intelligent, and independent jurors. The former often proves of essential service to the bench in the King's courts, by able expositions of the law as applicable to every case, by great acuteness in cross-examining witnesses, and in the detection of false evidence; while the importance of the jury is universally acknowledged.

Formerly, when the judges of the Provincial Courts of Appeal did the duties of the circuit, one or two of them used to remain at the station, to attend the necessary current business, while the others (one or sometimes, two) were on circuit. But under the present system, the Commissioner of Revenue being also Judge of Circuit, when he goes on circuit, all references to him, by the collectors under his jurisdiction, often remain unanswered, and the most important matters in the revenue business are entirely suspended for months together. Although the former Mohammedan governments were subject to the charge of indifference about the administration of justice, they yet perceived the evils liable to arise from a union of revenue and judicial duties. No judge or judicial officers empowered to try capital crimes (as *Kazees* or *Muftis*) was ever suffered to become a collector of revenue.

The separation of these two offices has also been established by long practice under the British Government, being one of the leading principles of the system introduced by Lord Cornwallis. Accordingly, those young civilians who attached themselves to the revenue line of the service, have advanced by successive steps in that line; while those again who preferred the judicial, have been in like manner continued and promoted through the different grades in that department of public duty. Therefore, by overturning this system, a gentleman may now be appointed to discharge the highest judicial duties, who never before tried the most trivial cause; and another to superintend the collectors of revenue, to whose duties he has been all his life a stranger. Mr. B.R. Barewell, Revenue Commissioner and Judge of Circuit of the 24 Parganas, Baraset, Jessore and Barisal, is an example of the former case: and Mr. H. Braddon, Revenue Commissioner and Judge of Circuit of Burdwan, Jungul Mahal, and Hughly is an instance of the latter.

The remedy I beg to propose, without further expense attending the establishment, is to separate the duties between two distinct sets of officers, and double the jurisdiction of each. By this arrangement each gentleman discharging one class of duties would find them more easy and simple, though the field embraced was more extensive, and the expense would be the same as under the present system.

The duties of Judges and Magistrates are not so incompatible as those of the Judges of Circuit and the Commissioners of revenue; but still separation of these duties is advisable on account of the great weight of the business in the zillah and city courts. Therefore these two offices (the office of judge and that of magistrate) should be exercised by different individuals. However, the magistrates should assist the judges in the execution of their decrees of orders as they have hitherto done in those districts where the offices of judge and magistrate are separate.

Q. In what manner do you think a Code of Criminal Law could be framed suitable to the wants of the country?

A. A Code of Criminal Law for India should be founded as far as possible on those principles which are common to, and acknowledged by, all the different sects and tribes inhabiting the country. It ought to be simple in its principles, clear in its arrangements, and precise in its definitions so that it may be established as a standard of criminal justice in itself, and not stand in need of explanation by a reference to any other books of authority, either Mohammedan or Christian. It is a subject of general complaint that persons of a certain high rank, however profligate some of them may be, are, from political considerations, exempted from the jurisdiction or control of the courts of the law. To remedy this inconvenience, in the proposed Code, so as to give general satisfaction, without disregarding the political distinctions hitherto observed, it may perhaps be expedient for government to order such persons to be tried by a special commission, composed of three or more persons of the same rank. This very regulation, when once known to them, would, in all probability, deter them from committing any very gross act of tyranny or outrage upon their dependants or others.

Q. What period of time would it take to frame such a Code, and by whom could it be done satisfactorily?

A. It must require at least a couple of years to do it justice; and it ought to be drawn up by persons, thoroughly acquainted with Mohammedan and Hindu law, as well as the general principles of British law.

Q. Would not the detention of the young civilians in England to obtain a regular legal education be injurious by delaying their proceeding to India for several years, at that period of life, when they are best capable to acquire the native languages? Do you conceive that any disadvantages arise from civilians going out at an early age?

A. This is a subject which merits the deepest consideration of the legislature. Young men sent out at an early age, before their principles are fixed, or their education fully matured, with the prospect of the highest power, authority, and influence before them, occupying already the first rank in society immediately on their arrival, and often without the presence of any parent, or near relative to advise, guide or check them, and surrounded by persons ready, in the hope of future favours and patronage, to flatter their vanity and supply money to almost any extent to their too easily excitable passions—are evidently placed in the situation calculated to plunge them into many errors; make them overstep the bounds of duty of their fellow creatures and fellow subjects, and to relax whatever principles of virtue may have been implanted in their yet inexperienced minds. The excuse made for so injudicious an arrangement, that it is favourable to the acquisition of the native languages, is of no weight; for it may be observed that the missionaries, who are usually sent out at the age of from 25 to 35 years, acquire generally in two or three years so thorough a knowledge of these languages as to be able to converse freely in them and even to address a native audience with fluency in their own tongue. In fact the languages are easily acquired at a mature as well as at an immature age by free communication with the people. Moreover, by the system of native assessors, juries and other helps to the judges and magistrates, and by the gradual substitution of English for Persian, above proposed, so extensive and minute a knowledge of the native languages would not be requisite. In short, from the present system of sending out youths at so early an age, very serious evils arise to themselves, as well as to the government, and to the public. *Firstly,* with respect to themselves, they are too often seduced into habits which prove ruinous to their health and their fortunes, becoming thereby involved in debts from which many of them are never afterwards able to extricate themselves without having recourse to improper means. *Secondly,* these embarrassments interfere very seriously with their duty to government and the public, as the persons to whom they are indebted generally surround them, and seize every opportunity of enriching themselves which their situation and influence put in their way. *Thirdly,* their indiscreet choice of native officers from youthful partialities, and the thoughtless habits acquired in early days, amidst power and influence, prove very injurious to the community. Therefore, no civil servant should be set to India under 24 or at least 22 years of age; and no candidate among them should be admitted into the judicial line of service, unless he can produce a certificate from a professor of English Law to prove that he possesses a competent knowledge of it. Because, though he is not to administer English Law, his proficiency therein will be a proof of his capacity for legal studies and judical duties, and a knowledge of the principles of jurisprudence as developed in one system of law, will enable him to acquire more readily any other system; just as the study of the ancient and dead languages improves our knowledge of modern tongues. This is so important that no public authority should have the power of violating the rule by admitting to the exercise of judicial functions any one who has not been brought up a lawyer.

Q. Is there any mode by which the law authorities, now so voluminous and perplexing, might be simplified in such a manner as to prevent the native lawyers from misleading the courts and confounding the rights of property?

A. To effect this great and pre-eminently important object, a Code of Civil Law should be formed on similar principles to those already suggested for the Criminal Code; and this, as well as the former, should be accurately translated and published under the authority of government. By printing off large impressions and distributing them at prime cost in the current languages of the people, they might render the rights of property secure; since these being clear and well-known to the whole community, it would be impossible for any designing man to induce an intelligent person to enter upon litigious suits. The law of inheritance should, of course, remain as at present with modifications peculiar to the different sects, until by the diffusion of intelligence the whole community may be prepared to adopt one uniform system. At present when a new regulation drawn up by any officer of government and submitted to it is approved of, it immediately becomes law when promulgated, the same as an Act of Parliament in this country, when approved of, discussed, and sanctioned by King, Lords and Commons. From the want of sufficient local knowledge and experience on the part of the framers of such regulations, they are often found not to answer in practice; and the local government is thus frequently obliged to rescind the whole or part of them. I would, therefore, suggest that if any new regulation be thought necessary before the completion of the Civil and Criminal Codes above proposed, great care and precaution should be observed in its enactment. With this view every such project of law, before it is finally adopted by the government, should be printed and a copy sent directly from government, not only to the Judges of the Sudder Dewanne Adawlat, and the members of the Board of Revenue etc., but also to the Advocate-General on the part of the Honourable Company, to the principal zamindars, such as the Rajahs of Burdwan, Behar, Banaras etc., and to the highly respectable merchants such as Jaggat Seth at Murshidabad, Baboo Baijnath at Patna, and the representatives of Baboo Manohar Das at Banaras, also to the Muftis of the Sudder Dewanee Adawlat, and the head native officers of the Board of Revenue, for their opinion on each clause of the regulation to be sent in writing within a certain period. Because these being the persons who are affected by the regulations, they will be cautious of recommending any that is injurious. It should still be optional, however, with government to be guided or not by their suggestions. But a copy of the minutes made by the different parties above-named should accompany the regulations, when these are to be transmitted to England for the consideration of the Court of Directors, and Parliament; and there should be a standing Committee of the House of Commons, to take the whole regulations and minutes into consideration, and to report to the House from time to time on the subject, for their confirmation or amendment.

In such matters as those of war and peace, it may be necessary that the local government should act on its own discretion and responsibility according to existing circumstances, notwithstanding the opinion of the government in England. But as the affairs of India have been known to the authorities in Europe, for such a series of years, in matters of legislation, the local government should be bound to carry into effect any regulations or order in judicial and revenue matter sent out, formally enacted by the British Government, or the Court of Directors under the express sanction of the Board of Commissioners for the control of the affairs of India, although the local government might still remonstrate against them to the home authorities.

The attention thus shown by the government at home and abroad, to the feelings and interests of the zamindars, and merchants, as principal members of the community, though it would not confer upon them any political power, would give them an interest in the government, and inspire them with greater attachment to it, and also the whole community, as being under their influence, and in general receiving its opinions from them.

Q. Should the civil servants, in the judicial and revenue departments, be educated expressly for the particular line of the service in which they are engaged, or is it advantageous to transfer them from one branch of it to another?

A. It is found by experience that persons, by long habit in the performance of any particular duties, become not only more dexterous in but more reconciled and even attached to them, and find them less irksome than others to which they have not been accustomed. In my humble opinion, the duties of a judge are not inferior in difficulty to those of any other profession whatever, nor is the qualification requisite for them to be acquired with less experience. It has been alleged that the revenue officers, when converted into judicial officers, must be better judges of revenue causes. But on this principle, commercial officers ought to become judges for the sake of commercial causes, agriculturists, for agricultural causes, as matters of revenue, commerce, agriculture, etc. are decided on the general principles of law and justice, any such special preparation has never been found necessary; therefore these two classes of duties should be kept quite distinct, if it is wished that either of them be performed well.

Q. Can you offer any other suggestions for the improvement of the judicial establishment?

A. Firstly, in order to keep the judicial officers above temptation, their salaries should not be reduced. Secondly, with the additional aids and checks of joint native judges, assessors, and juries above proposed, all Civil Courts of Appeal may be dispensed with, except the Supreme Civil Court (Sudder Dewanee Adawlat) and thus a very considerable saving may be effected by the government. One-tenth of this saving will suffice to support all the native assessors, juries etc., above recommended. Thirdly, by gradually introducing the natives into the revenue departments under the superintendence of European officers, and in the judicial department in co-operation with them, the natives may become attached to the present system of government, so that it may become consolidated, and maintain itself by the influence of the intelligent and respectable classes of the inhabitants, and by the general goodwill of the people, and not any longer stand isolated in the midst of its subjects, supporting itself merely by the exertion of superior force.

Should the gradual introduction of the natives into places of authority and trust as proposed, be founded not to answer the expectations of government, it would then have the power of stopping their further advancement, or even of reversing what might have been already done in their favour. On the contrary, should the proposed plan of combining native with European officers have the effect of improving the condition of the inhabitants and of stimulating them with an ambition to deserve the confidence of the government, it will then be enabled to form a judgement of the practicability and expedience of advancing natives of respectability and talent to still higher situations of trust and dignity in the state, either in conjunction with or separately from their British fellow subjects.

—Rammohun Roy

8

Rights of Women

Women are in general inferior to men in bodily strength and energy; consequently the male part of the community, taking advantage of their corporeal weakness, have denied to them those excellent merits that they are entitled to by nature, and afterwards they are apt to say that women are naturally incapable of acquiring those merits. But if we give the subject consideration, we may easily ascertain whether or not your accusation against them is consistent with justice. As to their inferiority in point of understanding, when did you ever afford them a fair opportunity of exhibiting their natural capacity? How then can you accuse them of want of understanding? If, after instruction in knowledge and wisdom, a person cannot comprehend or retain what has been taught to him, we may consider him as deficient; but as you keep women generally void of education and acquirements, you cannot, therefore, in justice pronounce on their inferiority. On the contrary, Lilavati, Bhanumati, the wife of the prince of Karnat, and that of Kalidas, are celebrated for their thorough knowledge of all the Shastras; moreover in the *Vrihadaranyak Upanishad* of the *Yajur Veda* it is clearly stated that Yagnavalkya imparted divine knowledge of the most difficult nature to his wife Maitreyi who was able to follow and completely attain it.

Secondly, you charge them with want of resolution, at which I feel exceedingly surprised: for we constantly perceive, in a country where the name of death makes the male shudder, that the female, from her firmness of mind, offers to burn with the corpse of her deceased husband; and yet you accuse those women of deficiency of resolution.

Thirdly, with regard to their trustworthiness, let us look minutely into the conduct of both sexes, and we may be enabled to ascertain which of them is the most frequently guilty of betraying friends. If we enumerate such women in each village or town as have been deceived by men, and such men as have been betrayed by women, I presume that the number of the deceived women would be found ten times greater than that of the betrayed men. Men are, in general, able to read and write, and manage public affairs, by which means they easily promulgate such faults as women occasionally commit, but never consider as criminal the misconduct of men towards women. One fault they have, it must be acknowledged, which is, by considering others equally void of duplicity as themselves, to give their confidence too readily, from which they suffer much misery, even so far that some of them are misled to suffer themselves to be burnt to death.

In the fourth place, with respect to their subjection to the passions, this may be judged of by the custom of marriage as to the respective sexes; for one man may marry two or three, sometimes even ten wives and upwards; while a woman, who marries but one husband, desires at his death to follow him, forsaking all wordly enjoyments, or to remain leading the austere life of an ascetic.

Fifthly, the accusation of their want of virtuous knowledge is injustice. Observe what pain, what slighting, what contempt, and what affliction their virtue enables them to support. How many Kulin Brahmins are there who marry ten or fifteen wives for the sake of money, that never see the greater number of them after the day of marriage, and visit others only three or four times in the course of their life. Still amongst those women, most, even without seeing or receiving any support from their husbands, living dependent on their fathers or brothers, and suffering much distress, continue to preserve their virtue; and when Brahmins, or those of other tribes bring their wives to live with them, what misery do the women not suffer? At marriage the wife is recognised as half of her husband, but in after conduct they are treated worse than inferior animals. For the woman is employed to do the work of a slave in the house, such as, in her turn, to clean the place very early in the morning, whether cold or wet, to scour the dishes, to wash the floor, to cook night and day, to prepare and serve food for her husband, father and mother-in-law, brother-in-law, and friends and connections (for amongst Hindus more than in other tribes relations long reside together, and on this account quarrels are more common amongst brothers respecting their wordly affairs). If in the preparation or serving up of the victuals they commit the smallest fault, what insult do they not receive from their husband, their mother-in-law, and the younger brothers of their husband. After all the male part of the family have satisfied themselves, the women content themselves with what may be left, whether sufficient in quantity or not. Where Brahmans or Kayasthas are not wealthy, the women are obliged to attend to their cows, and to prepare cowdung for firing. In the afternoon they fetch water from the river or tank; and at night perform the office of menial servants in making the beds. In case of any fault or omission in the performance of those labours, they receive injurious treatment. Should the husband acquire wealth, he indulges in criminal amours to her perfect knowledge, and almost under her eyes, and does not see her, perhaps once a month. As long as the husband is poor she suffers every kind of trouble, and when he becomes rich she is altogether heart-broken. All this pain and affliction, their virtue alone enables them to support. Where a husband takes two or three wives to live with him, they are subjected to mental miseries and constant quarrels. Even this distressed situation they virtuously endure. Sometimes it happens that the husband, from a preference for one of his wives, behaves cruelly to another. Amongst the lower classes, and those even of the better class who have not associated with good company, the wife, on the slightest fault or even on bare suspicion of her misconduct, is chastised as a thief. Respect to virtue and their reputation generally makes them forgive even this treatment. If, unable to bear such cruel usage, a wife leaves her husband's house to live separately from him, then the influence of the husband with the magisterial authority is generally sufficient to place her again in his hands;

when, in revenge for her quitting him, he seizes every pretex to torment her in various ways, and sometimes even puts her privily to death. These are facts occurring every day, and not to be denied. What I lament is, what, seeing the women thus dependent and exposed to every misery, you feel for them to compassion that might exempt them from being tied down and burnt to death.

—Raja Rammohun Roy

9

Demand for English Education

The establishment of a new Sangscrit school in Calcutta evinces the laudable desire of government to improve the natives of India by education—a blessing for which they must ever be grateful; and every well-wisher of the human race must be desirous that the efforts made to promote it should be guided by the most enlightened principles, so that the stream of intelligence may flow into the most useful channels.

When this seminary of learning was proposed, we understood that the government in England had ordered a considerable sum of money to be annually devoted to the instruction of its Indian subjects. We were filled with sanguine hopes that this sum would be laid out in employing European gentlemen of talents and education to instruct the natives of India in mathematics, natural philosophy, chemistry, anatomy, and other useful sciences, which the Nations of Europe have carried to a degree of perfection that has raised them above the inhabitants of other parts of the world.

While we looked forward with pleasing hope to the dawn of knowledge thus promised to the rising generation, our hearts were filled with mingled feelings of delight and gratitude; we already offered up thanks to Providence for inspiring the most generous and enlightened of the nations of the West with the glorious ambitions of planting in Asia, the arts and sciences of modern Europe.

We now find that the government are establishing a Sangscrit school under Hindoo pundits to impart such knowledge as is already current in India. This Seminary (similar in character to those which existed in Europe before the time of Lord Bacon) can only be expected to load the minds of youth with grammatical niceties and metaphysical distinctions of little or no practicable use to the possessors or to society. The pupils will there acquire what was known two thousand years ago, with the addition of vain and empty subtleties since produced by speculative men, such as is already commonly taught in all parts of India.

The Sangscrit language, so difficult that almost a lifetime is necessary for its perfect acquisition, is well known to have been for ages a lamentable check on the diffusion of knowledge; and the learning concealed under this almost impervious veil is far from sufficient to reward the labour of acquiring it. But if it were thought necessary to perpetuate this language for the sake of the portion of valuable information it contains, this might be much more easily accomplished by other means than the establishment of a new Sangscrit college; for there have been always and are now numerous professors of Sangscrit in the different parts of the country, engaged in teaching this language as well as the other branches of literature which are to be the object of the new Seminary. Therefore, their more diligent cultivation, if desirable, would be effectually promoted by holding out premiums and granting certain allowances to those most eminent professors, who have already undertaken on their own account to teach them, and would by such rewards be stimulated to still greater exertions.

From these considerations, as the sum set apart for instruction of the natives in India was intended by the Government in England, for the improvement of its Indian subjects, I beg leave to state, with due deference to your Lordship's exalted situation, that if the plan now adopted be followed, it will completely defeat the object proposed; since no improvement can be expected from inducing young men to consume a dozen of years of the most valuable period of their lives in acquiring the niceties of *Byakurun* or Sangscrit grammar. For instance, in learning to discuss such points as the followings: *khad*, signifying 'to eat'. *Khaduti*, 'he, or she, or it eats'. Query, whether does the word *khaduti,* taken as a whole, convey the meaning 'he, she, or it eats', or are separate parts of this meaning conveyed by distinct portions of the word? As if in the English language it were asked, how much meaning is there in the *eat,* how much in the *s*? and is the whole meaning of the word conveyed by those two portions of it distinctly, or by them taken jointly?

Neither can much improvement arise from such speculations as the following, which are the themes suggested by the Vedant? In what manner is the soul absorbed into the deity? What relation does it bear to the divine essence? Nor will youths be fitted to be better members of society by the Vedantic doctrines, which teach them to believe that all visible things have no real existence; that as father, brother, etc., have no actual entirety, they consequently deserve no real affection, and, therefore, the sooner we escape from them and leave the world the better. Again, no essential benefit can be derived by the student of the *Meemangsa* from knowing what it is that makes the killer of a goat sinless on pronouncing certain passages of the Vedas, and what is the real nature and operative influence of passages of the Veda, etc.

Again the student of the *Nyaya Shastra* cannot be said to have improved his mind after he has learned from it into how many ideal classes the objects in the universe are divided, and what speculative relation the soul bears to the body, the body to the soul, the eye to the ear, etc.

In order to enable your Lordship to appreciate the utility of encouraging such imaginary learning as above characterised, I beg your Lordship will be pleased to compare the state of science and literature in Europe before the time of Lord Bacon, with the progress of knowledge made since he wrote.

If it had intended to keep the British nation in ignorance of real knowledge the Baconian philosophy would not have been allowed to displace the system of the schoolmen, which was the best calculated to perpetuate ignorance. In the same manner the Sangscrit system of education would be the best calculated to keep this country in darkness, if such had been the policy of the

British legislature. But as the improvement of the native population is the object of the government, it will consequently promote a more liberal and enlightened system of instruction, embracing mathematics, natural philosophy, chemistry and anatomy, with other useful sciences which may be accomplished with the sum proposed by employing a few gentlemen of talents and learning educated in Europe, and providing a college furnished with the necessary books, instruments and other apparatus.

—Raja Rammohun Roy

10

Sri Rāmakrishna: Mystic and Spiritual Teacher

Sri Rāmakrishna (1836-1886) was among the most saintly of the many religious leaders to whom modern India has given birth. A son of Bengal, like Debendranāth and Keshub, he was, unlike them, a child of the soil and never lost his rustic simplicity. Like Dayānanda, he personified the rebirth of an ancient tradition in the midst of an era of increasing Westernization and modernization. But unlike that militant Gujarātī, he practised and preached a gentle faith of selfless devotion to God and of ultimate absorption in Him.

Rāmakrishna imbibed from his boyhood days as the son of a village priest the spirit of devotion to Kālī, the divine mother, which the songs of Rāmprasād had made popular in rural Bengal in the eighteenth century. Ecstatic communion with the Divine, an aspect of this tradition, came naturally to the attractive young Brāhman, and at the age of seven he experienced his first mystical trance. He received no formal education in Sanskrit or English, and could read and write Bengali only moderately well. Yet this "God-intoxicated" man attained to a wisdom that was the envy of many of his enlightened, English-educated contemporaries.

His elder brother took him at sixteen to Calcutta, where they were eventually installed as priests of a new temple on the Hooghly river, a branch of the Ganges. For the next twelve years Rāmakrishna put himself through every known type of spiritual discipline in an agonized search for God. Finally his efforts were rewarded with a series of mystical experiences during which he saw God in a variety of manifestations—as a Divine Mother, as Sītā, as Rāma, as Krishna, as Muhammad, as Jesus Christ, and worshipped Him in the manner of Muslims, Jains, and Buddhists—in each case suiting his dress, food and meditation to the particular religious tradition concerned.

Through the aid of Keshub Chundra Sen, who greatly admired him, Rāmakrishna began to attract disciples from among the Westernized middle class of Calcutta. His keen insight into the hearts of men made him an excellent teacher, and his natural simplicity and purity made a profound impression on these young men. From him they learned to draw strength from the living traditions of popular Hinduism; through them his teachings became known to all India and the world at large.

RĀMAKRISHNA

The World as seen by a mystic

Rāmakrishna lived in a state of consciousness so close to continual meditation that he was able to see great meaning in the smallest incidents. One of his disciples collected his sayings and anecdotes as he related them. They show us the world as he saw it—a world permeated by the presence of the Divine.

[From *The Gospel of Rāmakrishna*, pp. 207-14]

I practised austerities for a long time. I cared very little for the body. My longing for the Divine Mother was so great that I would not eat or sleep. I would lie on the bare ground, placing my head on a lump of earth, and cry out loudly: "Mother, mother, why dost thou not come to me?" I did not know how the days and nights passed away. I used to have ecstasy all the time. I saw my disciples as my own people, like children and relations, long before they came to me. I used to cry before my mother, saying: "O mother! I am dying for my beloved ones (bhaktas); do Thou bring them to me as quickly as possible."

At that time whatever I desired came to pass. Once I desired to build a small hut in the Panchavati[1] for meditation and to put a fence around it. Immediately after I saw a huge bundle of bamboo sticks, rope, strings, and even a knife, all brought by the tide in front of the Panchavati. A servant of the temple, seeing these things, ran to me with great delight and told me of them. There was the exact quantity of material necessary for the hut and the fence. When they were built, nothing remained over. Everyone was amazed to see this wonderful sight.

When I reached the state of continuous ecstasy, I gave up all external forms of worship; I could no longer perform them. Then I prayed to my Divine Mother: "Mother, who will now take care of me? I have no power to take care of myself. I like to hear thy name and feed thy bhaktas and help the poor. Who will make it possible for me to do these things? Send me someone who will be able to do these for me." As the answer to this prayer came Mathura Bābu,[2] who served me so long and with such intense devotion and faith! Again at another time I said to the mother: "I shall have no child of my own, but I wish to have as my child a pure bhakta, who will stay with me all the time. Send me such a one." Then came Rākhāl (Brahmānanda).

Those who are my own are parts of my very self.

II

In referring to the time of joyous illumination which immediately followed His enlightenment, He exclaimed:

What a state it was! The slightest cause aroused in me the thought of the divine ideal. One day I went to the Zoological Garden in Calcutta. I desired especially to see the lion, but when I beheld him, I lost all sense-consciousness and went into samādhi. Those who were with me wished to show me the other animals, but I replied: "I saw everything when I saw the king of beasts. Take me home." The strength of the lion had aroused in me the consciousness of the omnipotence of God and had lifted me above the world of phenomena.

Another day I went to the parade ground to see the ascension of a balloon. Suddenly my eyes fell upon a young English boy leaning against a tree. The very posture of his body brought before me the vision of the form of Krishna and I went into samādhi.

Again I saw a woman wearing a blue garment under a tree. She was a harlot. As I looked at her, instantly the ideal of Sītā[3] appeared before me! I forgot the existence of the harlot, but saw before me pure and spotless Sītā, approached Rāma, the incarnation of divinity, and for a long time I remained motionless. I worshipped all women as representatives of the Divine Mother. I realized the Mother of the universe in every woman's form.

Mathura Bābu, the son-in-law of Rāshmoni, invited me to stay in his house for a few days. At that time I felt so strongly that I was the maidservant of my Divine Mother that I thought of myself as a woman. The ladies of the house had the same feeling; they did not look upon me as a man. As women are free before a young girl, so were they before me. My mind was above the consciousness of sex.

What a Divine state it was! I could not eat here in the temple. I would walk from place to place and enter into the house of strangers after their meal hour. I would sit there quietly, without uttering a word. When questioned, I would say: "I wish to eat here." Immediately they would feed me with the best things they had.

III

Once I heard of a poor Brāhmin who was a true devotee and who lived in a small hut in Bāghbāzār. I desired to see him, so I asked Mathura Bābu to take me to him. He consented, immediately ordered a large carriage, and drove me there. The Brāhmin's house was so small that he scarcely had room to receive us, and he was much surprised to see me coming with such a rich man in such a carriage!

At another time I wished to meet [Debendranāth] Tagore. He is a very rich man, but in spite of his enormous wealth he is devoted to God and repeats his holy name. For this reason I desired to know him. I spoke about him to Mathura Bābu. He replied: "Very well, Bābā,[4] I will take thee to him; he was my classmate." So he took me and introduced me to him, saying: "This holy man has come to see you. He is mad after God." I saw in him a little pride and egotism. It is natural for a man who has so much wealth, culture, fame, and social position. I said to Mathura Bābu: "Tell me, does pride spring from true wisdom or from ignorance? He who has attained to the highest knowledge of Brāhman cannot possess pride or egotism, such as 'I am learned,' 'I am wise,' 'I am rich,' and so on." While I was speaking with [Debentranāth] Tagore, I went into a state from where I could see the true character of every individual. In this state the most learned pandits and scholars appear to me like blades of grass. When I see that scholars have neither true discrimination nor dispassion, then I feel that they are like straws; or they seem like vultures who soar high in the heavens, but keep their minds on the charnel-pits below on the earth. In [Debendranāth] I found both spiritual knowledge and worldly desire. He has a number of children, some of whom are quite young. A doctor was present. I said: "When you have so much spiritual knowledge, how can you live constantly in the midst of so much worldliness? You are like Rājā Janaka;[5] you can keep your mind on God, remaining amid worldly pleasures and luxury. Therefore I have come to see you. Tell me something of the Divine Being." [Debendranāth] then read some passages from the Vedas and said: "This world is like a chandelier, and each jiva (individual soul) is like a light in it." Long ago, when I spent nearly all my time meditating at the Panchavati, I saw the same thing. When [Debendranāth's] words harmonized with my experience, I knew that he must have attained to some true knowledge. I asked him to explain. He said: "Who would have known this world? God has created man to manifest His glory. If there were no light in the chandelier, it would be all dark. The chandelier itself would not be visible." After a long conversation [Debendranāth] Tagore begged me to come to the anniversary of the Brāhmo-Samāj. I answered: "If it be the will of the Lord. I go wherever He takes me."

Fix your mind on god

During one of his visits with Keshub Chundra Sen and his disciples, Rāmakrishna advised the Brāhmos to cultivate the liberating powers of the mind.

[From *The Gospel of Rāmakrishna*, pp. 158-60]

A Brāhmo: Revered Sir, is it true that God cannot be realized without giving up the world?

The Bhagavān,[6] smiling: Oh no! You do not have to give up everything. You are better off where you are. By living in the world you are enjoying the taste of both the pure crystallized sugar and of the molasses with all its impurities. You are indeed better off. Verily I say unto you, you are living in the world, there is no harm in that; but you will have to fix your mind on God, otherwise you cannot realize Him. Work with one hand and hold the feet of the Lord with the other. When you have finished your work, fold His feet to your heart with both your hands.

Everything is in the mind. Bondage and freedom are in the mind. You can dye the mind with any colour you wish. It is like a piece of clean white linen: dip it in red and it will be red, in blue it will be blue, in green it will be green, or any other colour. Do you not see that if you study English, English words will come readily to you? Again, if a pandit studies Sanskrit, he will readily quote verse from sacred books. If you keep your mind in evil company, your thoughts, ideas, and words will be coloured with evil; but keep in the company of bhaktas, then your thoughts, ideas and words will be of God. The mind is everything. On one side is the wife, on the other side is the child, it loves the wife in one way and the child in another way, yet the mind is the same.

By the mind one is bound; by the mind one is freed. If I think I am absolutely free, whether I live in the world or in the forest, where is my bondage? I am the child of God, the son of the king of kings; who can bind me? When bitten by a snake, if you assert with firmness: "There is no venom in me," you will be cured. In the same way, he who asserts with strong conviction: "I am not bound, I am free," becomes free.

Someone gave me a book of the Christians. I asked him to read it to me. In it there was only one theme—sin and sin, from the beginning to the end. (To Keshub) In your Brāhmo-Samāj the main topic is also sin. The fool who repeats again and again: "I am bound. I am bound," remains in bondage. He who repeats day and night: "I am a sinner, I am a sinner," becomes a sinner indeed.

Beware of the wicked

Rāmakrishna's advice to his disciples was often of a very practical nature, as this example shows.

[From *The Gospel of Rāmakrishna*, pp. 42-44]

One of the devotees present said: But when a person is annoyed with me, Bhagavān, I feel unhappy. I feel that I have not been able to love every-one equally.

Rāmakrishna: When you feel that way, you should have a talk with that person and try to make peace with him. If you fail after such attempts, then you need not give it further thought. Take refuge with the Lord. Think upon Him. Do not let your mind be disturbed by any other thing.

Devotee: Christ and Chaitanya have both taught us to love all mankind.

Rāmakrishna: You should love everyone because God dwells in all beings. But to wicked people you should bow down at a distance. (To Bijoy, smiling): Is it true that people blame you because you mix with those who believe in a personal God with form? A true devotee of God should possess absolute calmness and never be disturbed by the opinions of others. Like a blacksmith's anvil, he will endure all blows and persecutions and yet remain firm in his faith and always the same. Wicked people may say many things about you and blame you; but if you long for God, you should endure with patience. One can think on God even dwelling in the midst of wicked people. The sages of ancient times, who lived in forests, could meditate on God although surrounded by tigers, bears, and other wild beasts. The nature of the wicked is like that of a tiger or bear. They attack the innocent and injure them. You should be especially cautious in coming in contact with the following: First, the wealthy. A person who possesses wealth and many attendants can easily do harm to another if he so desires. You should be very guarded in speaking with him; sometimes it may even be necessary to agree with him in his opinion. Second, a dog. When a dog barks at you, you must not run, but talk to him and quiet him. Third, a bull. When a bull chases you, you should always pacify him by talking to him. Fourth, a drunkard. If you make him angry, he will call you names and swear at you. You should address him as a dear relative, then he will be happy and obliging.

When wicked people come to see me, I am very careful. The character of some of them is like that of a snake. They may bite you unawares. It may take a long time and much discrimination to recover from the effects of that bite. Or you may get so angry at them that you will wish to take revenge. It is necessary, however, to keep occasionally the company of holy men. Through such association right discrimination will come.

Parables and sayings

There is much in Rāmakrishna's homely yet charming wisdom that reminds the reader of the teachings of Jesus. Both men took experiences from everyday life and used them to illustrate profound moral and religious truths. But despite the many similarities in the sayings and parables of the two teachers, it is clear that there remains a basic difference between the Hindu and the Judeo-Christian conception of the nature and means of salvation.

[From *Teachings of Sri Rāmakrishna*, pp. 31-94, 351]

The vegetables in the cooking pot move and leap till the children think they are living beings. But the grown-ups explain that they are not moving of themselves; if the fire be taken away they will soon cease to stir. So it is ignorance that thinks "I am the doer." All our strength is the strength of God. All is silent if the fire be removed. A marionette dances well, while the wires are pulled; but when the master's hand is gone, it falls inert. [p. 31].

The guru said: "Everything that exists is God," and the disciple understood this literally. Passing along the road, he met an elephant. The driver shouted from his high place: "Move away, move away!" But the disciple thought: "Why should I move away? I am God and so is the elephant. What fear can God have of himself?" Thinking thus he did not move. At last the elephant took him by his trunk and dashed him aside. He was severely hurt, and going back to his guru, he told his story. The guru said: "It is quite true that you are God. It is true that the elephant is God too, but God was also in the form of the elephant-driver. Why did you not listen to the God on top?" [p. 46].

. . . .

At a game of chess the onlookers can tell what is the correct move better than the players themselves. Men of the world think they are very clever; but they are attached to things of this world—money, honours, pleasure, etc. Being actually engaged in the play it is hard for them to hit upon the right move. Holy men who have given up the world are not attached to it. They are like the onlookers at a game of chess. They see things in their true light and can judge better than the men of the world [p. 68].

. . . .

As a nail cannot be driven into a stone, yet it enters easily into the earth, so the advice of the pious does not affect the soul of a worldly man, while it pierces deep into the heart of a believer [p. 94].

. . . .

A man woke up at midnight and desired to smoke. He wanted a light, so he went to a neighbour's house and knocked at the door. Someone opened the door and asked him what he wanted. The man said: "I wish to smoke. Can you give me a light?" The neighbour replied: "Bah! What is the matter with you? You have taken so much trouble to come and [awaken] us at this hour, when in your hand you have a lighted lantern!" What a man wants is already within him; but he still wanders here and there in search of it [p. 351].

[From Müller, *Rāmakrishna, His Life and Sayings*, pp. 134-80]

. . . .

A disciple, having firm faith in the infinite power of his guru, walked over a river even by pronouncing his name. The guru, seeing this, thought within himself: "Well, is there such a power even in my name? Then I must be very great and powerful, no doubt!" The next day he also tried to walk over the river pronouncing "I, I, I," but no sooner had he stepped into the waters than he sank and was drowned. Faith can achieve miracles, while vanity or egoism is the death of man [p. 134].

. . . .

A man after fourteen years of hard asceticism in a lonely forest obtained at last the power of walking over the waters. Overjoyed at this acquisition, he went to his guru, and told him of his grand feat. At this the master replied: "My poor boy, what thou hast accomplished after fourteen years' arduous labour, ordinary men do the same by paying a penny to the boatman" [p. 154].

. . . .

When a wound is perfectly healed, the slough falls off it itself but if the slough be taken off earlier, it bleeds. Similarly, when the perfection of knowledge is reached by a man, the distinctions of caste fall off from him, but it is wrong for the ignorant to break such distinctions [p. 147].

. . . .

The light of the gas illumines various localities with various intensities. But the life of the light, namely, the gas, comes from one common reservoir. So the religious teachers of all climes and ages are but as many lamp-posts through which is emitted the light of the spirit flowing constantly from one source, the Lord Almighty [p. 148].

. . . .

The difference between the modern Brãhmaism [of the Brãhmo Samãj] and Hinduism is like the difference between the single note of music and the whole music. The modern Brahmas are content with the single note of Brahman, while the Hindu religion is made up of several notes producing a sweet and melodious harmony [p. 153].

. . . .

As it is very difficult to gather together the mustard-seeds that escape out of a torn package, and are scattered in all directions; so, when the human mind runs in diverse directions and is occupied with many things in the world, it is not a very easy affair to collect and concentrate it [p. 167].

. . . .

He who would learn to swim must attempt swimming for some days. No one can venture to swim in the sea after a single day's practice. So if you want to swim in the sea of Brahman, you must make many ineffectual attempts at first, before you can successfully swim therein [p. 175].

. . . .

As the village maidens carry four or five pots of water placed one over the other upon their heads, talking all the way with one another about their own joys and sorrows, and yet do not allow one drop of water to be spilt, so must the traveller in the path of virtue walk along. In whatever circumstances he may be placed, let him always take heed that his heart does not swerve from the true path [p. 177].

. . . .

When an elephant is let loose, it goes about uprooting trees and shrubs, but as soon as the driver pricks him on the head with the goad he becomes quiet; so the mind when unrestrained wantons in the luxuriance of idle thoughts, but becomes calm at once when struck with the goad of discrimination [p. 180].

. . . .

Know thyself, and thou shalt then know the non-self and the Lord of all. What is my ego? Is it my hand, or foot, or flesh, or blood, or muscle, or tendon? Ponder deep, and thou shalt know that there is no such thing as I. As by continually peeling off the skin of the onion, so by analyzing the ego it will be found that there is not any real entity corresponding to the ego. The ultimate result of all such analysis is God. When egoism drops away, Divinity manifests itself [p. 180].

. . . .

SWĀMI VIVEKĀNANDA: HINDU MISSIONARY TO THE WEST

Among Sri Rāmakrishna's disciples was a young Calcutta-born student on whom he showered special attention and praise.

This boy Narendranāth Datta (1863-1902) came from a Kāyastha family of lawyers and received a good Western-style education. When he first visited Rāmakrishna he was planning to study law in England and then follow the profession which was the high road to success in British India. Within a year's time his interviews with the master mystic had changed the course of his life. He resolved to give up worldly pursuits and adopt the life of a sannyāsī. After twelve years of ascetic discipline he became famous as Swāmī Vivekānanda, the apostle to the world of his master's philosophy of God-realization.

Vivekānanda's meteoric career as missionary of Vedantic Hinduism to the West began in 1893 when he addressed the First World Parliament of Religions at Chicago. After four years of lecturing in America and England he returned to India a national hero and took up the task of regenerating his fellow-countrymen. He literally burned himself out in their service, dedicating the Rāmakrishna Mission to both social work and religious education, and rousing young men with his fiery speeches to devote themselves to uplifting the poor and starving millions of India.

Although he died at thirty-nine, Vivekānanda's example had a powerful impact on the thinking of his own and later generations. Despite his scorn for politics, his success in preaching to the world the greatness of Hinduism gave his countrymen an added sense of dignity and pride in their own culture. His zeal to serve the downtrodden masses opened a new dimension of activity to Indian nationalist leaders, whose Western outlook had, heretofore, isolated them from the vast, majority of their countrymen. Gāndhi, the greatest to work in this new field, acknowledged his debt to the Swāmī in this respect.

Vivekānanda called India to become great by realizing her own possibilities and by living up to her own highest ideals. The heart and soul of his teaching was the message of his beloved master, Rāmakrishna: That each man was potentially divine, and so should both work to unleash the infinite power within himself, and should help other men to do the same.

VIVEKĀNANDA

Man is God

In his series of lectures entitled "Practical Vedanta," delivered in London in 1896, Vivekãnanda set forth the teachings of his master, Rãmakrishna. The central point of his message was that God is within man, that in his inmost being, man is God.

[From *The Complete Works of the Swami Vivekananda*, II, 324-25]

Do you not remember what the Bible says: "If you cannot love your brother whom you have seen, how can you love God whom you have not seen?" If you cannot see God in the human face, how can you see Him in the clouds, or in images made of dull, dead matter, or in mere fictitious stores of your brain? I shall call you religious from the day you begin to see God in men and women and then you will understand what is meant by turning the left cheek to the man who strikes you on the right. When you see man as God, everything, even the tiger, will be welcome. Whatever comes to you is but the Lord, the Eternal, the Blessed One, appearing to us in various forms, as our father, and mother, and friend, and child; they are our own soul playing with us.

As our human relationships can thus be made divine so our relationship with God may take any of these forms and we can look upon Him as our father or mother or friend or beloved. Calling God Mother is a higher idea than calling Him Father, and to call Him Friend is still higher, but the highest is to regard Him as the Beloved. The highest point of all is to see no difference between lover and beloved. You may remember, perhaps, the old Persian story, of how a lover came and knocked at the door of the beloved and was asked: "Who are you?" He answered: "It is I," and there was no response. A second time he came, and exclaimed: "I am here," but the door was not opened. The third time he came, and the voice asked from inside: "Who is there?" He replied: "I am thyself, my beloved," and the door opened. So is the relation between God and ourselves. He is in everything, He is everything. Every man and woman is the palpable, blissful, living God. Who says God is unknown? Who says He is to be searched after? We have found God eternally.

We have been living in Him eternally. He is eternally known, eternally worshipped.

The rationale of caste and idol-worship

In contrast with the Brāhmo reformers and Dayānanda, Vivekānanda justified the caste system as good and the worship of idols as useful for those who need them and follow these ancient practices in a way that brought them into harmony with the western ideals of social and religious equality.

[From *The Complete Works of the Swami Vivekananda,* III, 245-46, 460]

Caste is a natural order. I can perform one duty in social life, and you another; you can govern a country, and I can mend a pair of old shoes, but there is no reason why you are greater than I, for can you mend my shoes? Can I govern the country? I am clever in mending shoes, you are clever in reading Vedas, but there is no reason why you should trample on my head; why if one commits murder should he be praised, and if another steals an apple why should he be hanged! This will have to go. Caste is good. That is the only natural way of solving life. Men must form themselves into groups, and you cannot get rid of that. Wherever you go there will be caste. But that does not mean that there should be these privileges. They should be knocked on the head. If you teach Vedanta to the fisherman, he will say, I am as good a man as you, I am a fisherman, you are a philosopher, but I have the same God in me as you have in you. And that is what we want same privileges for anyone, equal chances for all; let everyone be taught that the Divine is within, and everyone will work out his own salvation [pp. 245-46].

This external worship of images has, however, been described in all our Shastras as the lowest of all the low forms of worship. But that does not mean that it is a wrong thing to do. Despite the many iniquities that have found entrance into the practices of image-worship as it is in vogue now, I do not condemn it. Aye, where would I have been, if I had not been blessed with the dust of the holy feet of that orthodox, image-worshipping Brahmana [Rāmakrishna]!

Those reformers who preach against image-worship, or what they denounce as idolatry—to them I say: "Brothers! If you are fit to worship God-without-Form discarding any external help, do so, but why do you condemn others who cannot do the same? A beautiful large edifice, the glorious relic of a hoary antiquity has, out of neglect or disuse, fallen into a dilapidated condition; accumulations of dirt and dust may be lying everywhere within it; may be, some portions are tumbling down to the ground. What will you do to it? Will you take in hand the necessary cleansing and repairs and thus restore the old, or will you pull the whole edifice down to the ground and seek to build another in its place, after a sordid modern plan whose permanence has yet to be established? We have to reform it, which truly means to make ready or perfect by necessary cleansing and repairs, not by demolishing the whole thing. There the function of reform ends." [p. 460].

India and the West

Vivekānanda developed the idea, put forth by Keshub, that India should take practical knowledge from Europe, and in exchange should teach religious wisdom to the world. In a speech about Rāmakrishna delivered in New York he stated most emphatically his claim that the Orient (by which he primarily meant India) was superior to the West in spiritual matters.

[From *The Complete Works of the Swami Vivekananda*, IV, 150-52].

"Whenever virtue subsides and vice prevails, I come down to help mankind," declares Krishna, in the *Bhagavad Gītā*. Whenever this world of ours, on account of growth, on account of added circumstances, requires a new adjustment, a wave of power comes, and as man is acting on two planes, the spiritual and the material, waves of adjustment come on both planes. On the one side, of the adjustment of the material plane, Europe has mainly been the basis during modern times, and of the adjustment, on the other, the spiritual plane, Asia has been the basis throughout the history of the world. Today, man requires one more adjustment on the spiritual plane; today when material ideas are at the height of their glory and power, today when man is likely to forget his divine nature, through his growing dependence on matter, and is likely to be reduced to a mere money-making machine, an adjustment is necessary; the voice has spoken, and the power is coming to drive away the clouds of gathering materialism. The power has been set in motion which, at no distant date, will bring unto mankind once more the memory of its real nature, and again the place from which this power will start will be Asia. This world of ours is on the plan of the division of labour. It is vain to say that one man shall possess everything. Yet how childish we are! The baby in its ignorance thinks that its doll is the only possession that is to be coveted in this whole universe. So a nation which is great in the possession of material power thinks that that is all that is to be coveted, that that is all that is meant by progress, that that is all that is meant by civilization, and if there are other nations which do not care for possession, and do not possess that power, they are not fit to live, their whole existence is useless! On the other hand, another nation may think that mere material civilization is utterly useless. From the Orient came the voice which once told the world, that if a man possesses everything that is under the sun and does not possess spirituality, what avails it? This is the Oriental type; the other is the Occidental type.

Each of these types has its grandeur, each has its glory. The present adjustment will be the harmonizing, the mingling of these two ideals. To the Oriental, the world of spirit is as real as to the Occidental is the world of senses. In the spiritual, the Oriental finds everything he wants or hopes for; in it he finds all that makes life real to him. To the Occidental he is a dreamer; to the Oriental, the Occidental is a dreamer, playing with ephemeral toys, and he laughs to think that grown-up men and women should make so much of a handful of matter which they will have to leave sooner or later. Each calls the other a dreamer. But the Oriental ideal is as necessary for the progress of the human race as is the Occidental, and I think it is more necessary. Machines never made mankind happy, and never will make. He who is trying to make us believe this, will claim that happiness is in the machine, but it is always in the mind. The man alone who is the lord of his mind can become happy, and none else. And what, after all, is power of machinery? Why should a man who can send a current of electricity through a wire be called a very great man, and very intelligent man? Does not nature do a million times more than that every moment? Why not then fall down and worship Nature? What avails it if you have power over the whole of the world, if you have mastered every atom in the universe? That will not make you happy unless you have the power of happiness in yourself, until you have conquered yourself. Man is born to conquer Nature, it is true, but the Occidental means by "Nature" only the physical or external Nature. It is true that external Nature is majestic, with its mountains, and oceans, and rivers, and with the infinite powers and varieties. Yet there is a more majestic internal Nature of man, higher than the sun, moon, and the stars, higher than this earth of ours, higher than the physical universe, transcending these little lives of ours; and it affords another field of study. There the Orientals excel, just as the Occidentals excel in the other. Therefore it is fitting that, whenever there is a spiritual adjustment, it should come from the Orient. It is also fitting that when the Oriental wants to learn about machine-making, he should sit at the feet of the Occidental and learn from him. When the Occident wants to learn about the spirit, about God, about the soul, about the meaning and the mystery of this universe, he must sit at the feet of the Orient to learn.

Indian thought to conquer the world

In a lecture in Madras Swāmī Vivekānanda challenged his audience to conquer the West with India's spirituality. Through such speeches as this he instilled a feeling of self-confidence in the youth of the country, thus contributing to the later movement for national independence.

[From *The Complete Works of the Swami Vivekananda*, III, 276-77].

This is the great ideal before us, and every one must be ready for it—the conquest of the whole world by India—nothing less than that, and we must all get ready for it, strain every nerve for it. Let foreigners come and flood the land with their armies, never mind. Up, India, and conquer the world with your spirituality! Aye, as has been declared on this soil first love must conquer hatred, hatred cannot conquer itself. Materialism and all its miseries can never be conquered by materialism. Armies when they attempt to conquer armies only multiply and make brutes of humanity. Spirituality must conquer the West. Slowly they are finding out that what they want is spirituality to preserve them as nations. They are waiting for it, they are eager for it. Where is the supply to come from? Where are the men ready to go out to every country in the world with the messages of the great sages of India? Where are the men who are ready to sacrifice everything, so that this message shall reach every corner of the world? Such heroic souls are wanted to help the spread of truth. Such heroic workers are wanted to go abroad and help to disseminate the great truths of the Vedanta. The world wants it; without it the world will be destroyed. The whole of the Western world is on a volcano which may burst tomorrow, go to pieces tomorrow. They have searched every corner of the world and have found no respite. They have drunk deep of the cup of pleasure and found it vanity. Now is the time to work so that India's spiritual ideas may penetrate deep into the West. Therefore, young men of Madras, I specially ask you to remember this. We must go out, we must conquer the world through our spirituality and philosophy. There is no other alternative, we must do it or die. The only condition of national life, of awakened and vigorous national life, is the conquest of the world by Indian thought.

America and India's poor

While he was preaching the philosophy of the Vedanta to the people of the West, Vivekānanda was worrying about the poverty of his own countrymen. In 1894 he wrote from Chicago to the Mahārāja of Mysore, one of India's most enlightened princes, giving his opinion of American materialism, and asking for help in his new-found ambition to educate their nation's poor.

[From *The Complete Works of the Swami Vivekananda,* IV, 307-9].

Sri Narayana bless you and yours. Through your Highness' kind help it has been possible for me to come to this country. Since then I have become well-known here, and the hospitable people of this country have supplied all my wants. It is a wonderful country and this is a wonderful nation in many respects. No other nation applies so much machinery in their everyday work as do the people of this country. Everything is machine. Then again, they are only one-twentieth of the whole population of the world. Yet they have fully one-sixth of all the wealth of the world. There is no limit to their wealth and luxuries. Yet everything here is so dear. The wages of labour are the highest in the world; yet the fight between labour and capital is constant.

Nowhere on earth have women so many privileges as in America. They are slowly taking everything into their hands and, strange to say, the number of cultured women is much greater than that of cultured men. Of course, the higher geniuses are mostly from the rank of males. With all the criticism of the Westerners against our caste, they have a worse one—that of money. The almighty dollar, as the Americans say, can do anything here.

No country on earth has so many laws, and in no country are they so little regarded. On the whole our poor Hindu people are infinitely more moral than any of the Westerners. In religion they practise here either hypocrisy or fanaticism. Sober-minded men have become disgusted with their superstitious religions and are looking forward to India for new light. Your Highness cannot realize without seeing, how eagerly they take in any little bit of the grand thoughts of the holy Vedas, which resist and are unharmed by the terrible onslaughts of modern science. The theories of creation out of nothing, of a created soul, and of the big tyrant of a God sitting on a throne in a place called heaven, and of the eternal hell-fires, have disgusted all the educated; and the noble thoughts of the Vedas about the eternity of creation and of the soul, and about the God in our own soul, they are imbibing fast in one shape or other. Within fifty years the educated of the world will come to believe in the eternity of both soul and creation, and in God as our highest and perfect nature, as taught in our holy Vedas. Even now their learned priests are interpreting the Bible in that way. My conclusion is that they require more spiritual civilization, and we, more material.

The one thing that is at the root of all evils in India is the condition of the poor. The poor in the West are devils; compared to them ours are angels, and it is therefore so much the easier to raise our poor. The only service to be done for our lower classes is, to give them education, *to develop their lost individuality.* That is the great task between our people and princes. Up to now nothing has been done in that direction. Priest-power and foreign conquest have trodden them down for centuries and at last the poor of India have forgotten that they are human beings. They are to be given ideas; their eyes are to be opened to what is going on in the world around them, and then they will work out their own salvation. Every nation, every man, and every woman must work out their own salvation. Give them ideas—that is the only help they require, and then the rest must follow as the effect. Ours is to put the chemicals together, the crystallization comes in the law of nature. Our duty is to put ideas into their heads, they will do the rest. This is what is to be done in India. It is this idea that has been in my mind for a long time. I could not accomplish it in India, and that was the reason of my coming to this country. The great difficulty in the way of educating the poor is this. Supposing even your Highness opens a free school in every village, still it would do no good, for the poverty in India is such, that poor boys would rather go to help their fathers in the fields, or otherwise try to make a living, than come to the school. Now if the mountain does not come to Mahomet, Mahomet must go to the mountain. If the poor boy cannot come to education, education must go to him. There are thousands of single-minded, self-sacrificing Sannyasins in our own country, going from village to village, teaching religion. If some of them can be organized as teachers of secular things also, they will go from place to place, from door to door, not only preaching but teaching also. Suppose two of these men go to a village in the evening with a camera, a globe, some maps, etc. They can teach a great deal of astronomy and geography to the ignorant. By telling stories about different nations, they can give the poor a hundred times more information through the ear than they can get in a lifetime through books. This requires an organization, which again means money. Men enough there are in India to work out this plan, but alas! they have no money. It is very difficult to set a wheel in motion, but when once set, it goes on with increasing velocity. After seeking help in my own country and failing to get any sympathy from the rich, I came over to this country through your Highness' aid. The Americans do not care a bit whether the poor of India die or live. And why should they, when our own people never think of anything but their own selfish ends?

My noble prince, this life is short, the vanities of the world are transient, but they alone live who live for others, the rest are more dead than alive. One such high, noble-minded, and royal son of India as your Highness can do much towards raising India on her feet again, and thus leave a name to posterity which shall be worshipped.

That the Lord may make your noble heart feel intensely for the suffering millions of India sunk in ignorance, is the prayer of:

Vivekānanda

Modern India

In one of his last essays, written in Bengali in 1899, Vivekānanda declared India's independence of Western standards. Scouting blind imitation of foreign models as unmanly, he called on his compatriots to take pride in their past and to unite rich and poor, high and low castes, in order to make their nation strong.

[From *The Complete Works of the Swami Vivekananda,* IV, 408-13].

It has been said before that India is slowly awakening through her friction with the outside nations, and, as the result of this little awakening is the appearance, to a certain extent, of free and independent thought in modern India. On one side is modern Western science, dazzling the eyes with the brilliance of myriad suns, and driving in the chariot of hard and fast facts collected by the application of tangible powers direct in their incision; on the other are the hopeful and strengthening traditions of her ancient forefathers, in the days when she was at the zenith of her glory—traditions that have been brought out of the pages of her history by the great sages of her own land and outside, that run for numberless years and centuries through her every vein with the quickening of life drawn from universal love, traditions that reveal unsurpassed valour, superhuman genius, and supreme spirituality, which are the envy of the gods—these inspire her with future hopes. On one side, rank materialism, plenitude of fortune, accumulation of gigantic power, and intense sense pursuits, have through foreign literature caused a tremendous stir; on the other, through the confounding din of all these discordant sounds, she hears, in low yet unmistakable accents, the heart-rending cries of her ancient gods, cutting her to the quick. There lie before her various strange luxuries introduced from the West—celestial drinks, costly well-served food, splendid apparel, magnificent palaces, new modes of conveyance—new manners, new fashions, dressed in which moves about the well-educated girl in shameless freedom; all these are arousing unfelt desires in her; again, the scene changes and in its place appear, with stern presence, Sîtã, Sãvitrī,[7] austere religious vows, fastings, the forest retreat, the matted locks and orange garb of the semi-naked Sannyasin. Samadhi, and the search after the Self. On one side, is the independence of Western societies based on self-interest; on the other, is the extreme self-sacrifice of the Aryan society. In this violent conflict, is it strange that Indian society should be tossed up and down? Of the West, the goal is—individual independence, the language—money-making education, the means—politics; of India, the goal is—Mukti, the language—the Veda the means—renunciation. For a time, modern India thinks, as it were: I am running this worldly life of mine in vain expectation of uncertain spiritual welfare hereafter, which has spread its fascination over me; and again, lo! spellbound she listens: "Here, in this world of death and change, O man, where is thy happiness?"

On one side, New India is saying: "We should have full freedom in the selection of husband and wife; because, the marriage in which are involved the happiness and misery of all our future life, we must have the right to determine, according to our own free will." On the other, Old India is dictating: "Marriage is not for sense enjoyment, but to perpetuate the race. This is the Indian conception of marriage. By the producing of children, you are contributing to, and are responsible for, the future good health of the society. Hence, society has the right to dictate whom you shall marry and whom you shall not. That form of marriage obtains in society, which is conductive most to its well-being; do you give up your desire of individual pleasure for the good of the many."

On one side New India is saying: "If we only adopt Western ideas, Western language, Western food, Western dress and Western manners, we shall be as strong and powerful as the Western nations"; on the other, Old India is saying: "Fools! By imitation, other's ideas never become one's own—nothing, unless earned, is your own. Does the ass in the lion's skin become the lion?"

On one side, New India is saying: "What the Western nations do are surely good, otherwise how did they become so great?" On the other side, Old India is saying: "The flash of lightning is intensely bright, but only for a moment; look out, boys, it is dazzling your eyes. Beware!"

Have we not then to learn anything from the West? Must we not needs try and exert ourselves for better things? Are we perfect? Is our society entirely spotless, without any flaw? There are many things to learn, we must struggle for new and higher things till we die—struggle is the end of human life. Sri Rāmakrishna used to say: "As long as I live, so long I learn." That man or that society which has nothing to learn is already in the jaws of death. Yes, learn we must many things from the West, but there are fears as well.

A certain young man of little understanding used always to blame Hindu Shastras before Sri Rāmakrishna. One day he praised the *Bhagavad Gītā*, on which Sri Rāmakrishna said: "Methinks some European pandit has praised the *Gītā*, and so he has also followed suit."

O India, this is your terrible danger. The spell of imitating the West is getting such a strong hold upon you, that what is good or what is bad is no longer decided by reason, judgement, discrimination, or reference to the Shastras. Whatever ideas, whatever manners the white men praise or like, are good; whatever things they dislike or censure are bad! Alas! What can be a more tangible proof of foolishness than this?

The Western ladies move freely everywhere—therefore, that is good; they choose for themselves their husbands—therefore, that is the highest step of advancement; the Westerners disapprove of our dress, decorations, food, and ways of living—therefore, they must be very bad; the Westerners condemn image-worship as sinful—surely then, image-worship is the greatest sin, there is no doubt of it!

The Westerners say that worshipping a single Deity is fruitful of the highest spiritual good—therefore, let us throw our Gods and Goddesses into the river Ganges! The Westerners hold caste distinctions to be obnoxious—therefore, let all the different castes be jumbled into one! The Westerners say that child-marriage is the root of all evils—therefore, that is also very bad, of a certainty it is!

We are not discussing here whether these customs deserve countenance or rejection; but if the mere disapproval of the Westerners be the measure of the abominableness of our manners and customs, then it is our duty to raise our emphatic protest against it.

The present writer has, to some extent, personal experience of Western society. His conviction resulting from such experience has been that there is such a wide divergence between the Western society and the Indian as regards the primal course and goal of each, that any sect in India, framed after the Western model will miss the aim. We have not the least sympathy with those who, never having lived in Western society and, therefore, utterly ignorant of the rules and prohibitions regarding the association of men and women that obtain there, and which act as safeguards to preserve the purity of the Western women, allow a free rein to the unrestricted intermingling of men and women in our society.

I observed in the West also, that the children of weaker nations, if born in England, give themselves out as Englishmen, instead of Greek, Portuguese, Spaniard, etc., as the case may be. All drift towards the strong, that the light of glory which shines in the glorious may anyhow fall and reflect on one's own body; i.e., to shine in the borrowed light of the great is the one desire of the weak. When I see Indians dressed in European apparel and costumes, the thought comes to my mind—perhaps they feel ashamed to own their nationality and kinship with the ignorant, poor, illiterate, downtrodden people of India! Nourished by the blood of the Hindu for the last fourteen centuries, the Parsee is no longer a "Native"! Before the arrogance of the casteless, who pretend to be and glorify themselves in being Brãhmans, the true nobility of the old, heroic, high-class Brãhman melts into nothingness! Again, the Westerners have now taught us that those stupid, ignorant, low-caste millions of India clad only in loin cloths are not bretherns! They are therefore no more our kith and kin!

Oh India! Wither this mere echoing of others, with this base imitation of others, with this dependence on others this slavish weakness, this vile detestable cruelty, wouldst thou, with these provisions only, scale the highest pinnacle of civilization and greatness? Wouldst thou attain, by means of thy disgraceful cowardice, that freedom deserved only by the brave and the heroic? Oh India! Forget not that the ideal of thy womanhood is Sîtã, Sãvitrî, Damayanti;[8] forget not that the God thou worshippest is the great Ascetic of ascetics, the all-renouncing Shankara, the Lord of Uma;[9] forget not that thy marriage, thy wealth, thy life are not for sense pleasure, are not for thy individual personal happiness; forget not that thou art born as a sacrifice to the *Mother's* altar; forget not that thy social order is but the reflex of the Infinite Universal Motherhood; forget not that the lower classes, the ignorant, the poor, the illterate, the cobbler, the sweeper, are thy flesh and blood, thy brothers. Thou brave one, be bold, take courage, be proud that thou art an Indian, and proudly proclaim: "I am an Indian, every Indian is my brother." Say: "The ignorant Indian, the poor and destitute Indian, the Brãhman Indian, the Pariah Indian, is my brother." Thou too clad with but a rag round thy loins proudly proclaim at the top of thy voice: "The Indian is my brother, the Indian is my life, India's gods and goddesses are my God, India's society is the cradle of my infancy, the pleasure-garden of my youth, the sacred heaven, the *Vārāṇasi*,[10] of my old age." Say, brother: "The soil of India is my highest heaven, the good of India is my good," and repeat and pray day and night: "O Thou Lord of Gauri,[11] O Thou Mother of the Universe, vouchsafe manliness unto me! O Thou Mother of Strength, take away my weakness, take away my unmanliness, and—*Make me a Man!"*

—***A.C. Basham***

REFERENCES

1. Five sacred trees planted together to form a grove used for contemplation.
2. A wealthy disciple. Bābu is a respectful Bengali form of address.
3. The consort of Rāma, hero of the *Rāmāyana.* She exemplifies the Hindu ideal of womanhood.
4. An affectionate form of address.
5. King Janaka, the father of Sītā.
6. Blessed One.
7. Sāvitrī, celebrated in Indian legend, for having saved her doomed husband from the God of Death.
8. Damayanti, celebrated in Indian legend for her devotion to her husband Nala.
9. Umā, a name of the wife of Shiva or Shankara (the Gracious One).
10. Banaras.
11. A name for the wife of Shiva.

11

Separate Movements among the Muslims

RECONSTRUCTION OF INDIAN ISLAM

While these intellectual and reform movements were shaking Hindu society to its foundations, the Indian followers of Islam were also experiencing something similar. Syed Ahmad Khan (1817-1898) was the outstanding Muslim leader of the nineteenth century who was strongly in favour of Indian Muslims accepting Western culture and reconstructing their social and religious life in accordance with it. It is significant that he also based his reforms on religious books. In the field of religion he undertook to show the basic similarity of Islam and Christianity, and hence to advocate a reconciliation of their followers. He wrote defending social intercourse with Christians and justified the point theologically. More daring, he published a study of the Bible, beginning with a sympathetic commentary, and—against the dogma that it had been corrupted—declaring that it was authentic. By reporting from each religion what is essential and what is accretion, he arrived at the concept of 'Religion' itself, as that which is common to all, a practical morality. He himself was genuinely tolerant, deeming that man's religion was his private affair which should not be obtruded from and not to be even discussed between those of different faiths, lest friendship be weakened. Even the slightest sign of religious bigotry distressed him.[1]

His opposition to miracles and supernatural authority was expressed vigorously in the following manner: "...it has become a habit with men that they ascribe miracles and supernatural attributes to an object or a person whom they consider to be holy or sacred. This is why men have interpolated supernatural factors into Islam, which are not worthy of belief, but such credulous persons believe in them. However, this is a grievous mistake. Any religion which is true, or claims to be true, cannot contain such elements in it as are contrary to nature and offend human reason, so that a sensible person would find it impossible to believe in them. A true faith in its pristine purity is absolutely free from such supernatural and irrational elements."[2]

There were others who also wanted the Muslim society in India to modernise itself and who based their arguments on the claim that Islam was the very source of Western liberalism and that modern science and civilisation owed their origin to it. Syed Amir Ali (1849-1928), an eminent jurist and prolific writer, was a typical representative of this group. He maintained that Islam was a dynamic religion commensurate with modern ideas and that its teachings released the very spirit which promoted those ideas. In his book, *Anglo-Muhammadan Law,* Amir Ali attempted to codify and interpret Islamic laws and institutions so as to bring them in harmony with modern legal concepts.

The Ahmadiya Movement, founded by Mirza Ghulam Ahmad (1839-1908), belongs to a different category inasmuch as it was apparently a protest movement directed against Christianity and Westernisation. But it also contained some liberal ideas and some reforms directed against many superstitions and corruptions.

REVIVALISM AMONG THE INDIAN MUSLIMS

The turn towards the past was not confined to the Hindus: Indian Muslims too were affected. The author of *Modern Islam in India,* who saw in Sir Syed's emergence as a leader the signs of arrival of a Muslim bourgeoisie in the social, economic and professional fields of India, thus explains the emergence of the revivalist spirit among Indian Muslims: "Sir Syed's Islam gave them permission to be bourgeois. They needed also a courage, confidence and drive to be bourgeois; and eventually, solace."[3]

Like the parallel movements among the Hindus, these Islamic movements tried to assert the superiority of their religion and their past and succeeded, at least, in spreading that their religion and philosophy of life were not inferior to others. These trends in Islam in India can be traced back to 1891, when Amir Ali published his book, *The Spirit of Islam.* Amir Ali recognised the interrelations between religious reform and the progress in other directions. He noted: "In the Western world, the Reformation was ushered in by the Renaissance and the progress of Europe commenced when it threw off the shackles of Ecclesiasticism. In Islam also, enlightenment must precede reform; and, before there can be a renovation of religious life, the mind must first escape from the bondage which centuries of literal interpretation and the doctrine of 'conformity' have imposed upon it. The formalism that does not appeal to the heart of the worshipper must be... subordinated to the inner feelings; and the lessons of ethics must be impressed on the plastic mind; then alone can we hope for that enthusiasm in the principle of duty taught by the prophet of Islam. The reformation of Islam will begin when once it is recognised that divine words rendered into any language retain their divine character and that devotions offered in any tongue are acceptable to God."[4]

Here, as well as in the following quotation, Amir Ali reminds one of Dayananda Saraswati, the founder of the Arya Samaj, both in regard to the questioning of the authority of orthodox priests and in the claims that their religions, in their early phases, were in line with the scientific spirit of the modern times: "For five centuries, Islam assisted in the free intellectual development of humanity but a reactionary movement then set in, and all at once the whole stream of human thought was altered. The cultivators of science and philosophy were pronounced to be beyond the pale of Islam. Is it impossible for the Sunni church to take a lesson from the church of Rome?.... Islamic protestantism, in one of its phases—Mutazilaism—has already paved the way. Why should not the great Sunni church shake off the old trammels and rise to a new life?"[5]

There was, however, a contradiction in Amir Ali's ideas, as those of other religious movements which were progressive in content but revivalist in form. "They succeeded moderately well in making out Islam to be liberalism, rationalism, tolerance, etc.; but it must be noted that in so doing they produced a religion which is in fact less liberal, less rational and less tolerant, than Sir Syed's. They have written glowing and laudatory accounts of the brighter aspects of Islamic history, to parade its liberalism; but have produced almost no liberal scholarship to study that history impartially. They have quoted the Quran and the traditions voluminously to prove that Islam is rational, but have never subjected the Quran and the traditions to rational criticism. They have drawn a picture of their Prophet tolerant and teaching tolerance; and have murdered someone who drew another picture. Besides, now that they have such a fine religion and true prophet themselves, they have increasing contempt for other religious systems, in which it is not difficult for them to pick faults."[6]

Apart from developing such an exclusive outlook these revivalists performed another disservice. Although they generally accepted the liberal values and tried to incorporate them in their social life, in some respects they defended orthodoxy. The defence of the seclusion of women and the consequent maintenance of their low status was an instance of this, although they verbally claimed that Islam positively gave women the highest possible position and tried to answer their critics by saying that there existed in Europe and America a situation of total moral depravity.

Another school of thought prevalent among the Indian Muslims went a step further in manifesting this revivalist tendency. They were the conservative group who established the institution *Nadvatul Ulema* at Lucknow in 1894. In their view Syed Ahmad and Amir Ali had made too many concessions to Western thought. The avowed object of the *Nadva* was to achieve a synthesis of the old and the new opinions, and its establishment, as well as early development, was encouraged by various leaders of the Aligarh movement, "but soon it became, in opposition to the Aligarh College, a centre of revivalist, if not reactionary, activity."[7]

The Ahmadiya Movement, the progressive features of which we have already referred to, also manifested a high degree of revivalism. The following summing up of the career of the founder of the movement, by one of his disciples, explains this character: "Thus ended an eventful life which in the short space of eighteen years—1890 to 1908—not only had revolutionised many of the existing religious ideas but had even taken definite steps in an entirely new direction—the preserving of Islam to, and the spiritual conquest of, the West. Deep religious mysteries which had baffled human minds for centuries had been unravelled. The second advent of Christ, the tribulation of the Anti-Christ, the prevalence of God and Megog, the coming of the Mahdi and similar other topics were mysteries which affected the two great religions of the world. Christianity and Islam, both contending for the mastery of the world, and an inspired man was indeed needed to lift the veil from the face of these mysteries. Such a man was Mirza Ghulam Ahmad. He was gifted not only with inspiration to elucidate the deepest mysteries, but also with the faith and energy which enabled him to give a new direction to the dissemination of Islam which had hitherto found the West deaf to its message. Christianity was out to conquer the Muslim world; in temporal matters it had ousted Islam, but, in the spiritual domain, Mirza Ghulam Ahmad made a bold start and gave a challenge to Christianity in its very home. It is as a result of that challenge that mosques are being built in the great centres of Christianity, that a vital change is being brought about in the attitude of Europe towards Islam, and that thousands of cultured and advanced Europeans are finding a haven of peace under its banner."[8] Here we have the same aggressive attitude of teaching the west as was evident in the speeches of Swami Vivekananda.

Very few students of modern India will deny that these religious movements, though primarily concerned with the social and religious questions, had a political significance insofar as they affected the thinking processes of large sections of people. It is said that "the Hindu response to the Christian challenge had now come full circle, from resistance, through defence by imitation, to proud self-confidence."[9] This analysis applies not only to the Hindu and Muslim religious movements but to the political movements; only in the political field they came a bit later than in the religious field. Moreover, while Hindus went back to their religious and historical past to assert their self-confidence, the Muslims went back to early Islam and the past history of Arabia. This led not only to a conflict between Indians and Westerners, whose cultural and religious invasion they wanted to resist, but also to a schism between the Hindus and the Muslims, as the two relied on separate sources of spiritual and intellectual sustenance.

REFERENCES

1. W.C. Smith, *Modern Islam in India* (London, 1946), p. 17.
2. Wm. Theodore de Bary and others, *The Sources of Indian Tradition* (New York, 1958), p. 743.
3. W.C. Smith, n. 1, p. 48.
4. Amir Ali, *The Spirit of Islam* (London, 1949), pp. 185-6.
5. *Ibid.*, p. 454.
6. W.C. Smith, n. 1, p. 57.
7. Ikram and Spear, *The Cultural Heritage of Pakistan* (London, 1955), p. 191.
8. M. Ali, *The Founder of the Ahmadiya Movement* (Lahore, no date), pp. 80-1.
9. Wm. Theodore de Bary, n. 2, p. 603.

12

In Support of Western Education, Art and Science

About thirty years have now elapsed since the despatch of 1854. During this period the condition of India has undergone a considerable change. In 1854, when the despatch was written, India was certainly in a condition which might justify our thinking that the acquisition of knowledge through the medium of the vernaculars of the country would be enough to meet our immediate wants. But now such is not the case. Vernacular education is no more regarded as sufficient for our daily affairs of life. It is only of use to us in our private and domestic affairs, and no higher degree of proficiency than what is acquired in primary and middle vernacular schools is requisite for that purpose; nor is more wanted by the country. It is English education which is urgently needed by the country, and by the people in their daily life. We see that an ordinary shopkeeper who is neither himself acquainted with English, nor has any English-knowing person in his employment, feels it a serious hindrance in the progress of his business. Even the itinerant pedlars and boxwalas, who go from door to door selling their articles, keenly feel the necessity of knowing at least the English names of their commodities, and of being able to tell their prices in English. It is high time that government as well as the people should exert themselves to their utmost in extending this popular education, if I may be allowed so to call it.

In vernacular and English primary and middle schools, the object of which is to impart instruction up to that standard only, and not to prepare scholars for a higher standard of education, the interests of the country will no doubt be furthered by teaching the Western sciences to the standard laid down for those institutions in vernacular. But in English elementary schools, which have been established with the object of serving as a stepping-stone for higher education, the tuition of European sciences through the medium of the vernacular is calculated to ruin the cause of education.

I confess I am the person who had first entertained the idea that the acquisition of the knowledge of European sciences through the medium of the vernacular would be more beneficial to the country. I am the person who had found fault with Lord Macaulay's Minute of 1835 for exposing the defects of oriental learning, and recommending the study of Western science and literature, and had failed to consider whether the introduction of European sciences by means of the vernaculars would bring any advantage to the native community.

I did not confine my opinion to theory alone, but tried to put it into practice. I discussed the matter at various meetings, wrote several pamphlets and articles on the subject, and sent memorials to local and supreme governments. A society, known by the name of 'The Scientific Society, Allygurh', was established for the very purpose, and it translated several scientific and historical works from the English language into the vernacular. But I could not help acknowledging the fallacy of my opinion at last. I was forced to accept the truth of what an eminent liberal statesman has said, that "what the Indian of our day wanted, whether he was Hindu or Mohammedan, was some insight into the literature and science which were the life of his own time, and of the vigorous race which were the representative of all knowledge and all power to him." I felt the soundness and sincerity of the policy adopted by Lord William Bentinck when he declared that "the great object of the government ought to be the promotion of European literature and science among the natives of India".

I am personally of opinion that the duty of Government, in relation to public instruction, is not to provide education to the people, but to aid the people in procuring it for themselves.

But the public feeling seems to differ widely from this view. The people base their argument on the fact that in India all matters affecting the public weal have always rested with Government. They see no reason why the education of the people, which is also a matter of public weal, should not rest with Government. After a full consideration of the question in all its bearings, I have come to the conclusion that the native public cannot obtain suitable education unless the people take the entire management of their education into their own hands, and that it is not possible for Government to adopt a system of education which may answer all purposes and satisfy the special wants of the various sections of the population. It would, therefore, be more beneficial to the country if Government should leave the entire management of their education to the people, and withdraw its own interference. The public opinion is not in favour of this view. A very able and intelligent native gentleman said to me some time ago that the idea that we should ourselves procure our education was an entire mistake; that the use of the word 'ourselves' in any national sense, with reference to the people of India, was out of place, for no nation could undertake any great work without the co-operation of all classes, high and low, whether in point of wealth or political and administrative power. He added that the higher order of political and administrative power in India was held by Government and its European officers, and that those who benefited most by commerce in India were also Europeans; and, therefore, they formed in reality the most important section of the Indian population.

Apropos of this, I may be allowed to relate an incident which has happened to myself. At the time when the Mohammedan Anglo-Oriental College was established at Allygurh, I asked a European gentleman, holding a high office under Government, to grant some pecuniary aid to the institution. He replied that he was not bound to help us in the matter, that the institution was a child of ours and not his, and that he would rather be inclined to spurn it than to hug it with paternal affection.

It may be briefly stated that the causes which have kept the Mohammedans aloof from English education may be traced to four sources—to their political traditions, social customs, religious beliefs, and poverty. An insight into the political causes can be obtained by studying the history of the last two centuries. The Mohammedan public was not opposed to the establishment of British rule in India, nor did the advent of British rule cause any political discontent among that people. In those days of anarchy and oppression, when the country was in want of paramount power, the establishment of British supremacy was cordially welcomed by the whole native community; and the Mohammedans also viewed this political change with feelings of satisfaction. But the subordinate political change which this transition naturally involved as a consequence, and which proved a great and unexpected blow to the condition of the Mohammedans, engendered in them a feeling of aversion against the British, and against all things relating to the British nation. For the same reason they conceived an aversion for the English language and for the sciences that were presented to them through the medium of that language. But this aversion is now declining in the same degree in which education is spreading among Mohammedans.

The Mohammedans were proud of their socio-political position, and their keeping aloof from English education may in some measure be ascribed to the fact that the Government colleges and schools included among their pupils some of those whom the Mohammedans, with an undue pride and unreasonable self-conceit and vanity, regarded with social contempt. They could never be brought to admit that sound and useful learning existed in any language except Arabic and Persian. They had given a peculiar form to moral philosophy, and had based it on religious principles, which they believed to be infallible; and this circumstance had dispensed, as they thought, with the necessity of European science and literature. I still remember the days when, in respectable families, the study of English, with the object of obtaining a post in Government service or securing any other lucrative employment, was considered highly discreditable. The prejudice has now, however, much slackened.

The religious aspect of the question I have already described. The poverty of the Mohammedan community is only too obvious to require any comment. I am, however, of opinion that the above-mentioned socio-political causes, though still extant, have been mitigated to a considerable extent, and the Mohammedans are gradually freeing themselves of old prejudices and taking to the study of English literature and science.

—*Syed Ahmad Khan*

13

Muslims and the Early Phase of the Congress*

I have referred to the fact that my association with the Congress is of very recent date; but this admission is not merely personal. It involves the political history of the community to which I belong, and if I give a brief outline of it to you, it is only for the purpose of elucidating a problem which is the most vital of all the problems we have to solve today. When, in 1885, some Indian leaders, assisted by their British sympathisers, founded the Indian National Congress, the Muslims of India did not participate in the movement except in a few individual cases. If their lack of Western education made them unfit to take part in a movement essentially that of the classes educated according to Western notions, their political temper made them an element that was not unlikely to prove dangerous to any political movement. They had already lost the rule of India, but the tradition of that rule had survived. This had increased the aversion they had always felt for the new type of education. The rule of India had finally passed from Muslim into English hands by slow and hardly perceptible degrees in the hundred years that intervened between the battle of Plassey and the Indian Mutiny; but the Muslims had not ceased to regard the new rulers of India as something very inferior to themselves in civilisation and culture. This storm of ill-will and disdain had been gathering force for a whole century and was at last precipitated in 1857. The Mutiny began near Calcutta as an affair of the Indian Army,

* Extracts from Maulana Mohammed Ali's Presidential Address at the Annual Session of the Indian National Congress.

but in the storm-centre of Delhi and of my own province, where it had to be fought out, if English rule was to continue in India, it soon attracted to itself many forms of discontent, and religion was inextricably mixed up with politics. Although so many Muslims had, at enormous risk to themselves, assisted the British at a time when hardly anyone could have predicted their eventual success with any degree of assurance, it was the Muslim aristrocracy in those parts that suffered most from the terrible aftermath of the Mutiny. In fact, in its permanent results, even more than in some of its terrors, it could, without any great exaggeration, be compared to the social upheaval that the French Revolution meant to the old nobility of France. The remnants of Muslim aristocracy, deprived of all influence and of many of its possessions, certainly did not expect the return of Muslim rule. Nevertheless, a whole generation of Muslims kept sullenly aloof from all contact with the culture of the new rulers of India which in their heart of hearts they still despised. They were in no mood to take advantage of the education provided by the Universities of Calcutta, Bombay and Madras, founded in the very year in which the Mutiny convulsed the regions which formed the political centre of Muslim India. It was a natural consequence of this attitude of Muslims who sulked in their tents that when, nearly thirty years later, a new generation of Indians, who owed their education to the English, inaugurated a political movement on Western lines, Indian Muslims should be unfit by lack of such education to participate in that movement. Nevertheless, the Congress which called itself 'Indian' and 'National' felt the need of Muslim participation, for it could not justify its title without it.

SYED AHMAD KHAN OPPOSES MUSLIM PARTICIPATION

Efforts were, therefore, made early enough to enlist Muslims as delegates. But at this juncture Sir Syed Ahmad Khan, the great pioneer of Western education among Muslims, stepped into the political arena, and in two historic speeches, one delivered at Lucknow on the 28th December, 1887, and the other at Meerut on the 16th March, 1888, decisively checked whatever signs the Muslims had shown of political activity in support of the Congress movement. It is by no means a difficult task to criticise those speeches, for they contained many fallacies to which no politically minded Muslim could subscribe today. But I am not one of those who declare, merely on the strength of some ill-advised expressions, characteristic of so militant a controversialist as Syed Ahmad Khan, that he was opposed to the cooperation of Hindus and Muslims.

Although his own public career after retirement from public service was identified with a movement for the uplift of his own community, he was a good Indian as well as a good Muslim and many of his speeches prove him to have been an ardent patriot inspired with the love of Indian unity. And those who knew him personally can testify to the staunchness of his friendship with many Hindus, which could not have survived the narrow prejudices of which he has sometimes been accused.

No more true is the charge that he was opposed to Muslim participation in politics for all time. Whatever arguments he may have used in the two political utterances to which I have referred, to convince his Muslim hearers, there were two arguments and two only, that had obviously convinced Syed Ahmad Khan himself of the undesirability of Muslim participation in the Congress at the time. He realised to the full that nothing would suit the temper of the Muslims of his day better than the vocation of critics of their British supplanters in the governance of India; and he also realised that such a pursuit would be as dangerous to the continuance and progress of a peaceful political movement like the Congress as it was easy. This was the first argument that impelled Syed Ahmad Khan to keep his community under restraint in politics. The second argument was no less potent. The Muslims must educate themselves if they desired the uplift of their community, and yet it was no easy task to reconcile Muslims to Western education even in an institution of their own, which unlike government colleges and schools, would not divorce religious from secular learning. The easy pursuit of a policy in which the Muslims could act as destructive critics of the hated infidel government was sure to offer superior attractions to the dull and drab constructive programme of the educationalist, and he, therefore, set himself to oppose all diversion of Muslim activities into the more attractive, but for the time being less useful, political channel. Reviewing the actions of a bygone generation today when it is easier to be wise after the event, I must confess I still think the attitude of Syed Ahmad Khan was eminently wise, and much as I wish that some things which he had said should have been left unsaid, I am constrained to admit that no well-wisher of Muslims, nor of India as a whole, could have followed a very different course in leading the Muslims.

Be it remembered that the man who enunciated this policy was not at the time a *persona grata* to the major portion of the community which he sought to lead. He was hated as a heretic because of the heterodoxy of his aggressive rationalism in interpreting the Holy Quran, and his militant opposition to popular superstitions believed in by the bulk of the orthodox and to shackling customs consecrated by time, though wholly authorised by Islam. He was abused and vilified by hundreds of thousands of his co-religionists, and for long the college that he had founded at Aligarh was the *bete noire* of the pious Muslim. And yet the entire community followed his political lead without a murmur. Neither fallacious arguments nor even political clap-trap could have possessed such potency, and it is my firm belief that his advocacy succeeded mainly because of the soundness of the policy advocated.

For two decades thereafter the Muslims had hardly any politics or any political institution worth the name. On important occasions when Syed Ahmad Khan, and, of course, his British supporters, thought any demand of the Congress if satisfied would not be productive of good for the Muslims, he would call together a few of his friends, mostly trustees of the Aligarh College, who used to form a society bearing some such name as the 'Muslim Defence Association', and a resolution of this body would be published in the *Pioneer* and in Syed Ahmad Khan's own local weekly newspaper in due course. That was all that the Muslims would do in those days in the field of politics.

I am far from denying that Syed Ahmad Khan knew perfectly well that his policy was more than acceptable to his official supporters, who would have in all likelihood put every possible obstruction in the way of his college and his Educational conference if he followed another less acceptable to them. But a very close study of his character leads me to declare that he was far from possessing the sycophancy with which some of his political critics have credited him. Indeed, even the opportunism of which his policy savoured could not have been entirely palatable to a nature so independent as his. In the year 1907, soon after the commencement of a new era in Muslim politics inaugurated by the foundation of the Muslim League, to which I shall presently refer, there occurred a strike of the students of Syed Ahmad Khan's College at Aligarh, owing to the support given against them by their own English Principal and Professors to the police that had picked up a quarrel with one of them. Just about that time fell the anniversary of Syed Ahmad Khan's death, celebrated annually in the College as the 'Founder's Day'. For that occasion I had written in Urdu an ode addressed to the late founder of my college, and referring to this unmistakable indication of the students' self-respect and of their willingness to make the necessary self-sacrifice demanded of the haughty disdain of the foreigner, I had said:

> "It is you that had taught the community all this 'mischief'; if we are its culmination, you are its commencement."

That I am not alone in this estimate of Syed Ahmad Khan's character and policy will be proved by an interesting conversation that I shall relate. Once when my brother was still in the public service, an old English official asked him who he thought was the greatest rebel in India against British rule. And, correcting my brother's answer, that experienced official had declared that it was no other than Syed Ahmad Khan, loyalist of loyalists! When my brother protested against this astonishing judgement, he said: "Do you think young Muslims who are being taught at Aligarh almost as well as our own boys at Harrow and Winchester, who live their lives and can beat them at their own games, would obsequiously serve them when they come out as Indian civilians or members of such other superior services. No. Mr. Shaukat Ali, the days of British rule in India are numbered, and it is your loyal Syed Ahmad Khan that is the arch-rebel today!"

Like only too many of us, this British official too had failed to realise the paralysing effect of the education given in the colleges and schools established or favoured by this foreign Government and had only foreseen the dissatisfaction and discontent that it must inevitably produce. With a Muslim University, chartered, aided and controlled by government still flourishing at Aligarh, so far as the numbers of the teachers and the taught and a university chest filled with the contributions of the rich are concerned, though robbed of all generous ideals and national and communal ambition, and existing side by side with another, poor in everything save its ideals and its dreams, into which my old college had seemed to have transformed itself three years ago, I cannot boast that the 'arch-rebel' of Aligarh has altogether succeeded in his 'rebellious' endeavour. But it is my firm conviction that he had always aimed and intended to produce staunch Muslims and patriotic Indians even if he could not perhaps contemplate a near enough future for India in which his 'young barbarians all at play' could be other than 'loyal British subjects.'

ALIGARH AND THE MUSLIM LEAGUE

Nearly thirty years after the foundation of the universities in the three presidency towns of India—a period which corresponds with the growth of a new generation—the Congress had inevitably come into existence. It was no easy task that Syed Ahmad Khan had accomplished in founding an Anglo-Oriental College of his own community within two decades of the Indian Mutiny in the very regions which had formed the storm-centre in 1857. In obedience, as it were, to a law of nature, once more nearly thirty years after the foundation of this college, there came into being a political institution of the Muslims who had not availed themselves of the educational facilities provided by the state universities, and could not consequently share in the political awakening which those universities had indirectly brought about. And it is not without significance that fairly prominent among the founders of the Muslim League at Dacca at the end of 1906 were some alumni of Syed Ahmad Khan's own college.

This inaugurated a new era in the political life of the Indian Muslims. Some months previously a Muslim deputation had waited at Simla on the Viceroy, Lord Minto, to place before him and his government a statement of the Muslim demands in connection with the Minto-Morley reforms then foreshadowed. To follow the fashion of British journalists during the war, "there is no harm now in saying" that the deputation's was a 'command performance! It was clear that government could no longer resist the demands of educated Indians and, as usual, it was about to dole out to them a morsel that would keep them gagged for some years. Hitherto the Muslims had acted very much like the Irish prisoner in the dock, who, in reply to the judge's inquiry whether he had any counsel to represent him in the trial, had frankly replied that he had certainly not engaged counsel, but that he had 'friends in the jury'! But now the Muslims' 'friends in the jury' had themselves privately urged that the accused should engage duly qualified counsel like others. From whatever source the inspiration may have come, there is no doubt that the Muslim cause was this time properly advocated. In the common territorial electorates the Muslims had certainly not succeeded in securing anything like adequate or real representation, and those who denounced and deplored the creation of separate electorates for which the Muslims had pleaded, should have remembered that separate electorates were the consequence, and not the cause, of the separation between Muslims and their more numerous Hindu brethren.

—Mohammed Ali

14

Islam—Neither Violent nor Dogmatic

The remark that "the sword is the inevitable penalty for the denial of Islam", is one of the gravest charges falsely imputed to this faith by the professors of other religions, and arises from the utter ignorance of those who make the accusation. Islam inculcates and demands a hearty and sincere belief in all that it teaches; and that genuine faith which proceeds from a person's heart cannot be obtained by force or violence. Judicious readers will not fail to observe that the above-quoted remark is entirely contrary to the fundamental principles of the Moslem faith, wherein it is inculcated in the clearest language possible: "Let there be no forcing in religion; the right way has been made clearly distinguishable from the wrong one" (chap. x, 98). And also: "If the Lord had pleased, all who are on the earth would have believed together; and wilt thou force men to be believers? No man can believe but by the permission of God, and He will pour out His indignation on those who will not understand" (chap. ii, 257).

The principle upon which Moses was allowed to use the sword to extirpate all idolaters and infidels, without exception of one single individual, is by no means applicable to Islam. Mohammedanism grasped the sword, not to destroy all infidels and pagans, not to force men to become Moslems at the sword's point, but only to proclaim that eternal truth, the unity of the Godhead, throughout the whole extent of the then known globe.

According to Islam, the best and the most meritorious act is the preaching and making generally known existence of one invisible God. It could hardly be expected that, in the infidel countries, there could be sufficient personal security for such Moslems who might choose to inculcate by precept, exhort by preaching and practise open the worship of the unity of God; and, therefore, appeal was at once made to the sword in order to establish the superiority of the Moslem power, and to ensure security and tranquillity for such Mohammedans as might choose to preach the whole—some doctrine of their faith, and to live in peace in those countries, so that their habits, conduct and manner of living might serve as an example for the unbelievers. The effect so desirable—viz., that the Moslems might live in peace and preach the worship of the one only true God—was only attainable by one of three ways. First, the voluntary conversion of the people; secondly, the establishment of peace and security by means of alliances, offensive and defensive; and thirdly, by conquest. As soon as the desired object was secured, the sword was immediately sheathed. If tranquillity was established by either of the last two methods, the parties had no authority to interfere with the religious observances of the subject or of each other; and every person was at liberty to observe, unmolested by any one, all the ceremonies and rites, whatever they might be, of his creed.

The preceding observations likewise show clearly the gross mistake into which some writers have fallen, when they assert that in Islam 'toleration is unknown'. But in saying this, we do not mean to deny that some of the later Mohammedan conquerors were guilty of cruelty and intolerance, but that the doctrines of our religion ought not to be judged from their actions. We must, however, inquire, in order to discover whether they acted according to it or not, and we shall then arrive at an undeniable conclusion that their actions were in opposition to the doctrines of their religion. But at the same time, we find that those conquerors who were anxious to act according to the doctrines of their religion did practise tolerance, and granted amnesty, security and protection to all their subjects, irrespective of caste or creed. History furnishes us with innumerable instances of the tolerance of Moslem conquerors, and we shall here quote a few remarks made by various Christian writers, which prove the tolerant spirit of Islam.

Though we are told that the Moriscoes were banished because they would not turn Christians, I suspect there was another cause. I suspect they, by their arguments, so gained upon the Christians, that the ignorant monks thought that the only way their arguments could be answered was by the Inquisition and the sword; and I have no doubt they were right, as far as their wretched powers of answering them extended. In the countries conquered by the Caliphs, the peaceable inhabitants, whether Greeks, Persians, Sabeans, or Hindus, were not put to the sword as the Christians have represented, but after the conquest was terminated, were left in the peaceable possession of their properties and religion, paying a tax for the enjoyment of this latter privilege, so trifling as to be an oppression to none. In all the history of the Caliphs, there cannot be shown anything half so infamous as the Inquisition, nor a single instance of an individual burnt for his religious opinion, nor, do I believe, put to death in a time of peace for simply not embracing the religion of Islam. No doubt, the later Mohammedan conquerors, in their expeditions, have been guilty of the great cruelties Christian authors have sedulously laid to the charge of their religion; but this is not just. Assuredly religious bigotry increased the evils of war, but in this the Mohammedan conquerors were not worse than the Christians....

John Davenport, in his 'Apology', writes in the following strain: "It was at the Council of Nicea that Constantine invested the priesthood with that power whence flowed the most disastrous consequences, as the following summary will show: the massacres and devastations of nine mad crusades of Christians against unoffending Turks, during nearly two hundred years, in which many millions of human beings perished; the massacres of the Anabaptists; the massacres of the Lutherans and Papists, from the Rhine to the extremities of the North; the massacres ordered by Henry VIII and his daughter Mary; the massacre of St. Bartholomew in France; and forty years more of other massacres, between the time of Francis I, and the entry of Henry IV into Paris; the massacres of the Inquisition, which are more execrable still, as being judicially committed; to say nothing of the innumerable schisms, and twenty years of popes against popes, bishops against bishops; that poisonings, assassinations; the cruel rapines the insolent pretensions of more than a dozen popes, who far exceeded a Nero or a Caligula in every species of crime, vice, and wickedness; and lastly, to conclude this frightful list, massacre of twelve millions of the inhabitants of the New World, executed crucifix in hand. It surely must be confessed that so hideous and almost uninterrupted a chain of religious wars, for fourteen centuries, never subsisted but among Christians, and that none of the numerous nations stigmatised as heathen ever spilled a drop of blood on the score of theological arguments."

The celebrated Mr. Gibbon, the greatest of the modern historians, and whose authority cannot be doubted or questioned, writes as follows: "The wars of the Mohammedans were sanctified by the Prophet; but, among the various precepts and examples of his life, the Caliphs selected the lessons of toleration that might tend to disarm the resistance of the unbelieving. Arabia was the temple and patrimony of the God of Mohammed; but he beheld with less jealousy and affection the other nations of the earth. The polytheists and idolaters who were ignorant of his name might be lawfully extirpated; but a wise policy supplied the obligations of justice, and, after some acts of intolerant zeal, the Mohammedan conquerors of Hindustan have spared the pagodas of that devout and populous country. The disciples of Abraham, of Moses, and of Jesus were solemnly invited to accept the more perfect revelation of Mohammed; but if they preferred the payment of a moderate tribute, they were entitled to the freedom of conscience and religious worship.'

The author of an article entitled 'Islam as a Political System,' inserted in the *East and the West,* thus expresses himself on the subject under consideration: 'Mohammed was the only founder of a religion who was at the same time a temporal prince and a warrior. Their power lay exclusively in restraining violence and ambition; his temptation was ambition, and the sword was at his disposal. It is, therefore, to be expected that, making religion a means of temporal power, and having obtained that sway over the minds of his followers by which they accepted as law and right whatever he chose to promulgate, his code should be found at variance with all others, and even in opposition to those dictates of justice which are implanted in the breasts of all men. If, then, we find that it is not so—if we find him establishing maxims of right in international dealings, of clemency in the use of victory, moderation in that of power, above all, of toleration in religion,—we must acknowledge that, amongst men who have run a distinguished course, he possesses peculiar claims to the admiration of his fellow-creatures." Again he says: "Islam has never interfered with the dogmas of any faith, never persecuted, never established an Inquisition, never aimed at proselytism. It offered its religion, but never enforced it; and the acceptance of that religion conferred co-equal rights with the conquering body, and emancipated the vanquished States from the conditions which every conqueror, since the world existed up to the period of Mohammed, has invariably imposed."

—***Syed Ahmed Khan***

15

Marriage Reform among the Hindus

There is no doubt some basis for the trite observation that India is not a country but a continent and contains not a nation but a congeries of nations; and when a stranger reads or hears the vast extent of the country and of something like the three hundred millions who inhabit it, of the numerous religions and faiths which they profess and follow, Mahomedanism, Zoroastrianism, Sikhism, Buddhism, Jainism, Hinduism—with the almost countless sects which are included in it—he is apt to be impressed with the absolute correctness of the remark. But to one who belongs to the country or has a knowledge of the actual condition of Indian society, the facts appear otherwise; and undoubtedly so, as far as the Hindu community is concerned. From the Himalayas down to the Indian Ocean and from the Indus to the Brahmaputra the Brahmin, Kshatriya, Vaishya and Shudra classes have institutions, manners, customs, observations, ceremonies which in essential features are the same. The members of the Jain sects differ though they do in religious beliefs, dogmas and rituals from the orthodox sections of the Hindu community, are in the other matters which constitute their everyday life, so similar that it is impossible to say from outward appearances whether a person is a Jain or an orthodox Hindu. We may go one step further and say that, as far as the bulk of the Mahomedan community is concerned, excluding religious observances, their domestic life is in several respects similar to that of the Hindus, which by the way cannot be a matter for surprise; for, they consist of the descendants of converts to

Mahomedanism and come from the same stock as the Hindus. Hindus and Mahomedans can well, in spite of difference of religion, be called one nation. But leaving Mahomedans out of consideration, the Hindus, who form the majority of the population, possess socially as well as politically all the characteristics of a nation; and every question affecting their well-being is a question of national importance. Out of the total population of 287 millions returned by the census of 1891, over 222 millions are Hindus, Sikhs, Jains and Buddhists. Social reform in India, therefore, possesses a significance far greater than in other countries; and it is to be expected that every attempt to effect any alteration in the existing practices should in these days of free thought and free discussion excite the watchful jealousy and keen criticism of a highly intellectual people and often produce warm controversies.

There is no subject in regard to which there is greater difference of opinion productive of hot discussion than Marriage Reform. That phrase apparently giving expression to one idea denotes really speaking several subjects; many of them concern the very basis of social life. For an adequate treatment of them even a good-sized volume will not suffice.

In this paper the question of marriage reform is considered in some only of its most important aspects. It is proposed to deal chiefly with infant or early marriage, compulsory marriage and enforced widowhood; and even in regard to these it is hardly possible to give within the limits at my command anything more than a statement of the conclusions which the discussions that have taken place on the subjects suggest to me. Solicitous for the regeneration and progress of the great community to which I have the proud privilege to belong and believing firmly that its material and moral regeneration cannot be effected without a considerable readjustment of its marriage customs, I am not unmindful that there are amongst my countrymen several with knowledge, experience and abilities superior to what I may be allowed to possess, who with equal fervour believe that many of the views herein set forth are wrong and that Hindu society would suffer if the attempt to give effect to them succeeds. The number of such, however, is small among those who, having received the benefit of education in modern literature and science, are accustomed to subject every question to the test of reason.

According to the prevailing practice every girl must be married and the religious ceremonies which create the binding tie and irrevocably unite the wife to the husband must be performed before the girl attains puberty. As will be shown further on, there are a few sections of Hindus amongst whom girls are permitted to be kept unmarried sometimes for years after they reach womanhood. But the general practice insists upon marriage before that event. For the marriage of men no age is prescribed, but the general custom is to get them married at the age of 15 or 16, indeed very often at the age of 10 or 11 even. Thus throughout the whole society the spectacle is presented of boys of 17 and 18 and girls of 13 and 14 entering upon married life and subjected to all its responsibilities. Little children of 14 becoming mothers is a very common sight. It is now conceded by most thinking people that this is a very deplorable state of things; and it is unquestionable that serious evils have resulted from these early marriages. The general deterioration in physique universally noticeable is justly attributed to this baneful custom, the greatest sufferers being the poor girls who enter upon maternity before their bodies are properly developed. The progeny of such parents cannot be otherwise than weak and sickly.

Equally harmful, both to the individuals concerned and to the country generally, are the interference with education and the crushing out of all spirit of enterprise and adventure which result from these early marriages. Thousands of promising young men have been forced to give up their studies and seek employment because the means of their parents or guardians were exhausted in getting them married and the maintenance of the members of the family became itself a difficult question. In these days when so much thought is bestowed on the question of the poverty of the country and schemes for the restoration of the industrial eminence which India once enjoyed, are discussed, it should not be forgotten that some of the causes which have brought about pecuniary embarrassments and consequent ruin of many families can be removed by ourselves, if we only sufficiently exert ourselves and persevere in our efforts.

If the education of boys is interfered with and its progress hampered, that of girls in most cases completely ceases with her marriage, *i.e.*, from the age of 8 or 10. As it is, female education is in a most backward condition in this country and what of the so-called instruction is received is only till the age of 10 and after that there is complete cessation of it.

The want of enterprise and absence of love of adventure is phenomenal. Boy husbands burdened with family cares, with their education cut short, can hardly think of striking into new paths and going in quest of adventures either for fame or for money. The very restricted and low view taken of women's right and position can hardly be attributed to the notions about early or compulsory marriages, for they exist in communities which were or are free from these trammels. But there is no doubt that the elevation of woman to her proper position and her moral equipment for that position is greatly retarded by the existing marriage customs.

The information disclosed by the old Sanskrit literature in regard to the institutions of the ancient Hindus shows that, during the best period of Aryan history, neither compulsory nor early marriage was enjoined for women and it is during this period we find a high view taken of the dignity and rights of women and the wife was regarded as the half of her husband, not only figuratively, but participated in the glories and privations of war and peace and was his companion in the study of science and philosophy.

Closely connected with early and compulsory marriage is its expensiveness. The presents to the bridegroom and his relations in cash and in kind, the feasts and parties, the vain displays and processions which a man who gets his daughter married to the son of a person of his social position has to provide, not merely strain his resources, but in many cases absolutely bring about his bankruptcy. This absurd costliness is which is mainly responsible for the disparagement and low estimate in which female children are regarded and for the dislike which the majority feel for them.

In some castes and sections the evil has gone so far as to pervert human nature and brought about female infanticide, turning loving parents into worse than human monsters. To check these atrocities government had to interfere and special methods had to be devised in the shape of the provisions of the Infanticide Act.

In the contemplation of human misery there is no more pathetic and heart-rending spectacle than the child widow of 8 or 10, hopelessly condemned to life-long misery and degeneration. And this exists only because there is compulsory child marriage. Even the staunchest and most orthodox upholders of the current Hindu beliefs admit that the lot of the child widow is most pitiable. A Hindu father, howsoever devout he might be, curses his fate and the harsh customs which bind him down, when he sees his child reduced to such a condition. A few figures will show the extent of the evils and the harms they produce. In 1891 there were amongst Hindus, Sikhs, Jains and Buddhists 89,051 boys below the age of 4 who were married and 223,560 married girls of the same age. The number of widows below the age of 4 was 10,641. The number of married boys between 5 and 9 years of age is nearly six lakhs and two thousand and that of girls over 18½ lakhs. The total number of married males below the age of 14 is 2,725,124 and that of girls is 6,871,999. The number of widows between 5 and 9 years of age is 52,759 and of those between 10 and 14 years of age is 143,100. Of these two lakhs and more of widows below the age of 14 all but some four thousand are Hindus proper.

These evils are recognised by almost all educated and thinking persons, whether they belong to the old or to the new school. But while the Progressive Party urges and active steps should be taken for removing them altering the existing customs, the orthodox party resist their demands as untenable on the ground that they are opposed to religion.

The reform advocated is mainly on the following lines:

1. Option of marriage to be allowed to women in the same way as to men.

2. No girl to be married before 18 or at the earliest 16.

3. No man to be married till he is at least 20 and in no case till he is able to maintain himself and his family.

4. Abolition of customs which bring about unnecessary expenditure on occasions of marriage.

5. Removal of the religious and social prohibition against the remarriage of a widow and the recognition of her claim to be socially treated in the same way as any other married woman of her caste.

As things stand, the greatest difficulty is about the general acceptance of the changes set forth in points 1, 2, 3 and 5.

One of the features common to all the innumerable castes and sub-castes into which the Hindus are divided is the firm acceptance of the doctrine that marriage is absolutely necessary in the case of a female. Amongst the higher castes, *i.e.*, those who are comprised under the three original main castes of Brahmins, Kshatriyas and Vaishyas there is another common feature and that is the prohibition of the remarriage of a widow. The feeling against widow-remarriage amongst the members of the castes is so great that even amongst seceders and dissenters from orthodox Hinduism like the Jains (who are classed as Vaishyas) there is the same horror of women's contracting a second marriage as amongst Brahmins and Kshatriyas. Nay, in the Shudras amongst whom widow-remarriage is recognised and considered lawful, the general sense of the community, whatever the law might lay down, accords a much lower status to a remarried widow than to a woman who was married when she was a virgin.

The Progressive Party, while anxious for the removal of evils, are conscious that no change which is not supported by authority or precedents has any chance of being considered by their countrymen. Their efforts have, therefore, been directed towards such only as can receive these supports. In spite, however, of this attitude of theirs, they have not yet succeeded in securing the acceptance of their proposals by the majority of the Hindus. They believe, however, that reason and justice are on their side, and they expect to win their battle by the weapons drawn from the ancient scriptures and ancient history.

In regard to compulsory and early marriage the position of the orthodox party is this. There are certain sacraments ordained as necessary for every person male or female. In the case of males of the three regenerate classes, this necessary sacrament is the *upanayana* or *thread* ceremony. For females and Shudras the place of this necessary sacrament is supplied by marriage. Relying on a text contended to be that of Ashwalayana, one of the highest authorities on ceremonial law, it is advanced that certain ceremonies constituting the consummation of marriage must be performed immediately after a young woman attains puberty. Great reliance is also placed on various texts and dicta of writers of eminence laying down that the father of a girl who attains puberty before marriage goes to hell. The chief recognised test is from Parashara which says, "a girl in her eighth year is a *Gauri*, in the ninth year a *Rohini*, in her tenth year a *Kanya* and above that a *Rajaswala*. The giving in marriage of a *Gauri* will lead to *Nak* (the celestial region belonging to Indra), of a *Rohini* to *Vaikuntha* (the one belonging to Vishnu), of a *Kanya* to *Brahmaloka* and a *Rajaswala* to hell". The prevailing and accepted belief is that no Hindu can, without imperilling the future of his soul, keep his daughter unmarried after puberty. The social penalty for the disregard of this injunction is excommunication, perhaps the severest punishment which a community can inflict.

On the other hand, the advocates of reform urge that there is no Vedic text or anything in the works of any of the *Smriti* writers except the one attributed to Ashwalayana, which some question as spurious, which lays down that every girl ought to be married and the marriage consummated at the very first appearance of womanhood. Passages from Manu and other authorities of equal position are pointed out by them as distinctly opposed to the alleged heinousness of keeping a girl unmarried at puberty. One passage of Manu states that a girl is to wait for three years after attainment of puberty to see if her father gets her married. If he does not, then at the end of that period, she may look out for a suitable husband for herself and select and marry one. Baudhayana states similarly. This, it is urged with great force, evidently means that a girl does not lose her caste or social position by being kept unmarried after puberty. The great medical authority Sushruta says: "A woman is considered to be a child till the sixteenth year of her age and afterwards to be in her youth till the thirty-second year. If a man of less than 25 years begets a child on a woman of less than 16 years, it remains in the womb. If it is born it does not live long, and if it lives at all, it is weak."

It deserves to be noted that in ancient times not only was it not considered necessary to marry women before puberty, but at times they even remained unmarried their whole life. The names and memory of the Brahmavadinis, Gargi Vachaknavi, Sulabha Maitreyi, Vadava Pratitheyi who never married at all and passed their whole life in celibacy are still regarded with veneration by the most orthodox Hindus. Judging from the instances of Draupadi, Shakuntala, Damayanti and several others, it would seem that it was quite an ordinary thing for girls to remain unmarried till considerably after they attained the years of discretion. The orthodox party urges that the instances are all those of women of the Kshatriya caste. To this the other side replies that the laws of marriage are the same for all three regenerate classes.

The facts stand thus: formerly it was as much in the option of women as of men to marry or not to marry and the tie itself was contracted generally after the attainment of the years of discretion. The sentiment of the community, however, became changed in course of time and not only did the old practice of women remaining unmarried or marrying considerably after they came of age fell into disuse, but it came to be regarded that it was unallowable for women to pass an unmarried life and further they ought to be married before they reach puberty. This accounts for the apparently conflicting texts and dicta to be found in works on ceremonial law.

There can be no question that the prohibition of the remarriage of widows is of comparatively recent origin. Manu says:

"If the husband has disappeared and cannot be found, if he is dead, if he is banished or is neuter or becomes an outcaste: in the case of the occurrence of these five misfortunes a second husband is ordained for women."

The same or similar permission is accorded in the Smritis of Narada and Parashara. About the comparative authority of the Smriti writers the orthodox rule is (the Smriti of Parashara is the guiding authority in the *Kaliyuga, i.e.,* the present age). Katyayana, Vasistha, Shatatapa and Prajapati accord this permission to women whose marriage was not consummated. All the same there is the recognition of the right of a woman who has lost her husband to contract a second marriage. And yet there is no matter which the orthodox regard with greater horror than the remarriage of widows. Neither the weight of authorities, nor the accordance of the demand with the principles of natural justice, nor compassion for the hard fate of the child widow, seems to diminish that horror.

Amongst the three regenerated classes, or rather amongst Hindus who do not belong to the Shudra caste, both the widow who contracts a remarriage, as also the man who marries her, are considered as degraded, polluted and as having lost caste. It is not permissible to eat food prepared or touched by them; nay it is not allowed, what in English would be called, to dine with them at the same table. Those who dine with them are excommunicated. At one time even those who attended a remarriage were subjected to the same penalty. The very sight of a remarried woman is regarded with aversion. The orthodox will condone a widow, however scandalously she misbehaves herself if she makes penance; but a remarried woman as also her husband are beyond the pale of the most extreme penance. Shunned in life they are execrated after death. Still more wonderful, these sentiments are more strongly held by women than by men. One of the main reasons which is at the bottom of this is the extreme reverence in which the husband is held by the wife, whose highest conception of womanly dignity and felicity is to be united with her husband not only in her life-time but after her death also."

Whatever the origin, the sentiment is there. A mother who is grieving over the widowhood of her child, if asked whether she would agree to her remarriage, would, in the majority of cases, unhesitatingly say that she would rather wish the child were dead than remarried.

Though there is a mass of authorities and historical instances in support of widow-remarriage, the obstacles in the path of its recognition by the community generally are far greater than in that of late marriages. Even amongst Shudras in certain sub sections widow-remarriage is considered prohibited. The ordinary Kunbis also amongst whom it is permitted to look upon a *Pat* wife (a woman married after she became a widow) as lower in status and dignity than other married women who were married virgins. Though our courts have accorded to the son by a *Pat* wife the same rights as to the son by the *Lagna* wife, it is well known that amongst the higher sections of the Shudras at any rate, the son by the *Lagna* wife is accorded precedence in all social and religious matters over the sons by the *Pat* wife. Some even go to the length of questioning the right of the *Pat* wife's sons to inheritance when there are sons from a *Lagna* wife.

It cannot be determined with any degree of exactness from what time compulsory marriage before puberty and enforced widowhood came into vogue. Nor is it known whether any efforts were made to remove these evils, or any protest raised against them till the last century. In the last quarter of that century, however, the injustice of enforced widowhood roused the attention.

The organised efforts made to raise the marriageable age of girls, if later than the remarriage movement, have, on the other hand, roused less violent opposition and have received a greater measure of success. Thirty years ago the age at which most girls were married amongst the Brahmins south of the Narmada was 7 or 8. It has now gone up to 10 and 12. Even the latter limit has in numerous cases been exceeded by a year or so by orthodox people without any reproach from their community. In Mysore the movement against infant marriages can show results hardly to be expected in British India. Being supported by an enlightened ruler and a sympathetic minister, it was able without much difficulty to obtain recognition from the *Acharyas* (the spiritual heads of the different sections of the community) and encountered less formidable opposition than it would have done otherwise. Proceeding cautiously, the Mysore

Government first ascertained whether the general sense of the people was in favour of progress or against it, and when it was satisfied from the proceedings which took place in the Representative Assembly in 1892 that there was a fairly large volume of public opinion behind it, it introduced and in 1894 passed a Bill regulating the age of marriage, which prohibits under pain of criminal prosecution the marriage of girls below the age of 8, and men above the age of 55 to girls below the age of 14. In the regulation as passed there is no minimum limit for boys. Some ardent reformers may not regard the results achieved as remarkable or even satisfactory. But when it is borne in mind that the heads of all the three great divisions of Brahmins, the Smarta, Madhva and Ramanuja sects have laid down that 10 is the proper age and marriages below 8 are sinful, that is a matter of no small moment where there are 2,32,276 girls below the age of 4 who are married or are widows and 19,04,915 between the ages of 5 and 9. Equally valuable is the measure as a precedent to be followed by the other Indian States if not by the British Government.

A few years later two Bills were prepared, one by the Hon'ble Mr. Jambulingam Mudaliar and the other by the Hon'ble Mr. Ratnasabhapaty Pillai of the Madras Legislative Council, for obtaining a similar enactment for the Hindus of the Madras Presidency generally. But there is no likelihood of proposals for the introduction of measures of this kind being entertained by the British Government, unless the demand comes from the majority of the people. The extent to which the British Government would interfere in matters connected with the religious observances and social customs of the people of this country, has been over and over again authoritatively laid down and was restated only the other day by the present Viceroy. The regulation of the age of marriage is a matter which is clearly outside that sphere, unless the bulk of the people desire legislative sanction for what they have come to agree amongst themselves. The right and duty of the government to take suitable action in a matter like that covered by the Age of Consent Bill stands on a different footing. Besides, the social controversies of the last sixteen years have satisfied many members of the party of progress who were first disposed to welcome outside help, particularly that of government, that any proffer of such help or any demand for it, far from furthering the cause of progress, distinctly retards it by injuring the susceptibilities of the people and rousing their suspicions.

The administrations of the Native States occupy a more advantageous position in this respect and an enlightened policy, calculated to educate public opinion and give effect to reforms proceeding on the lines of least resistance, if adopted by them is far less likely to encounter active hostility than any similar measure of the Government of India. The Baroda Government in 1893 formulated certain proposals of a purely permissive character in regard to marriage reform, but these were abandoned later on. It is trusted that this does not betoken an intention on the part of that State to leave social reform severely alone.

But whether in British India or in Native States, the great factor, the one on which chief reliance has to be placed, for bringing about the desired transformation, is the education of public opinion. According to the strict letter of the text of Parashara every Hindu father who gives his daughter in marriage after the tenth year goes to hell. Numerous fathers, who claim to be orthodox and are treated as such, commit this heinous sin of marrying their daughters after the age of 10, and yet they are not excommunicated or subjected to any social inconvenience. Of the Hindu female population between the ages of 10 and 14 over 38½ lakhs are unmarried. Taking the higher castes among whom this rule prevails to be only 8 per cent of the total Hindu population, there would be 3 lakhs unmarried girls between the ages of 10 and 14 belonging to these classes. The plain inference to be deduced from this is that the injunction about marrying a girl before she completed her tenth year is not in practice at least regarded as mandatory. If all the reformers 'hot and cold', instead of carping at each other, were to combine, would they not be able to obtain a similar relaxation in regard to the injunction about the marriage of girls before puberty? Amongst the Nambudri Brahmins of Malabar, who are most staunch in their orthodoxy, it is permissible to defer marriages of girls till after the attainment of womanhood. Amongst the

Kulin Brahmins of Bengal the same thing exists. Amongst the Patane Prabhus of Bombay and among the Mudaliar and other castes of the Madras Presidency claiming to hold an intermediate position between Kshatriyas and Shudras, the general practice is to marry girls after the age of 12. The position of the advocates of change is that it is beyond question that our forefathers exercised the right, which every community has, of altering their customs and institutions according to change of circumstances to bring them into conformity with their notions of what was proper or improper. If in doing so they could not be considered transgressors of religion and law, it would hardly be just to regard as irreligious the proposals of those who after all are merely asking for a return to the earlier and better traditions of their race.

The change can be effected by the community alone. No compulsion from outside is feasible or desirable. It would be unprofitable to go into the controversies which were raised by the Ages of Consent Bill or Mr. Malabari's proposals. At present there is certainly no proposal which calls for the legislative or executive action of government. The appeal is to the community. As in all matters so in this, neither the formation of correct opinions nor their articulate expression, nor the devising of methods for putting them into practice, can be expected from the masses. It is on the leaders that this task devolves. It is the duty of men of light and leading, of thought and reason, of culture and refinement.

The question naturally arises who are these men of light and leading and what is the recognition to be extended to the numerous spiritual heads (Gurus, Swamis, Maharajas or whatever else they be called) of the different sections and sub-sections of the community. It is not claimed for a moment that thought, reason or culture is confined to the recipients of western education merely. But it is submitted that no one, whatever stores of bookish lore he may have laid by, can justly claim to possess these who blindly and without examination accepts a thing on the principle of scriptumest, who declines to consider the justice or injustice, propriety or impropriety of existing institutions and customs, forbidding his reason to sit in judgement on them to determine whether they are harmful or serve any useful purpose, whose imagination is not fired and whose sympathies are not moved by the spectacle of the misery he sees around him, misery which is self-inflicted and is preventible. It is devoutly to be wished that all angry recriminations about hot reformers and cold reformers will cease and that all reference be avoided and that both those who advocate action from within and those who demand help from without will combine and devote their energies to obtain the recognition and acceptance of the principles which they hold in common.

The attitude of the Acharyas except in one or two matters has not been such as to encourage the Progressive Party in expecting help from them in the solution of the great problem of social reform. It is, therefore, natural that there should be among them if not a disposition to ignore these dignitaries, at any rate an indifference to secure their co-operation. It is not the Reform Party alone who does not attach great value to the authority of the Acharyas. The orthodox party are as prompt in questioning it whenever any of these spiritual heads show any disposition to make a concession to the demand for reform. Their position is, it is true, rather anomalous. But it is sincerely hoped that they and all people of the orthodox party will study the signs of the times and show a more liberal and sympathetic spirit to remedy admitted grievances than they have done till now. The cause of progress will not wait for them. By their uncompromising opposition to it, it is their position which is being imperilled.

For the extravagance in marriage expenditure no blame attaches to the *Shastras* and it is the custom and the innate variety of man which is responsible for it. There being no difficulties about the Shastras to be overcome in this matter, one would have thought that reform here would be easily accomplished. But except in certain places and in certain sections, where the evil had reached extraordinary proportions, little change is noticeable. On the contrary the expensiveness of marriage has increased in almost all grades of the community, particularly in the middle and well-to-do classes during the last thirty years.

Formerly there were inter-marriages between the four castes—the Brahmins, Kshatriyas, Vaishyas and Shudras—with certain restrictions. A Brahmin could marry a Brahmin, Kshatriya, Vaishya or Shudra woman; and a Kshatriya could marry a Kshatriya, Vaishya or Shudra wife and so on; and the issues by all the marriages were legitimate and the wives all lawfully married. This was *Anuloma* marriage. But if a woman of a higher caste married a man of a lower caste, it was *Pratiloma* marriage or a mesalliance. But though reprobated, such marriages were not unlawful. Devayani's marriage with Yayati was never questioned. When and how this old system disappeared, it is not easy to say. We have the fact that in the present day, the restrictions on marriage have become absurdly unreasonable and intolerable. Not only has not inter-marriage between the original four main castes gone out of fashion, but persons belonging to the different sub-sections of the same caste cannot intermarry without danger of social ostracism and reprobation. For instance, the three main sections of the Maharashtra Brahmins, Deshastha, Kokanastha, Karhada—do not intermarry. Among the Deshasthas again, the Rigvedis, Madhyandinis, Kanvas, Maitrayanis cannot intermarry. The same is the case between the Madhvas, Smartas and Ramanujas in Southern India, the Nagars and the Audich and other Brahmins in Gujerat, the Kashmiris, Saraswats, Kanyakubjas etc. in Northern India, the Shenavis and the western coast Saraswats in Western India. From the original four castes have sprung the present thousand and one castes ranking below the Brahmins and sub-castes. These numerous castes and their sections observe similar prohibitions in regard to inter-marriages with sections of equal rank. The result is restriction in the field of choice, creation of unnecessary difficulties and increase in marriage expenditure. The change advocated and which is the only one practicable is inter-marriage between those different sub-sections of a caste which interdine. How difficult to move Indian society is, is shown by what happened in regard to this matter. Deshasthas, Kokanasthas and Karhadas were some years ago allowed to intermarry by one of the Shankaracharyas, yet no action has followed this edict. In the last century some progress was sought to be made in this matter by the Maharashtra

Brahmins. Bajirao I had a Deshastha wife. But it does not appear that any other marriages of that kind took place.

Even dissenters from orthodox Hinduism have not escaped this influence. The Lingayats, who ought, according to the theory of their religion, to be all on a footing of equality, are as strict in their observance of prohibitions against inter-marriage between different sub-sections as the orthodox people. The same thing is to be seen amongst Jains. What is still more wonderful is that even converts to Christianity observe in some places caste distinctions in regard to marriage almost as rigorously as the Hindus.

Prejudice against mesalliances is common both to the East and the West. To expect the total removal of all restriction in regard to class in the matter of marriage is to expect an impossibility. It is not only against Indian nature but against human nature. Confining our efforts to the domain of the practicable, our action should be directed to the bringing about of inter-marriage between the sub-sections of the chief castes as now existing.

In this matter it is not the Shastraic ordinances which have to be surmounted but custom. But unreasoning custom is as difficult to change as any practice sanctified by express text of law.

To polygamy and to Kulinism the most serious form in which it exists, a passing reference only can be made. Polygamy though permitted by the *Shastras* is nowhere except in Bengal a serious evil. The number of men with more than one wife is in the other parts of India very small. But in Bengal among the Kulin Brahmins its extent and magnitude are even now shocking. Twenty, thirty, forty, sixty, eighty and even hundred women married to one man who seldom sees the majority of them for years as they are left to pine at their paternal houses by the husband who exacted the payment of large sums for condescending to marry and whose few and far between visits can only be obtained by the inducement of fresh presents for every such visit, ought to be a matter of great regret and humiliation to any civilized people. In 1866 an attempt was made to obtain its prohibition by law. But after a very careful and sympathetic enquiry it had to be abandoned as impracticable, unless the government was prepared to make departure from its settled policy, which it was not.

The Shastras do not permit the supersession of a wife by her husband except under very special circumstances. It is submitted that the reform party ought to take an even higher stand and agitate for the establishment of the principle that no man should marry another wife while one is living or continues united to him in marriage.

Education and the juster appreciation of right and wrong which flows from it are producing their effect, and even the polygamy of the Kulins is decreasing. The Polyandrous tribes who are coming under the operation of these beneficent influences and the Malabar Marriage Bill testify to the acceptance by the enlightened persons among them of a higher ideal of family life. On the Aryans the descendents of the old Rishis and the valiant warriors who created, spread and developed civilization in this vast land is imposed the sacred duty of restoring and enforcing the lofty views of life and duty enunciated by the great men of their race. The cause of reform is the cause of justice, of righteousness, of humanity. Shall we tolerate unequal laws? Shall we, while claiming every sort of liberty and licence for men, impose upon women restrictions and disabilities productive of the utmost misery and degradation in too many cases? On our reply to this and congnate questions and the attitude we adopt towards them depends the future of our race. If we want to recover our former greatness, we must set high in the sanctuary of our heart the goddess of truth and justice and paying entire devotion to her and vowing undivided homage to her, consecrate ourselves to establish her sway both in our houses and in our country in social matters as in political matters.

—Rao Bahadur R.N. Mudholkar

16

A Plea for Widow Re-Marriage

In India, religion, not content with unlimited control over spiritual concerns, gradually wormed itself into the details of daily life, however trifling and however removed from the generally accepted idea of religion. In extending its dominion it insensibly increased in power. A departure, never so slight, from the rules of everyday life as observed by the Hindus came to be looked upon as a sacrilege and as a consequence, to entail the penalty of excommunication. None can lay any claim to the name of a Hindu unless he endorses every practice sanctioned by the priestly class. Either a person must be a Hindu all over, or he cannot be a Hindu at all.

The Vedas troubled themselves only about particular religious performances like sacrifices. The Smritis extended their conquests and brought purely temporal things like apprenticeships, marriage, succession, adoption and the criminal law within the pale of religion; and its example was imitated by the *Puranas* in the work of extending the dominion of religion to regions which were not its legitimate objects. How far this extending process would have carried its operations had it been allowed to go its own way, it is idle to speculate. But it is amusing to note the fetters with which religion thought fit to bind the apparently trifling routine of life. The obsequious ceremonies, that have to be performed before the dead are allowed to be burnt, are an instance in point. A son must, after the death of his father, part with his mustachios, and the shaving business has to keep time with incantations uttered by a priest.

The adjustment of the pile of wood that is to consume the dead is accompanied by appropriate incantations. Even acts to which no ingenuity can attach the semblance of religious significance have their own religious appurtenances. On cremation grounds as near marriage altars, on death-beds as on hymenal beds, in dinner parties as on fast days, there is only one idea present to the mind of a Hindu, one idea alone runs through acts performed by him; and that all-engrossing idea is one of religion.

Fiction actively aids religion in its conquests. Comparatively recent works in order to claim the respect generally yielded to antiquity, are palmed off on the credulous reader as of ancient dates as the Vedas themselves. Even the Vedas are referred back to a fabulously old period. Mr. B. G. Tilak has, in a scholarly treatise on the antiquity of the Vedas, clearly shown that the greater part of the Vedas was written only about 4,000 years ago. The Smritis, which on the very face of them appear to be much more recent, are devoutly believed by all orthodox Hindus to be reminiscences of the Vedas. Works on mathematics which were evidently composed after the Greek invasion are credited with being emanation from Brahma. Even works of a couple of decades back are said to have been fathered on the famous Vyas with something like indecent haste. How far Vyas and others to whom these later works are imputed will like the several acts of filiation and what welcome the imposters will meet at their hands it is difficult to imagine. But it is beyond reasonable doubt that though in an age in which the mist of ages of superstition is being dispelled by the searching light of historical investigation they are not likely to find any credence, still they have done incalculable mischief by tightening the fetters with which superstitious India was manacled. The fact that great rulers like Shivaji who were in their time only great heroes have within the short period of a couple of centuries risen to the dignity of demi-gods illustrates the same credulous tendency. The result has been that antiquity which, in other countries, would be at best but extremely suspicious evidence, is in India conclusive proof of the desirability of a custom.

This process of extending the domain of religion, once understood, easily explains the subordinate position which has been assigned to Indian women. They were prevented by the physical irregularity of their lives from taking part in sacrificial performances which, in some not rare cases, extended over inconveniently long periods, and thus gradually lost the importance which they once enjoyed in the times of Gargi and Maitreyi, much as the warrior and merchant classes lost their occupations being inconsistent with an unimpeded participation in religious ceremonies. That these latter too once shared high privileges with the priestly class is borne out by the history of Viswamitra and by traces being found in the Vedas of a time when warriors could give lessons in religious matters to priests without scandalizing them.

That a widow had the right of remarrying is placed beyond the shadow of a doubt by several Smritis which have been already explained with remarkable lucidity by Pandit Ishwar Chandra Vidyasagar, Vishnu Shastri Pandit and Mr. Justice Ranade. The most important of them are the works of Manu, Narada and Parasara. Whatever legal force we may attach to the several taxts, we cannot escape the conclusion to which they point—that the custom of widow marriage was once in vogue in India. The ancient Indian law on the subject was, if anything, more liberal in its provisions than the modern English law. Of course, in the progress of time, as the extension of the range of religion began to contract on the liberty enjoyed by women, the above texts began to be tortured out of their natural significance by ingenious interpreters to fit in with a state of society that had of late come into being. This method being deemed of doubtful utility in cases of serious controversies, was later on given up in favour of the creation of new texts to be fathered on some ancient sage or other. This point in the history of the movement is represented by the Puranic period when the leaders of the Brahmanic community began to marshal their forces against the advocates of Buddha's religion which, from an insignificant sect, had been growing to gigantic proportions and which threatened at no distant date to swallow it up unless active steps were taken to represent the Brahmanic religion it tempting colours. To this period the great Indian epics belong. Even in the Purana, however, traces of the custom of re-marriage are found.

"The first on the list is the remarriage of Ulupi, the widowed daughter of a patriarch of the Naga tribe, who on the death of her first husband was given in marriage by her father to the famous Arjun, the hero of the *Mahabharat* story. Ulupi, in so many distinct words, is described to have become one of Arjun's many wives, the son she bore to him is emphatically described to be his legitimate-born son, and not one of the inferior sorts of sons. The entire narrative in the *Mahabharat* and still more emphatically Jaimini's continuation corroborates this assertion.

The second illustration is from the story of Nala and Damayanti. The latter princess, after having been abandoned by her husband in the forest, found her way after much suffering to her father's house. While there, she bided in hope for some time, but could get no news of her absent lord. Thereupon, with the consent of her mother she contrived a plan for finding out her long-lost Nala. She secured the services of a learned Brahman to advertise to all the neighbouring princes that she was going to have a second *Swayamvara* and make a second choice of a husband for herself in consequence of the disappearance and probable death of Nala, her first husband. This Brahman carried his message to the Court of the King of Ayodhya, with whom Nala had sought shelter in the disguise of an obscure charioteer. The king of Ayodhya, on hearing this news, prepared to go to the *Swayamvara* and Nala drove the chariot for him with extraordinary speed and the secret of which was known to him only. This display of skill and certain other circumstances led to his subsequent recognition, whereupon all idea of the second marriage was given up. This story has its importance, for it shows the received opinion among the people of the day, to whom such an invitation did not appear in any heinous light, did not appear more extraordinary than the invitation to the first marriage. That a woman like Damayanti, so renowned for her devotion to her husband, should, with the consent of her parents, try to discover the whereabouts of her lost husband by this stratagem, at once shows that remarriage did not strike people in those times as an abomination, but as an ordinary commonplace thing.

The third illustration is from *Padma Purana*, the story of the unfortunate daughter of the King of Benares who was married no less than twenty times, it being her peculiar misfortune that as soon as the marriage rites were all performed, the husband so married died, but though this happened over and over again, the father, with the consent of the sage Brahmans of his court, solemnly gave her in marriage as often as she became a widow. The emphatic words used in the text preclude the supposition contended for by some disputants, that the several husbands were removed by death before, and not after the binding marriage rites had been celebrated.

Soon after this followed the celebrated expulsion of the Buddhists from India. One of the impressions that the Buddha's religion left back was the further curtailment of the liberty of women. To this period is relegated the birth of the odious custom of disfigurement of widows in imitation of a similar custom of the Buddhistic ascetics. Once it obtained a vogue, marriage of widows was rendered practically impossible.

Along with the introduction of enforced widowhood there was springing up a hateful custom, *i.e.*, that of infant marriage, which was in the end to prove its worst enemy. The two customs thus brought together by a mere accident were diametrically opposed to each other. An infant widow is a pitiful result of their combined action, and in her turn, is wreaking a just vengeance on them by representing the evil consequences of each in their exaggerated form. A widowed infant has been the first to attract the sympathies of an advocate of late marriages as she has been the first to enlist the sympathies of all pioneers of widow marriage. This young and at the same time widowed creature is a favourite both with the reformers and the anti-reformers, and paradoxical though it may appear, nothing would please both the parties so much as a complete annihilation of her.

The reasons why, after being established as a sacred custom enjoying the privileges attending the idea of its sacerdotal birth, enforced widowhood continued in full swing for a period of nearly two thousand years, are not far to seek. Religious institutions are, as a rule, not so fragile of frame as other institutions. Systems based on temporal grounds can be discontinued at pleasure when no justification remains for their continuance. Obedience to government legislation can be enforced only so long as obvious blessings flow from it. It is true, as observed by an acute thinker, that a change in law never anticipates a change in popular sentiment. But it is equally true that it is never long in following it. The code of Manu, on the other hand, has been the law of the Hindus for a period of nearly two thousand years, and a construction of its texts inconsistent with their obvious meaning is to this day scarcely admitted except by a side wind. The rigidity of Hindu scared law thus made a disturbance in the Hindu social structure every corner of which breathed of nothing but religion, possible only by revolution. The minister and judges of Hindu kings were themselves priests, men of high principles and rigid morality and well versed in ancient lore if you please but incompetent for that very reason to the task of introducing a beneficial reform, where necessary, and incapable of understanding that widows in the full bloom of their youth could be in any need of a second marriage. A revolution in the religious ideas of the nation was a condition precedent to the introduction of salutary reforms. But such a revolution was by no means desirable or possible. It was impossible because, during the process of development from the rude material of universal pantheism to the highly subtle doctrine of absolute idealism, the Hindu religion had gathered on its way doctrines of a miscellaneous sort and restrained them with a firm grasp. It was not possible for any foreign religion, in competition within the indigenous product of India to present an exterior subtle enough to mystify, tempting enough to win, imposing enough to awe or gross enough to strike. The Hindu religion was itself calculated to humble the king in his palace, solace the peasant in his hovel, and satisfy the philosopher in his study.

The tendency of the Maya doctrine which came into fashion after the expulsion of the Buddhists was to confirm leaders of the Hindu community in their indifference towards women, especially towards widows, by making the world, widows included, as unreal one. This philosophical school maintained a stoic indifference of feeling to its disciples and cut the Gordion knot of the origin of evil by imputing unreality to worldly pleasures as well as worldly pains. The doctrine of fatalism, too, which had obtained a vogue among the Hindus tended to benumb their feelings and introduce among them a reckless indifference by teaching that all misery was inevitable. Though the subject of free will and necessity is doomed to remain a vexed question to the end of time, it is as plain as daylight that the prevalence of the doctrine of fatalism has introduced an unhealthy tone of thinking among those who hold it.

Foreign travel which always creates a respect for foreign customs through a sympathetic observation of them and thus acts as a check on the tendency of the customs of a country to stagnate, was not open to Hindus,. The priests were wise enough to anticipate the innovations that would follow in the train of foreign travel and accordingly forbade it on pain of doing penance.

Mahomedan conquest, instead of familiarizing the natives with foreign customs, only contributed materially to prejudice them against their conquerors. After it, the natives were solely occupied by the thought of their political regeneration and indefinitely postponed their social progress. Even had the conquerors been more sympathetic in their treatment, it is more than doubtful if they would have impressed the conquered with a favourable opinion of their customs, as the latter were their superiors in social matters. Indeed, it is suspected by some writers that many evil customs among the Hindus like the system of *Purdah* and early marriage owe their origin to Mahomedans. It was reserved for English conquerors alone to present a set of manners atonce foreign and civilized.

The pit of ignorance into which women fell after their degradation is also one of the potent reasons why their male partners who strove to rise superior to the existing state of society were often held in check in their upward march. This was as it should be. This is the fate of every nation in which one class, after obtaining the mastery over another equally numerous class, tries to crush it to the dust.

In Bengal the widow marriage movement was inaugurated by the late venerable Pandit Ishwar Chandra Vidyasagar who may be termed the great apostle of the cause.

In an able work on remarriage which he wrote in 1854, not content with proving its desirability on ground of justice and convenience, he maintained that it was not prohibited by the Vedas, but that on the contrary it was positively countenanced by them. He went on to show that those texts in the Smiritis which militated against the Vedic texts must yield the preference to them as being more recent in date. This book was written in Bengali and, therefore, was intelligible to all. His principal opponent, the then best grammarian in Bengal, wrote his rejoinders in Sanskrit in accordance with the tradition of Sanskrit scholars, which were, therefore, quite Greek and Latin to the masses. Later on Pandit Ishwar Chandra translated his work into English with a view to create interest in the subject in his English readers.

Once mooted, this question soon attracted public attention and rapidly grew in importance. Several meetings were held to discuss the subject in all its bearings. Many scholars from Bengal expressed views contrary to those held by the Pandit. Government consulted the Pandits of Benares on this point and they returned a verdict in favour of remarriage. The agitation led it last to the passing of act XV of 1856 which legitimatised the issue of remarried widows.

After removing the legal bar to the legitimacy of the offspring of remarried couples, the Pandit next turned his attention to giving the subject a practical turn.

"The first widow marriage celebrated by him took place in Calcutta on the 7th December 1865. This created a great sensation in the Hindu community. He was excommunicated himself and the same penalty was threatened upon all who joined him. Although he was deserted by his friends and countrymen, he firmly adhered to his plans. He succeeded in causing a number of widow marriages to be solemnized. He became heavily involved in debt on account of the expenses connected with them, but refused to accept any pecuniary assistance from others. He chose a widow as the bride of his son."

Tracing back the time when the attention of the Maharatta we come to a pamphlet on remarriage written in 1837. It was the fruit of the joint authorship of a Telugu Brahman and a resident of Ratnagiri. It was published in Bombay and many favourable and adverse criticisms appeared in the *Mumbai Darpan*, a weekly paper of that time. On this another book was written, but it was not printed, though copies of it were privately circulated among Shastris. The language of the book leads one to conclude that it was written by an old Shastri. The name of the author is not given. It appears to have been sent by the author to a wealthy and influential friend who, in his turn, published it. This book refers, among other things, to the stories of Parashuram Bhau's widowed daughter and thus confirms the facts which Mr. Ranade gathered from an independent source. The Rev. Baba Padmanji also wrote two works on remarriage—*"The Kutumba Sudharna* and *The Yamunaparyatana"*.

Thus in the Deccan, books on the subject appeared even prior to Pandit Ishwar Chandra's work. But this reform was far from being instantly carried into practice. The remarriages that were celebrated after this wordy warfare and before the movement was taken up by Vishnu Shastri were few and far between. Raghunath Janardan, a Gaud Brahman by caste and a clerk in the municipal office at Ahmedabad, married a widow, Chimabai by name, at Poona about the year 1853. The bridegroom had his first wife living at the time of the remarriage and consequently his remarriage was not hailed by the reformers with anything like enthusiasm. The second remarriage took place thirteen years after the first. The bride was a Gujarathi lady named Diwali Bai. The very next year, Narayan Jagannath Bhide, a Mahratta Brahman and an ancient pleader at Poona, married his wife's widowed sister at Bandra near Bombay. All these remarriages were celebrated privately and were not as fruitful and of any practical consequences as in Bengal. This may be accounted for partly by the fact that education of the masses in the Deccan had commenced later than in Bengal.

The Widow-Marriage Association was started in Bombay in the year 1866. Many educated natives enlisted themselves as its members. It had for its Chairman H. H. the Chief of Jamkhind and for its Vice-Chairman H. H. Raghunath Rao of Vinchur Vishnu Shastri Pandit acted as Secretary. Bal Mangesh Wagle K. T. Telang, M. G. Ranade, Janardhan Sakharam Gadgil, Gopal Rao, Hari Deshmukh Balaji, Pandurang Shantaram Narayana,

N. M. Parmanand, B. H. Bhagvat, A. V. Kathavate were some of its members. In antagonism to this association the orthodox party set up an association, the Hindu Dharma Vyavasthapaka Mandali, with the active cooperation of Vithoba Anna Daftardar and Nilkanth Rao Joshi. It held its meetings at Thakor Dwar. The wordy strife of these associations lasted for three years.

The widow-marriage movement had need of a champion like Ishwar Chandra Vidyasagar who should combine in his person sound scholarship, an intellect capable of understanding and harmonizing the several discordant texts in the Smritis, an eloquence powerful enough to move the masses and an honesty of purpose which never shrank from consequences, in short, one who should possess both the head to plan and the hand to execute. This champion of the reform party found at last in the celebrated Vishnu Shastri Pandit. As for many days the cause of widow-marriage was all but identified with his name, it would not be amiss to give a brief account of his life and doings. Curiously enough, the broad facts of his life coincide with those of Pandit Ishwar Chandra. After being educated according to the old system, he learnt English in the government school at Poona. When he left school, he entered government service, but was soon obliged to throw it up. He then became the editor of the *Indu Prakash,* an Indian paper. He had an intimate knowledge of Sanskrit, English and Marathi. The widow-marriage movement appears to have early attracted his notice. He translated Pandit Ishwar Chandra's work on the subject into Marathi, and tried to sow the seed of reform broadcast by writing able essays in his paper. This did not fail to elicit adverse criticism from his opponents, who were old Shastris well versed in Sanskrit lore. To carry the discussion to successful termination Vishnu Shastri had need of all his resources. He was equal to the occasion. He had to read a variety of Sanskrit works in order to face his opponents. Questions about the gotra of the remarried widow, the person who was to give her away in marriage, and about inheritance were readily put to him by his opponents or by interested lookers-on and were as readily answered by him in his eloquent and convincing manner. More-over, he was not sparing in using his elocutionary powers for the cause. He was justly reputed to be one of the best, if not the best orator of his time. The subject lent an additional charm to his eloquence. He lost no opportunity of delivering lectures and thus making the subject popular in provincial towns though a variety of business detained him in Bombay oftener than he wished. He made several speeches at Nasik which was then, as it still is, a city of scholars and priests. Lectures were followed by disputes. Placards signed by Vishnu Shastri and inviting discussion were to be seen in all the principal streets of large towns. The defiant challenge was accepted by the celebrated Vithoba Anna Daftardar who was atonce a great scholar and a great poet. He came to Poona in 1868 and expressed his desire that the controversy should take place in that city. Vishnu Shastri assented to the proposal and came to Poona with his friends. But the controversy did not come off as expected. While the terms on which the controversy was to take place were being settled to the satisfaction of both parties, Vithoba Anna commenced a series of lectures against remarriage in the Pachhapurkar's Wada, Budhwar. Vishnu Shastri was not invited to the meetings that were held there. Seeing the opposite party busy with arousing popular opinion in their favour, he commenced a similar series of lectures at Sonia Bapu Mande's house in the Narayan Peth. He refuted in his lectures those very arguments which had been advanced by the Daftardar in his lectures and summaries of which were being published as soon as they were delivered. The novelty of the subject and his claims on popular sympathy raised public excitements of the highest pitch. A little incident may serve as well as another to show what absorbing interest the subject had created. On the first day of Vishnu Shastri's series of lecture, the audience was no large owing to no previous intimation having been given to the public. But on the very next day the crowd literally crammed the place of meeting. The meeting was accordingly adjourned from the principal hall to the courtyard. The yard was not in proper order and the servants were bid to sweep it clean and to spread carpets. An eminent friend of Vishnu Shastri who had accompanied him from Bombay, impatient of the delay, commenced the sweeping operation himself. Bandu Nana Ranade, who was himself no mean scholar and who was himself present on the occasion, expressed his satisfaction with the masterly way in which Vishnu Shastri handled his subject, with the lucidity with which he made his meaning plain.

So far everything went on very well. But the really arduous task still remained to be accomplished—that of breaking through the barriers of custom. The reform party had had more than enough of disputes and were tired of them. A hero was required who would break the ice by marrying a widow and face the opprobrium that always attaches to innovation, in a word, who would transfer the question from speculation to reality. There were not many persons among the foremost reformers who were unfortunately for themselves widowers (adult bachelors were out of question) and fortunately for the cause brave souls. In India bravery in social matters means more than it does in more liberal countries. Religion being the basis of all Hindu customs, and it being naturally conservative in its tendency, every innovation, however trifling, comes to be looked upon as something opposed to religion and therefore to be discouraged by every means. Poverty of reformers in particular cases lends a peculiar bitterness to the hardship of social ostracism which more resembles Robinson Crusoe's solitary life in the desert island than the isolation of reformers like Wilberforce and Bradlaugh, who, differing in a single point, retained in their personality sufficiently numerous points of resemblance to those among whom they moved, to be but little affected by a difference of opinion. The absorption of individual life in religion makes it indispensable to yield a wholesale allegiance to it or eschew it altogether. An Englishman in a similar predicament would seek to forget his misery in the excitement of foreign travei. But an excessive love of the country and lack of adventure have made foreign travel a forbidden fruit to the Hindus. What are the pangs of the black hole compared to these? Let not, therefore, those of us who are more conservative gloat over the weakness of those reformers who failed in the necessary amount of courage to carry out their principles into practice and thus to run the gauntlet of popular disfavour and of whose weakness such merciless floating would be the best justification, if any were wanted. Moral weakness is the heritage common to all Hindus and nobody has the right to laugh at another's weakness unless he himself has shown signal courage in identical circumstance. We must make allowance for weakness which is constitutional with us all.

The much needed man of courage was not long in making his appearance. Two brothers, Waman Rao and Narayan Rao Paranjpe, who belonged to the reform party, had a young widowed sister, Venu Bai, whom they wished to see remarried, and were in search of a suitable match. They had the full sympathy and co-operation of their sister. They made their intentions known to the remarriage association who advertised in the *Indu Prakash* paper for a man willing to marry a widow. The advertisement elicited a response from one Pandurang Vinayak Karmarkar, a teacher in the vernacular school at Saoda in the Khandesh district who signified his willingness to risk a marriage with the widowed girl. The association had him examined as to his *bona-fides* and fitness and then gave its sanction to the remarriage. The bridegroom took a few days' leave and went to Bombay. The celebration was to be public and measures were taken accordingly. The day and place of the marriage were fixed and invitation cards were sent over the signatures of the following gentlemen—

1. Vishnu Parsharam Pandit,
2. Gopal Hari Deshmukh,
3. M. G. Ranade,
4. Vishnu Moreshwar Bhide,
5. Vishnu Parsharam Ranade,
6. Shri Krishna Shastri Talekar, and
7. Janardan Sakharam Gadgil.

The marriage was to take place at the house of Rao Bahadoor Moroba Kantoba near the Gowalia Tank. The host, one Pathare Prabhu, was a staunch adherent of the reform party and followed up this proof of his devotion to the cause by soon afterwards himself marrying a widow of his own caste. He had his house specially decorated on the occasion. The anti-reform party was naturally vexed to see the efforts of their opponents on the verge of being crowned with success. They left no stone unturned to prevent the remarriage. Anonymous letters were sent to Vishnu Shastri and open threats of setting the Indu Prakash Press building on fire uttered in his presence. Plans were laid to waylay and attack the bridegroom on his way to the marriage-hall. But Vishnu Shastri was not a person to mind such threats. Steps were taken to have recognisances for keeping public peace executed by those using the threats. Vishnu Shastri received succour at this juncture from an unexpected quarter. The master of a gymnastic school who took great interest in the progress of reform, hearing of the threats directed against Vishnu Shastri, sent a defiant warning to the leaders of the lawless of the adverse party that they would do well to desist from their efforts to prevent the remarriage taking place. Finding all their attempts at prevention baffled, the leaders of the anti-reform party proposed, a couple of days before the day fixed for the marriage, that a controversy should first take place and only in the event of a majority voting in favour of its legality and not otherwise, should the remarriage be solemnized. The orthodox party evidently hoped by this means to gain time. The reformers were not deceived by this appearance of anxiety on the part of their opponents to refer the matter to arbitration. They kept to their original resolution of celebrating the remarriage on the day fixed and took additional measures in anticipation of a riot taking place. Thus the first public celebration of a remarriage took place on the evening of 15th June 1869, without anything happening to mar the joy of the occasion. Many European and native gentlemen of distinction were present. Vishnu Shastri himself, assisted by some priests, conducted the marriage ceremonies. The marriage presents amounted to rupees three thousand which was deposited in the Bank of Bombay in the name of the bride. The marriage feast too was attended by a number of Hindus from different places.

Seeing all their intentions frustrated one by one, the infuriated opponents had recourse to excommunication. But at the very outset, a dilemma presented itself. A wholesale excommunication of persons who had attended the marriage ceremonies or the marriage feast without distinction would be too vague and would lose its strength by reason of the number of those included in it while one confined in its operation to the leading offenders would be too limited for the rage of the orthodox party which knew no bounds. At length after due deliberation, the latter course was adopted; and accordingly the seven signatories, the bridegroom, and bride and her brothers were excommunicated. The meeting held at Thakor Dwar, by which the resolution of excommunication was adopted, was a disorderly one—a fact which before long occasioned a dispute as to what was the precise wording of the resolution passed by the meeting. Before the question was satisfactorily decided circular letters were sent by the leaders of the orthodox party to different towns notifying the fact of excommunication. On this, four gentlmen, Bhaskar Shastri Tambankar, Sakharam Shastri Kale, Mahadeo Chemnaji Apte and Anna Moreshwer Kunte, issued a circular letter stating that no resolution had been unanimously come to the meeting at Thakor Dwar. These four gentlemen were forthwith summarily excommunicated.

Some partisans of the reform party who had attended the meeting at Thakor Dwar took for perusal a list from a partisan of the anti-reform party. This resulted in a dispute and the dispute in a prosecution of Vishnu Parsharam Ranade, Bal Mangesh Wagle and N. M. Parmanand which was, however, dismissed for want of sufficient evidence.

Soon after this, letters appeared in several papers with recommendations that the public should not respect the decree of excommunication, seeing that remarriage had not been proved to be invalid according to Hindu law by the orthodox party. These were signed by young educated gentlemen mostly from Poona. Their number at length went up to one hundred and seventy-two.

In 1884, the subject of remarriage acquired a fresh importance through the writings of Mr. Malabari, one of those Parsi gentlemen who have been doing yeomen's service to the country of their adoption in social, political and industrial matters and who have thus been more than discharging the debt of gratitude they owe to it. Being a non-Hindu and consequently not in a position to speak with authority and to be heard with unbiased minds, in constant danger of having his disinterestedness construed into meddlesomeness, his laudable efforts were far less successful than those of a Hindu of equal courage, sincerity, ability and knowledge would have been. After years of untiring labour he handed over his self-imposed and thankless task to Dewan Bahadoor R. Raghunath Rao as likely to prosper in orthodox hands. That his confidence was not misplaced has been amply proved by his worthy successor. Madras was rather late in the field, but it has more than made amends for its early indifference by its sustained enthusiasm for the cause of remarriage, thanks mainly to the indefatigable and zealous labours of Rao Bahadur K. Viresalingam Pantulu, than whom a more ardent worker in the cause of social reform does not breathe in the whole country and who is justly known as the Pandit Vidyasagar of Southern India. The Punjab is still in a backward condition and no wonder. Education has been there neglected to a degree which renders freedom of thought well-nigh impossible.

We must not ignore the influence of literature on widow marriage. The *Sudharak,* a paper started by the late lamented G. G. Agarkar, and the *Indian Social Reformer* have been the leading organs of the reformers in the Deccan and Madras respectively and been doing immense service to the cause of widow marriage. The widow homes of Shashipada Banerji and D. K. Karve have also had their share in the furtherance of the movement. Of late several pamphlets and plays have been written in favour of widow marriage and have been growing in popularity.

A statistical study of remarriages celebrated hitherto in the Maratha country leads to some curious conclusions. The largest number of bridegrooms is from the Kokanastha Brahman class and the largest number of brides from the Deshasthas. The ratio of Kokanastha bridegrooms to Kokanastha brides may be said very nearly to vary inversely as that of Deshastha bridegrooms to Deshastha brides. The number of remarriages among the Karhadas and the Deorakhas is too small to draw any conclusion. Out of 21 marriages, in 8 bridegrooms earned not more than Rs. 20 per month, in 2 they earned more than Rs. 25 but not more than Rs. 50; in 4 they earned more than Rs. 50 but not more than Rs. 75 and in 2 more than Rs. 75 and not more than Rs. 100. This falsifies the assertion often confidently made that most bridegrooms in remarriages are highly paid government officials. Among the Mahrattas, Brahmans appear to have taken the most prominent part while among the Gujarathis, the Banias have been the principal actors, and the Brahmans have been thrown in the background. The ages of the majority of Mahratta brides vary from 15 to 20 and those of the majority of Gujarathi brides from 20 to 25; while the age of an average Mahratta bridegroom varies from 30 to 35 and that of his Gujarathi brother from 25 to 30. The inequality arises from the fact that even in ordinary marriages among the Gujarathis the ages of the bride and the bridegroom are allowed to gravitate more towards each other than in ordinary Mahratta marriages.

The annual increase in remarriages is greater in Berar and the Central Provinces than in the Deccan proper. The reasons are obvious. Those who have migrated to those provinces observe a great difference between their own manners and those of the inhabitants of the provinces, and being thus impressed with the immateriality of differences in social customs find it easier to advance than those whom they have left behind.

Moreover, neither their old bonds nor their new connections are so strong as to materially affect their conduct in social matters. The annually growing number of remarriages in these provinces is also no unsure index to the sentiments of the Deccanites proper which are every year being more and more alienated from the old religion, and, though held in check by their surroundings for a time, wait only a transplantation to express themselves in action. Even in Poona, the seat of orthodoxy, old people who have witnessed the ravages of the terrible plague on thousands of Brahman families are heard openly to deplore the absence of the custom of remarriages. God grant that we learn to reform ourselves without the aid of misfortunes.

It has been observed by an acute Maratha thinker that the cause of reform was not a little compromised by the social reformers themselves posing as religious reformers. Perhaps this was. But one who is conscious of the part religion has played in the fossilizing of old customs need not be reminded of the necessity of religious reform being undertaken side by side with social regeneration. The educated people in India have outgrown their customs. To whatever reform they direct their energies they are met at every turn by the all-absorbing and tyrannical Hindu religion holding every custom tight with the iron grip of desperation. Naturally they feel an aversion from it and the odium is gradually transferred from its vulnerable parts to those that are lovely. The same religion that once trespassed upon the provinces of society and law is now, in its turn, exposed to the danger of having its merits confounded with its defects. Its blind mistakes recoil upon its head with a terrible fury; and after having taken undue liberty with its sister institutions it is now fast losing the respect that is its due.

The Bengali as well as the Maratha reformers thought fit to substitute in the place of the old religion a new one which was in reality nothing more or less than the self-same old religion shorn of its accidents and excrescences, the old religion in all its pure splendour. The religious movement in Bengal was far more successful than that in the Bombay Presidency. The result has been that in Bengal religious reform has kept pace with social reform while in the Bombay Presidency it has given place to skepticism and atheism. On the other hand, in Bengal social reform has been in a degree imposed by the tacit requirement of conformity with the principles of Brahmoism which is the religion of the reformers, while in Bombay the reformers, apparently continuing as they do in the religion of their ancestors, are not estranged from popular sympathy to the degree they have done in Bengal. In Bengal, social reform has assumed the shape of a caste question, while in Bombay the refusal of the reformers to claim a separate caste for themselves has set the whole society in a ferment. Reform is bound to live an isolated life in Bengal and to be general in Bombay. Whichever state of the two one is inclined to prefer to the other, one fact remains undisputed that neither social aristocracy nor religious anarchy is a thing to be congratulated upon. It is time the Shankaracharya reviewed his decision in the Poona controversy in a spirit of compromise and effected a reconciliation between the innovations that are knocking for admission and the old religion that is indignantly refusing them entrance.

The number of remarriages is bound to be small as compared to that of first marriages. Bearing this fact in mind, we find that the number of remarriages is steadily growing every year. Occasional inequalities can be accounted for by the recent terrible visitations that have relegated everything save the safety of life to a subordinate rank. A sudden increase is expected after society is restored to its equilibrium, which, it is fervently hoped, is at no distant date.

—Rao Bahadur Wamanrao Madhav Kolhatkar

17

Theosophy and Social Change in India: With Special Reference to Annie Besant's Contribution

Theosophical Society was established in America in 1875 by Madam Blavatsky and Col. H. S. Olcott. The founders of the society came to India in 1879. This was the period of rapid social changes in India. Christian missionaries had started some work to improve the position of the weaker and depressed sections of Indian society. Annie Besant joined the Theosophist group in India in 1893. Besant made her mission the saying:

They are slaves who fear to speak for the fallen and weak[1].

The main objective of Theosophy was brotherhood of man and acquisition of knowledge about the common truth of all the great religions. It advised their followers to remain within the religion to which they belonged and to deepen it, broaden it and spiritualize it.[2]

While the Western world had come full circle. While they had started realising the trials and tribulations of their materialistic existence. While they had started examining the spiritual aspects of the human existence, Indians looked for Western ideals to bring about social change. English manners, English behaviour, and English language became the means of their salvation. English ideals dominated their lives and thought.

Immorality, licentiousness, riotous living were the order of the day. Denationalising emasculation was the prevailing characteristic. Young men took delight in wounding the religious susceptibilities of their countrymen and in cutting their way to salvation through ham and beef and wading their way to liberalism through tumblers of beer.[3]

Much of the social change in the 19th and 20th centuries originated from secular motives based on rationalistic critiques of society and led to secular as well as religious movements for social reform. Caste was considered the root of all problems.[4] The reformers held that due to prevailing social evils in Indian society the land of virtue had become the land of depravity. K. T. Telang and M. G. Ranade felt that the system had become petrified[5]. Rammohun Roy and Keshub Chandra Sen attributed the decline to false religion and Dayananda Saraswati held the hypnotic control over society of corrupt Brahmins as the cause of India's downfall[6]. Indians were–a race, degenerated, paralysed in all their energies. *The Indian Social Reformer* declared:

> *'The Hindu civilization based on the ancient Aryan institutions is doomed.'*[7]

N. G. Chandavarkar and K. Natarajan admitted that Charistian missionaries had brought much social wisdom in India.[8] Vithal Ramji Shinde founded the Depressed Classes Mission of India in 1906, with the help of the Bombay Presidency Social Reform Association under Chandavarkar.[9] This mission and the Brahmo Samaj were the first examples of non-Christian efforts on an organized basis to improve the outcastes' conditions.[10] By 1913 the Depressed Classes Mission maintained thirty educational institutions throughout Bombay and Madras provinces. Efforts in this direction were also made by the Arya Samaj, the Dev Samaj, Sikh Associations and by some rulers.[11]

These were some of the illustrations of social change in India when the Theosophical Society and Annie Besant emerged on the scene in India with somewhat different ideas.

To begin with the Theosophical Society took an interest in the untouchables. The society established schools for them in 1890. Four such schools were in operation by 1902 under the direction of Miss E.E. Palmer of the University of Minnesota. The number of Olcott Pariah Schools, as they were called, was compared by their founder, in 1902, to the approximately four thousand Christian missionary institutions for pariahs which were then in operation.[12]

Annie Besant's work for women's upliftment in India which later developed in the form of all-India Women's Conference is a lasting testimony of her concern for women's upliftment in India. Throughout her life she stood committed to the true and not politicized elevation of the cause of weaker sections and depressed classes. She wrote that for a Theosophist the most dynamic idea was the universal brotherhood of humanity. Only imagine a world peopled in the majority with men and women who not only believe but have discovered the joys inherent in that principle; would a man or woman then care to ask to what race other belongs, to what God he or she bends the knee? The one joyous truth which the stranger brings with him is then: "You are my brothers. I am your brother." How could wars ever arise in such a civilization? How could poverty exist as contrasted with callous luxury? These human evils the source of the struggle for existence disappear, as the morning mists disappear with the rising of the sun.[13] Hence, for Annie Besant service and upliftment of the weaker sections and depressed classes of the colonial Indian society was the performance of the dharma and a duty also which she had to discharge for the sins her countrymen as rulers of the country had committed towards the Indian society by their exploitative and wanton acts.

An examination of the references made by scholars on Annie Besant's works and her activities in India show a lack of true grasp of the lady's personality and her ideas. She has been often denounced as a Hindu revivalist or as a 'Putna' who was playing an imperial game. But tons of literature available at Adyar, Madras, Nehru Memorial Museum and Library and the National Archives of India, New Delhi, alone give us different pictures of her works and antecedents, which is born out by many living Indians who directly or indirectly came in contact with her works and activities in India. To understand her ideas clearly let us go back a little and briefly.

Annie Besant was born with a total faith in God. After marriage, sufferings of children and separation from the husband she studied and reflected and turned non-believer and a stark rationalist—a free thinker with Charles Bradlaugh. Then an anti-imperialist, a birth control agitator and a Fabian socialist. She continued experimenting with truth and finally became Thesophist and claimed to have ultimately found her moorings.

Hence her ideas and activities do not need to be analysed on the basis of any Euro-centric methodologies and theoretical formulations. She was a humanitarian and social reformer according to her own light and not under any external pressures and motives as is often made out:

> *'Olcott and Leadbeater were joined in 1893 by Annie Besant, who within a few years established herself as the outstanding revivalist of Hinduism in south India.... Mrs. Besant held forth on the glories of ancient and modern Hinduism in all its facets. Social reformers stood nearly helplessly by while a great-voiced, cultivated English woman besought Hindus to avoid the pitfalls of so-called western advancement and revere their own great culture.'*[14]

Annie Besant was not the first nor the only advocate of the philosophy of social reform, discussed in the preceding paragraphs. Dayanand Saraswati had already given a call to go back to Vedas and the whole lot of orientalists who had by now drunk deep of the original and translated Indian classics had started examining them more carefully for a happy and healthy social order.

Annie Besant had herself read and written extensively on Upanishads. Gita and other Indian classics and through her varied experiments and experiences was fully convinced that any social change brought about on the basis of mere human rational was not enough, it must also conform to the perennial truth as revealed in the divine revelations.

Throughout her exhortations for social change in India she propounded and advocated Indian ideals, howsoever she was misunderstood or criticized by those for whom she lived and died at Adyar (Madras) on 20 September 1933. she believed:

> *Each truth can only be seen by a man as he develops the power of vision corresponding to it,*

—Raj Kumar

REFERENCES

1. Raj Kumar, *Annie Besant's Rise to Power in Indian Politics, 1914-1917*, New Delhi, 1989.
2. Annie Besant, *A Sketch of Theosophy*, T.P.H. Adyar, Madras, 1951, p. 6.
3. *Hindustan Review*, May 1907, p. 480.
4. M. G. Ranade, *The Miscellaneous Writings of Mr. Justice M. G. Ranade*, Bombay, 1915, p. 192. Also Rammohun Roy, The English Works of Rammohun Roy (ed. Jogendra Chunder Ghose), Allahabad, 1906, pp. 929-30.
5. Iswar Chandra Vidyasagar, *Marriage of Hindu Widows*, Calcutta, 1856, p. 94.
6. K.T. Telang, *Selected Writings and Speeches*, Bombay, 1916, p. 97.
7. *The Indian Social Reformer*, 8 March 1903, pp. 1, 112.
8. Fred B. Fisher, *India's Silent Revolution*, p. 85.
9. J. N. Farquhar, *Modern Religious Movements in India*, p. 372.
10. *Ibid.*, p. 372
11. S. Natarajan, *A Century of Social Reform in India*, Bombay, 1959, p. 156.
12. Henry S. Olcott, *The Poor Pariah, Madras*, 1902, p. 23.
13. Annie Besant, *A Sketch of Theosophy*, Adyar, Madras, 1951, p.
14. Charles H. Heimsath, *Indian Nationalism and Hindu Social Reform*, Princeton, 1964.

18

The Work of the Theosophical Society in India

Let us glance at India as she was when the Theosophical Society came to her; let us see whether the Theosophical Society has not had a large share in bringing about the change in India that we see on every side today; for this, after all, is the point of immediate interest to raise and it is this on which explanation and defence are needed.

Now the Theosophical Society in India consists of some five thousand men and women scattered over the country in something less than three hundred branches or lodges. Almost the whole of that number is made up of English educated men and women. We have scarcely touched the masses of the people and in truth our work lies more with the educated; for the religious can deal with the uneducated, if the advanced classes be enlightened and spiritual. Better to work among those who influence the masses than in the masses themselves as regards reformation and change. Changes should always begin above and work downwards: then they influence powerfully and healthily; but changes which begin in the masses tend to bring about revolutions rather than reforms. This is a small number you may say, in comparison with the population, though large regarded by itself. But it is an organized body and that adds enormously to its power. A very small body of disciplined people is far more effective and powerful than a vast mob of the undisciplined; and each group of these five thousand people is surrounded by a great mass of sympathizers who work with them everywhere and strengthen their power enormously, whether you think it wielded for good or harm.

So India has within her borders an organized mass or her own sons and daughters gathered under the banner of the Theosophical Society. The majority of them in India, naturally, are Hindus; in Ceylon and Burma there is a fair number of the daughter faith of Buddhism; there is a very considerable number among the Parsis; very few in the great faith of Islam and that is one reason why the gulf yawns so widely between the Hindu and Muhammadan populations. If we could only win a few hundreds in Islam to became members of the Theosophical Society, a bridge would be thrown across the gulf which threatens to grow wider and wider, the gulf which is fatal to the unity of the nation, an obstacle to advancement in the future. This body of men and women then, with a few Christians also, and a sprinkling of the descendants of Abraham, our Hebrew brothers, a fair number of Sikhs and not so many of the Jains—this makes up the composition of the Theosophical Society in India. The European element also enters into it—a handful in the great mass of eastern-born bodies.

Now against the Theosophical Society two accusations are made: first it tends to revive superstition and secondly that the Hindu theosophists are encouraged in inertia, laziness and sloth. It is said in an article in the *Hindustan Review:* "What does 'Theosophy' stand for in the new life of India? It stands for orthodoxy, for reaction, for inactivity, for sheer inertia." The writer is a 'pandit' but apparently identifies religion and superstition. He says that the Central Hindu College, the main object of his attack, "stands identified with 'Theosophy',"

I quite agree in this last point and will deal presently with the nature of that identification.

But let us compare the statement as to Theosophy standing for inertia with the fact. When Mme. H. P. Blavatsky and Col. H. S. Olcott, the earthly founders of the Theosophical Society, first set foot on Indian soil what was the condition of India and of Hinduism? Scepticism and materialism had eaten out the life of the nation. The crowds of the so-called English-educated class were followers of Huxley, Mill and Spencer and had entirely forgotten their own literature; were contemptuous of the past and hence hopeless for the future; they were copying English ways, English manners, filling their houses with English furniture to the destruction of Indian arts and crafts. They had lost all national spirit.

De-spiritualisation had brought about national degeneracy. There was no activity of national life, no pulsing of the national heart. Read the papers of the day and judge for yourselves. Even when I came to India, Indians told me that India was dead; they smiled sadly at my statement that India was not dead, but sleeping. She is not sleeping today.

In those past days of sleep accusations many and various were levelled against the founders of the Theosophical Society. They were suspected by the government, because they accepted Indians with the social courtesies shown to equals, because they did not pay proper attention to distinctions of colour, because they were trying to make the people proud of their ancient philosophy, were trying to make them aspire to ancient ideals, Everywhere the police dogged their steps and took down the Colonel's lectures, until at last the Colonel indignantly remonstrated; and not until after a most humiliating justification on the part of each of them—were showing their respective ranks in the countries they had quitted—the police removed from their track, at least openly, and they were permitted to travel undogged by spies over India. At least at that time the government theory was not that they were likely to increase Indian inertia.

Realising that spirituality must first be restored to its place in life, they began by the revival of religions. There was then no national life, no Congress, no industrial exhibitions, no idea of the unity of the Indian people. These things the young men have grown up amongst, not knowing whence they came, but among the elder generation not one of these activities was known. Colonel Olcott and Madame Blavatsky saw that not until India recognized the value of its ancient faith could there be any bond of unity among the Indians, separated by provincial jealousies and hatreds. So they began with the revival of religion; they pointed the value of Hindu teachings; they held up the Vedas and the Upanishads as the glory of India, proclaimed the value of Indian thought and the priceless heritage of the Indian people; until at last the Indians began once more to pride themselves on their past and to realise that the Hindu scriptures were not the babblings of children or the fancies of savages, but were the foundation of a mighty system, the glory of the past and the life of the future.

Both the founders joined Buddhism, because it was the only eastern religion that would accept them, and they wanted to emphasise the value of eastern religion. Buddhism offers an open door to those who desire to come and Colonel Olcott, with his leanings of the past to Buddhism, went into it heart and soul, Madame Blavatsky's joining was of a more superficial character. I once asked her why she had joined Buddhism and she answered: "Well my dear, I wanted to show that I thought a religion of the East was rather better than the religion of the West." This reason was quite enough for, and quite characteristic of, Madame Blavatsky. She was above all esoteric religions and valued them as far as they were true, rejecting all that ignorance had added. She became nominally a Buddhist and took Pansil. And so that great protest in favour of the superiority in spirituality of the East was made. With what result? With the result that everywhere this revival of the religions of East began to spread; Boys' Associations were formed by Colonel Olcott all over the land, in which the boys were helped to study their ancient faith and were taught to love and feel pride in their motherland. There were no cries of *'Bande Mataram'* in those days. The idea of a motherland was new and the time had not yet come. There were none to help, so that religious and moral education might be introduced into the schools. And so these Boys' Associations were formed; the elders were told that they were already spoiled, but that the young ones might grow up properly. And we can see the difference between them and the fathers from whom they sprang. Zoroastrianism began to throw off some of the shackles of its materialistic thought; Buddhism changed its character. A missionary lately complained that whereas formerly when a Buddhist of Ceylon was asked his religion in court he hung down his heads and whispered: 'Buddhist', he now holds up his head and says proudly: "I am a Buddhist", and he complained that this was the result of the work of the Theosophical Society in Ceylon. Gradually in that ancient Buddhist country the leaven of Theosophy has worked in transforming the inert into the active, not the active into the inert. When the Theosophical Society went there government and missionary schools alone existed. Now more than two hundred and twenty schools and three colleges are under Buddhist control, filled with Buddhist children who learn to reverence the Lord Buddha and to keep the precepts of the faith. Before Theosophy went there that Buddhist country was becoming a drunken country, and much of the revenue was drawn from drink. With the revival of Buddhism by the Theosophical Society and the constant repetition of the statement in the Pansil that no intoxicating liquor might be taken, came the revival of temperance in Ceylon, until the authorities complained that they would have to find some new way of raising the money hitherto drawn from the excise.

Now how far, think you, would this revival of religion—which is everywhere granted as the work of the Theosophical Society—tend to superstition? Are religion and superstition identical? If so, then Theosophy must plead guilty to reviving superstition. But we Thosophists strenuously deny this identity, and we proclaim religion—man's search for God—as the one sure foundation for national prosperity and stability, while superstition and scepticism are alike the foes of religion, born in ignorance and alike destructive to national life. Unless all history be false, religion has ever dominated the rise and strength of a civilization, while scepticism has ever been the sign of its coming decay. The unity of the self is the basis of religion and of morality; when this is forgotten, the warring selves tear society into pieces. Superstition, substituting the non-essential for the essential, grows strong with the decay of religion; in vain it is denounced, while the realities, it masks, are hidden. Superstition can only be destroyed by knowledge. It laid stress on the things in religion which are based on natural laws and so justified very often some old custom that otherwise would have died away. But in doing this, it has only anticipated western science. Europe is rediscovering some of these very laws and scientific men are beginning to insist on the careful rules of hygiene and sanitation that our Manu had taught thousands of years ago. The trifling things that cannot be justified fall away, but the customs based on natural laws begin to revive. Some modern Hindus, not knowing either the ancient scriptures or modern science scoff at these observances. Why, they say, insist on the Brahmanic superstition that the Brahmana alone should draw water from the village well and pour it into the village pots brought for filling? And yet an English inspector travelling through these provinces said that the custom checked disease, for you could take care of the one vessel and see that it was clean; whereas if any vessel brought perhaps from a dirty house were dipped into the well, the water would be made foul, disease would spread and health be injured. It is silly to throw away these hygienic rules when Europe is rediscovering them. I know only one man in the West who is as careful as a Brahmana and he is a doctor. He washes his hands before he eats and when asked the reason, he answers: 'Microbes'. Such rules of caring for food-vessels are not superstition; they are good hygiene; we have been blamed for justifying them, but the more you disregard them the more disease will spread. And so with many other customs and ceremonies, called superstitions by the ignorant.

I am, however, willing to grant that wherever there is a revival of religion there will be some recrudescence of superstition. So in re-lighting a smouldering fire, there will be some smoke. But the remedy for the smoke it to blow the fire into flame; then the smoke will vanish and the fire will burn bright and clear. As Theosophy spreads, the smoke of superstition will vanish, and the fire of knowledge will blaze up. But if you refuse knowledge, the smoke will continue, for men would rather have a smoke fire than none.

Let us now consider more closely this question of inertia. There is rather a long list of the ways in which Hindu Theosophists have demonstrated their inertia, their sloth, their inaction! To begin: the first industrial exhibition was held in Bombay at an early convention of the Theosophical Society, on the initiative of Colonel Olcott until the nation knew what it could produce, it was not possible to revive the national prosperity—so Colonel Olcott said. Hence he gathered together Indian products and placed them in a house in which they might be seen; and that first industrial exhibition was the parent of exhibitions now so popular all over India. The National Congress was founded by English and Indian Theosophists, working hand-in-hand. The first meeting which suggested it was held at a convention of the Theosophical Society at Adyar; it was under the shelter of the banner of Theosophy, when Mr. Hume and other Indian Theosophists were present, that the National Congress took birth. And in those early days its life came from the inert members of the Theosophical Society! It was the Hindu Theosophists who worked in the early days before the Congress was popular; later, it grew popular and strong; but it ought not to forget the days of its infancy, when it was cradled and nursed in the Theosophical Society, until it was able to stand and run alone. And as regards the Swadeshi Movement: the Colonel preached it and I preached it when it was very unpopular; and when everybody laughed at us; saying: "You will never get the people of this country to care." To princes and people I preached it, wherever I went, and always from the economic standpoint. It had then no echo in Bengal. It was not until the lash fell upon them in the partition of Bengal that Bengalis—the most anglicized of all the Indian peoples—were stirred into activity and the Swadeshi movement, as a political weapon rather than an economic reform, was triumphantly proclaimed everywhere But some of us, who are older and within the pale of Theosophy, remember how the seed was sown. While we admire the vigour of today, we do not see why the poor Theosophist should be shut out. So of that third great movement also you find the beginning in the inert Hindu Theosophists!

Then we come to the depressed classes. I cannot help remembering that outside the missionary work—and they did it more to attack Hinduism—that schools for the depressed Pariahs were founded round the theosophical headquarters at Adyar by Colonel Olcott and that it was theosophists who laboured there in order to make that education a success. Now, India is waking up to her duty to the oppressed, but this fourth great movement of the day was worked at patiently for years, before it became popular, by the members of the Theosophical Society.

Pass from this and look at the work of temperance in India. I know that it is a disgrace that this work should be necessary and that it has became a necessity largely from the example set by westerners. But it is an Indian Theosophist, Dr. Edal-Behram—whose name in Surat is a symbol of self-sacrifice—who has led in Gujerat the great temperance Crusade. Thousands of people who ate flesh and drank alcohol—the two go together—have been rescued. The initiative, as ever, came from the Theosophical impulse and others have joined to follow where it has taken the lead.

Take the question of child-marriage. Here again, Hindu Theosophists have been much more ready to take up a reform and carry it out than their critics. It is many years since we formed a league within the E. S.—attacked by those who know nothing about it—and took down the names of fathers who took a pledge not to marry their daughters until two or three years later than their caste custom demanded. They ask here, in the *Hindustan Review*, whether the Central Hindu College will give men who are physically robust. You will never have robust men with boy-fathers and girl-mothers and if you want strong men you must let your boys and girls grow up into reasonable maturity before you put upon them the burden of bringing children into the world. And the Central Hindu College is the only institution, so far, that has dared to refuse married boys up to the eighth class in the school and has asked for a pledge from the father not to marry the boy until he reaches the ninth class.* If those who attack us would do the same! If instead of assailing us they would imitate us, this great curse would be more rapidly removed from India. They have not attacked it as a defection from the Hindu religion. We have shown that the marriage of a student is against the Laws of Manu, who imposed celibacy on the student. If we had brought arguments from Spencer instead of from Manu, perhaps they would have approved us! At any rate the inert Hindu Theosophists have taken the lead in this great practical reform—the sixth—and have worked at it everywhere, until now there is a very general cry in its favour. It has been among Theosophists that men have

* The board has just closed the upper school classes also to married boys and has imposed double fees on married college students in the first and second year from July 1910.

been found to face the social odium of delaying the marriage of their children, who have not shrunk, in the words of our critic, "from braving the pain of new ideas".

With regard to girls' education a seventh movement: we have not enough schools, but we have some; and how many girls' schools have been opened by our critics? I know only of one body which is energetic in this field and that is the Arya Samaj; they have done all they could in favour of girls' education; but outside I do not see any other bodies who are working so hard, and I find Hindu Theosophists all over the country opening girls' schools and leading the way, as they have done in so many other cases, despite their inertia.

Now as regards religious and moral education: the Central Hindu College is the most marked institution in which Theosophists have been working, and as said by one of our critics: "You cannot disguise from yourself the fact that the Central Hindu College stands identified with Theosophy." I accept the fact. On this matter, some of our critics say we are too orthodox; that is the idea of the *Hindustan Review* article; the other side says we are not orthodox enough and should put an orthodox Hindu in the place of Mr. Arundale. I do not know which of these I ought to answer; perhaps I may be permitted to leave them to answer each other. But I may perhaps say, in passing, that you could not have any more orthodox Hindu than Mahamahopadhyaya Pandit Adityaram Bhattacharya—an inert Theosophist! I should add—who was here as the honorary Acting Principal of the College so long as his health permitted and on his finding the work too heavy at his advanced age, we asked him to take the post of Rector, so that he might still have a strong influence and voice in the conduct of the college. And if you can find another good Hindu as capable and as willing to sacrifice himself as the present English principal, I think I could find other work for my friend George Arundale. Other proofs of Theosophical inertia are the religious examinations in several great centres; I have given prizes for religion in Bombay in which hundreds of boys and girls have been taught and examined by Hindu Theosophists, who had given both money and time. I do not find that other bodies are willing to give the same money and time. But our inert Theosophists are constantly busy along these lines, trying to do the work while others talk about it. And then we have a number of affiliated schools. There is the great school in Aleppey; and the college in Kashmir is another due to Theosophical initiative. There are textbooks issued by the Central Hindu College giving, for the first time in Hindu history, a short clear outline of Hinduism, so that the boys and girls may understand their religion—and the books have been adopted by state after state and school after school. What right have those to criticize, who have nothing to show against these many works of the Hindu Theosophists? Another point as to our college: it is Theosophists, both English and Hindu, who have supplied the strong staff of honorary workers which enables us, despite the pressure put upon us, to keep down the fees. Who was the first honorary superintendent of the boarding house? Pandit Chheda Lal, an old Theosophist. And who followed him? Babu Rameshwar Prasad, another Theosophist. Who was the first honorary principal? An English Theosophist—Dr. Arthur Richardson, who has lost health and strength in the loving service given to the college. Who is helping us, by honorary professorships, to keep the college an Indian one? Professor Telang—a son of the late Mr. Justice Telang—a Hindu theosophist; and professor Dalal, a well-known Bombay chemist, also a Hindu Theosophist; and Rai Iqbal Narain Gurtu, our honorary headmaster; he indeed came to us without being a member, but he has joined the Society since, appreciating the value of the work that we have been doing. And it is the same with our honorary office-workers, who do daily drudgery: Babu Bhagavan Das, Babu Jnanendranath Basu, Babu Kali Charan Mitra, all Hindu theosophists. I might take name after name of Hindu Theosophists—leaving out our English Theosophical workers—who have given up money, health, time and life to the work. I think that their work, at least, might be respected by their countrymen, until Hindu non-Theosophists can show a similar roll of honorary workers for their motherland.

But why any English? Why not? The proof lies with the people who attack us for serving India, not with us. Love needs no difference; only hatred needs to be excused; the gulf between nation and nation, the antogonism between people and people, these need justification and the loving service freely given. And before I tell you—answering an unnecessary question—why there should be some English working among you, let me suggest that such an article as that in the *Modern Review*, entitled, 'The Social Conquest of the Hindu Race', can but bring fresh fruits of sorrow, new waves of hatred from those on either side who prefer hatred and isolation to love and brotherhood. It is said that if the English work with the Indian it is on an unequal footing and that "all the positions of trust, responsibility and social leadership are occupied by Englishmen and Englishwomen". Certainly that is not true in the Central Hindu College, nor within the limits of the Theosophical Society. In order to make that accusation apparently stand on a groundwork of fact, a statement is made as to some pretended 'Executive Committee' in 1906, but I cannot find any justification for it in our Annual Report for that year—or any other. To say that 'there is no Hindu occupying an important office on the Executive Committee' is only true because there is no Executive Committee! On the Managing Committee I am the only non-Indian in office. I find that Mr. Arundale worked under a Hindu, Mahamahopadhyaya Pandit Adityaram Bhattacharya, without any trouble. English ladies now work under a Hindu Headmaster, Pandit Iqbal Narain Gurtu, without the least trouble. Now that Mr. Arundale is Principal, a position he has won by good service and the love of his colleagues, I find that there is not one of his countrymen to be a second Englishman in the college. It is a little hard in some ways, that we have to resist pressure which would force us to engage other Englishmen in this college, and at the same time are attacked by some of our Indian brothers because there is one Englishman on our staff. Mr. Arundale was the one man who came forward to work without a salary as Principal, with the necessary capacity and the necessary university degree when Dr. Richardson had finally broken down and Pandit Adityaram withdrew because of age. If anyone cares to read our reports he will find Indians and English mixed up without reference to race. Even in the Athletic Association, where we might very well expect Englishmen to predominate, as the games are English, I find in this report of 1906 that the President was Mr. D. Kini, the General Secretary

Babu Kali Das Manik, Mr. A. W. Collie was the Cricket Secretary, Babu Brij Lal Prasad was the Football Secretary and Mr. Arundale the Hockey Secretary. The names are on a footing of absolute equality, with an Indian at the head. As regards the Governing Body I myself have been President and Chairman, because sometimes it needs an English mouth to speak out plainly. My colleague in all these long years has been Babu Upendra Nath Basu as Vice-President and Vice-Chairman and he takes my place during my long absences. The Secretary of the Board at the beginning was Babu Govinda Das. When he had to give it up, owing to ill-health, his brother Bhagavan Das resigned his government service to take up the Honorary Secretaryship, as well as being first Honorary Assistant Secretary and then Honorary Secretary to the Managing Committee and bearing the drudgery of the office work.

It may be an invidious and ungracious thing to point to all these facts, which anyone can verify, in answer to the falsehoods circulated in order to stir up strife and prevent co-operation between two nations brought together by Providence in this Indian land. But what can one do against the false but speak the true, when the false means ruin and the truth means peace?

For surely it cannot be well to circulate fabrications of this kind. To what end can they bring us? And what purpose can they serve? Let me put to you what seems to me to be the really serious matter regarding the whole of this; it means, if successful, the stirring up of strife, the rending of India, the explosion of war. I ask you why the English should not work with their Indian brothers? Why page after page in an important review—admirably conducted save for its wild hatred of the English should be filled with incitements to strife? Wwy should every Englishman who had tried to serve India be insulted, forgetting that in the changes which have made modern India, English and Indian have worked hand-in-hand? Is there any reason for this suspicion and this hatred? There is a justification and that we, who wear English bodies, should never forget under any insult. I who wear an English body have a right to say so. There is a justification for our Indian fellow-subjects regarding the English people with suspicion and even, perhaps, with hatred. There was so much of evil and of wrong, so much of treacherous betrayal and barbarous treatment in the past, that Indians may well suspect and hate. The memories of Clive, of Warren Hastings and of many other have cast a dark shadow of suspicion over many and many an Indian heart. Let Macaulay bear witness, who has written the story in deathless prose. When I see suspicions rise and read words of hatred such as these I read in this article, I say to myself: "Alas! the memory of wrong still remains, and the only way to root it out is the way of loving service, of quiet acceptance of now wrongful suspicion, until hatred is worn out of love." "Hatred ceaseth not by hatred at any time; hatred ceaseth by love." And will not you, my Indian brothers, allow the few of us in English bodies, who have given to the motherland our love, our work and our devotion, who have for her sake forsaken the country of our birth and the friends we have left behind, will you not allow us to pour out our love at Indian's feet and to give the service we count it honour and amends for the wrongs of the past? We will bear the *karma* of our country; we will bear the suspicion; we sill bear the hatred; and we will pay you back only in love and service, Even if, at the bottom of your hearts you do not trust us, even if you wrongly think that we have some ulterior motive, some personal aim, yet, for the sake of India's future, for the sake of the children of the future, who should work hand-in-hand and not in ever-perpetuated hatred and mutual wrong, forgive us what is wrong in the past of our countrymen, take us as willing offerings to make amends for the wrong. Do not drive us away until you have others to replace us: but let us work in love and harmony and let us help you towards that self-government, which can only come by English and Indians working hand-in-hand for the coming future and the motherland, to make the common tie, which shall bind these countries into one for evermore.

—*Annie Besant*

19

Society and Religion

State of Society and Religion in the Eighteenth Century

Society and religion in India have passed through numerous phases of change. In her long and chequered history, there have been periods of progress, regeneration and reform, as well as periods of decay, dissolution and degeneration. The eighteenth century witnessed the latter tendencies. While in Europe it was the age of enlightenment, in India, it was a period of stagnation.

With the death of the last great Mughal Emperor, Aurangzeb, in 1707, there began the speedy disintegration of a political fabric with ominous results for the whole country. In brief, the fall of the Mughal Empire inaugurated an era of unlimited political chaos. For considerable times and over vast areas there was no authority, no administration, no law and no security. There were prolonged struggle and conflicts among numerous small powers who were striving to make capital out of the decline of the Mughals. Society had to pass through a period of instability and insecurity, and suffered within itself from the stupefying effects. The strong prevailed over the weak, the poor suffered oppression, wayfarers endured plunder, and anarchy became the order of the day. Accounts left by eighteenth century foreign travellers and Indian writers present the picture of such a sad state of affairs.

Of course, Indian society as a whole remained detached from, and indifferent to, the political developments. The innumerable village communities over the length and breadth of the land led their self-contained and more or less secluded life as before. They endured the impact of the bad political times in a fatalistic mood and continued to remain unconcerned as far as possible. But their unconcern had unfortunate results, for the village communities became more and more isolated and closed, and their social life became more and more stagnant and static. Social institutions, customs and practices began to assume a rigid and petrified form.

Social rigidity and irrational social practices became conspicuous features of eighteenth century India. The disease was more aggravated by the outer aspects of contemporary religions which became even more dogmatic. In the fifteenth and sixteenth centuries India produced a number of seers and saints, preachers and religious reformers who played a vital role in rationalizing medieval religions. But the eighteenth century was a dark period in her religious history. There was no great religious, spiritual or moral preacher to preach enlightenment to the ignorant. Thus the eighteenth century religious outlook harked back to the outmoded practices and beliefs of bygone centuries. The echo of the social philosophy which the great medieval bhakti reformers like Kabir, Nanak, and Chaitanya had preached, was not heard again for two centuries.

Religion, the pivot of Indian life, had always exercised great influence on the people in their social ways and habits. That being the case, the condition of the society depended on the condition of its religion. The epochs in which religion stood for deeper philosophies in quest of the Absolute, were the epochs when society represented vitality and tolerance, vigour and elasticity, At other times, when religion meant only the outer form and rituals, the pattern of social outlook became stereotyped. In the eighteenth century, for most men, religion meant rigid rules and restrictions regarding what to eat and what not to eat, whom to touch and from whom to keep apart, in which pot to cook food and where to cook it and eat, how far to go, where to take one's bath, and which temples to visit. To maintain religious purity, people became intolerant of others and developed excessive sectarianism. Extreme dependence of people on the priestly class and of the priestly class on irrational practices made religion synonymous with bigotry and orthodoxy. It was a paradox of Hinduism that, while it tolerated all external religions with quiet indifference, it was intolerant within its own orbit towards anything which did not conform to established ritualistic details. Yet, Hinduism within itself was hydra-headed. It was amorphous enough to mean anything to anybody. It was complex and composed of numerous forms. Each form was subservient to a number of hard formalities. Deviation from formalities was unpardonable, though the meaning underlying them remained ever unintelligible and was seldom questioned or understood.

In the eighteenth century, idolatry and fetishism had been extended to extremes. Believers in monotheism and pantheism were there, but the mass of people were believers in sacrificial rites, witchcraft and sorcery, various pujas, festivities and ceremonies. In certain areas like Bengal, *tantric* rites and *sahajiyanist* practices were widely prevalent, and in some places, certain religious practices were dreadful. There was no escape from superstition, and surprisingly enough, there was hardly any protest even against inhuman practices.

Islam, too, had become an intolerant religion. In the heyday of Islamic glory, the Sufi preachers preached tolerance. But from the latter part of the seventeenth century the Muslim rulers assumed religious bigotry as a part of their state policy. In fact, the fall of the Mughal empire was due to the struggle of the Rajputs, Marathas, Sikhs and others against the oppressive laws which the orthodox Aurangzeb unwisely introduced. The bitterness between Muslims and Hindus became a legacy of the seventeenth century which continued into the eighteenth. The earlier understanding between the two communities had almost vanished with the consequent result of their indifference and antipathy towards each other. The days were gone when Muslim liberals like Akbar and Dara Shikoh had tried to appreciate the spiritual doctrines of the Hindu scriptures. Instead, religious animosity pervaded the mind of the Muslim ruling class. Instead of understanding between the two major communities in their socio-cultural life, there was more and more of separation.

Muslim society withdrew inside its own orthodox shell as Islam in India detached itself from other spiritual streams.

With religions attaching more importance to external form than to inner reality, religious superstitions began to pervade all aspects of social life. The more numerous the superstitious practices, the greater became the dominance of the priestly class. The bulk of that class seldom understood the scriptures, and cared little for spiritual values. But they practised the ceremonies in all earnestness and society obeyed them faithfully. Amid ignorance and blind belief, dangerous social customs appeared as religiously sound. Priests could explain any social evil as holy, with the apparent sanction of the scriptures behind it. Infanticide, child marriage, polygamy, the burning of widows, and other social evils, were all interpreted as scripturally and religiously valid, and hence there was no qualm of conscience even before the most horrible performance. Similarly, such social systems as caste, untouchability, seclusion of women and slavery were all considered as sanctified by the *shastras*, and therefore, absolutely valid and estimable.

Thus the eighteenth century was an age of intolerant institutions and irrational customs. In the following lines a brief reference is made to some of these social institutions and socio-religious customs.

CASTE

Hindu society was a caste society and the caste system was as old as Hinduism, if not as old as Rig Vedic Aryanism, Through the centuries, the history of the caste system was a record of ups and downs, of rigidity and liberalism. There had been periods of extreme caste exclusiveness, when the shadow of a Chandala was abominable to the Brahmin. Equally there were periods when the Chandala and the Brahmin embraced each other in emotional delight. In sixteenth century India, in the days of Chaitanya and the Bhakti preachers, caste rigidity had slackened greatly and God had been brought nearer to the Sudras through personal devotion which did not require priestly mediation. But the eighteenth century saw the reversal of the sixteenth century social ethics. In the nineteenth century there began the reform movements to liberalise the caste structure and rationalize the religious practices. Since there were no such progressive movements in the eighteenth century, the caste prejudices were at their height. In a sense, the rigidity of the caste system attained its strictest form in that epoch and continued to be dominant till the reform movements began in the nineteenth century.

It is difficult to determine the actual number of castes and sub-castes which existed in the society. There are different estimates, some of which even suggest the existence of two to three thousand castes and sub-castes. While such numbers might include all possible social divisions existing all over the subcontinent, in any particular area the number might only be a few. The merits and demerits of the caste system have been debated since the days of Buddha, but without any conclusion. It remains, therefore, one of the most controversial social institutions of human history. Its greatest demerit was that it divided the society into water-tight compartments. Without social unity, the country had to suffer many consequences including foreign domination. Much before the eighteenth century, the French traveller, Tavernier, described the great disadvantage of caste in the following words: "The idolaters of India are so numerous that for one Mahomedan there are five or six Gentiles. It is astonishing to see how this enormous multitude of men has allowed itself to be subjected by so small a number of persons, and has bent readily under the yoke of the Mahomedan princes. But the astonishment ceases when one considers that these idolators have no union among themselves, and that superstition has introduced so strange a diversity of opinions and customs that they never agree with one another."

The advantage of the caste system has been ascribed to its economic implications. An occupational function was allotted to each caste or sub-caste, however small it might have been. There was means of livelihood for everyone in the society and inside every group there was a place for every individual. It is this aspect of the caste system which has prompted even some modern thinkers to justify the system in that it preserved Hindu arts and craftsmanship, besides religion and morals. In the words of Monier Williams: "(ste has been useful in promoting self-sacrifice, in securing subordination of the individual to an organized body, in restraining vice and in preventing pauperism."

Its merits or demerits notwithstanding, the caste system stood on certain social formalities. It was a ladder from the highest to the lowest. While the highest caste contained God's men and claimed the utmost reverence, the members of the lowest groups were so inferior as to remain secluded, while of course doing their duty by society. Between the highest and the lowest, there existed numerous grades depending on the nature of caste profession. In such a system, the individual's life and occupation were determined at his birth irrespective of his inborn qualities. Thus a dullard born in a Brahmin family was accepted by the society as a sacred man, supposed to be well versed in the *shastras* and laws, whereas a genius born in the house of a Sudra had no opportunity for recognition, and society regarded him as nothing more than a washerman or tanner or scavenger. In the periods of liberalism, men from lower ranks had won recognition and distinction, but at other times, talent lay buried beneath the caste. Inter caste marriage was unthinkable. Eating with other castes was equally forbidden. Even to take water from the hands of many castes was a sin. Restrictions were so strictly enforced that anyone, who broke the rules, even unknowingly, faced social excommunication. The fear of losing one's own caste was great. The upper castes assumed greater and greater pretensions regarding caste purity. The practice of touch-me-not was an austere mode of maintaining personal purity.

On established forms, the caste system remained rigid. To the Hindus, it was a sure and settled way of existence, sanctified by time and religion. In the eighteenth century, the caste system was no problem to the society. But in the eyes of the Europeans of that time, as in the eyes of the Hindu rationalists of the nineteenth century, caste appeared degrading. The modernism of the nineteenth century became synonymous with a crusade against caste, and the most degrading evil of the caste system, untouchability.

UNTOUCHABILITY

Had the caste structure been merely an economic system of the division of labour, it could have been justified as useful. But the society was divided into touchables and untouchables in the most irrational way. The concepts of human equality, upheld by religions and preached by prophets, were valueless in the context of social relations. Untouchability was itself the supreme example of social inequality. But, more than that, there was the problem of injustice associated with it. The untouchables were denied certain basic privileges of living. They could not use tanks, wells, inns or schools meant for upper caste people, not to speak of places of worship or public institutions. In the eighteenth century, the old injunction of the *Tantra* dominated Hindu society. "Avoid the touch of the Chandala, and other abject classes. Whoever associates with them undoubtedly falls from his class; whoever bathes or drinks in wells or pools which they have caused to be made, must be purified by the five productions of kine."

The only redeeming feature of untouchability was that the untouchable belonged to a class of his own. Inside it, he was accustomed to the traditional ways of his forefathers and did not feel, or was not conscious of, the injustice to which his class had been subjected through the ages. In the words of Horace Hayman Wilson, who was an admirer of Hindu ways of life: "The lowest native is no outcaste, he has an acknowledged place in society; he is the member of a class; and he is invariably more retentive of the distinction than those above him.... The veriest Chandala, who is one of a community, is less miserable, less unhappy, than many of the paupers of the civilized communities of Europe, with whom no man owns companionship or kindred; they are the true outcastes—not the Pariah or Chandala."

Be that as it may, the eighteenth century society retained untouchability in its extreme form. That was the last great epoch of social inequality in India. With the impact of western ideas and the rise of Hindu reform movements in the subsequent century, caste was assailed and there began a slow slackening of rigid attitudes towards untouchability. However, in spite of reform movements, throughout the nineteenth century the caste inertia continued without any spectacular improvement in the position of the untouchables.

SECLUSION OF WOMEN

The position of women in the eighteenth century was far from being satisfactory. It was their total seclusion which brought about their physical and mental degeneration. In many parts of India, especially in the north and east, the *purdah* had long become an established system both among Hindus and Muslims. The general insecurity and lawlessness which prevailed at that time made the seclusion more tight. The freedom and status which the Indian women enjoyed in ancient times were beyond the range of imagination. For centuries under Muhammaden rule there had developed an apathy towards the lot of the women. The climax of that tendency was perhaps most marked on the eve of British rule.

There was hardly any opportunity for girls to attend educational institutions. Among the Rajputs, the girls belonging to richer sections received some kind of elementary education. Among the Vaishnava sects in Bengal, too, there was some inclination to educate girls so that they might read religious books. But apart from a few exceptions, as a general rule Indian women remained unlettered and ignorant.

Women in south India were not so much subjected to *zenana* as their counterparts in the north. Similary, mainly for economic reasons, the women belonging to the lower classes of society did not lead such a secluded life. They were called upon to work in their caste professions or in agricultural fields. Women in cities and towns were more confined to their homes than women in remote villages.

It was the complete dependence of women on men which reduced their position to one of abject surrender. "Their fathers protect them in childhood; their husbands protect them in youth; their sons protect them in age"—such was the ancient saying which dominated the Hindu mind through the centuries. Protection in this case meant making the female dependent on her father, husband and son in childhood, youth and old age respectively. It was the system of denying Hindu women any right to paternal property which made them economically completely dependent on men. Their economic status was a vital cause of their misery and suffering.

Much before the eighteenth century certain abominable socio-religious customs had entered Hindu society which affected Hindu women in the most horrible manner. The most iniquitous of these customs were five—infanticide, child marriage, polygamy, forced celibacy of widows, and last but not least, the burning of widows on the funeral pyre of their husbands. In eighteenth century India, the above-mentioned customs were, if not universal or widely prevalent, yet prominent enough to catch the attention of the new rulers. They survived through the eighteenth century, but were challenged in the nineteenth century both through legislation and reform movements. A brief reference to those customs is made below.

INFANTICIDE

Destruction of female children at their birth was not a common custom. But its worst aspect was that it was practised secretly. Surprisingly, it was more prevalent among the wealthier and upper sections of the people in certain areas. In 1789, Jonathan Duncan, at that time the British Resident at Benares, discovered the practice among the Rajkumars of that place. It was also discovered among the Jadejas of Kathiawar and Kutch. Subsequently it was seen that the custom was familiar among the Kuchwah Rajputs near Allahabad. The Chauhan Rajputs and the Pathak Ahirs of Mainpuri were addicted to the crime. In the Punjab, too, it was widely practised. The Bedis of Jullundur were so accustomed to it that anybody among them who kept a daughter was excommunicated. Certain Muslims of the Rat tribe also practised it.

The reasons for infanticide varied. Among the Chauhans it was primarily due to economic causes, veiled by ignorant pride. They killed their infant daughters as it was imperative to spend large sums of money for the marriage of a daughter. Among the Bedis, it was a matter of social pride not to give a daughter to an inferior caste. The practice was first enjoined upon them by Dharm Chand Bedi, the grandson of Guru Nanak. It arose out of a fit of temper of that religious leader, and consequently took on a superstitious colour and continued into posterity as a social custom. In Rajputana, the chief cause was the determination of the chiefs not to allow their daughters to remain unmarried beyond the age of ten. This feeling induced the fathers of the boys to demand heavy bribes for their consent. Hence it became a common custom to kill daughters to avoid difficulties in getting them married. Among Munha Rajputs, infanticide became a means of preserving the purity of their race.

Whether it arose from pride or poverty, superstition or ignorance, the custom was a crime. That the society tolerated it was itself a proot of the degradation to which it had stooped. The methods of killing the infants were extremely barbaric. At many places the child was destroyed immediately after birth by filling the mouth with cowdung or by immersing the head in cow's milk or by coiling the umbilical cord around the face. At certain other places, the infant was buried alive. Another method was to administer a small pill of opium. In the Kangra area, the juice of the Madar plant was administered, or death was brought about by causing injury to the navel. Such were the cruelties associated with the custom.

CHILD MARRIAGE

There were times in ancient India when girls selected their own husbands, if they were considered sufficiently grown up to exercise due discretion. Indeed, for a considerable period in ancient Hindu history, there was perhaps no system of early marriage, though there were probably exceptions to the rule. But by the time of the *Manusamhita* the custom had already become so familiar that the marriageable age for girls had been prescribed as twelve or even eight. Gradually, early marriage became an established custom. Various social factors operated to make the system popular. The influence of climatic conditions being what it is, social systems became regulated in the light of such influences, Maturity comes earlier in hot climates, and society, over-anxious to uphold its moral standards, laid particular emphasis on the chastity of girls. By giving them in marriage before they were of proper age, people felt assured that society would retain its moral purity. There were economic factors as well. To the poorer people, a girl was as much a burden to her parents as of use to her husband's family where she was required to remain in charge of the kitchen. The Hindu joint family system was no less responsible for encouraging the custom. The desire of the grandparents or even great grandparents to see the younger ones marry was a strong factor.

Whatever be the causes, child marriage was a widely prevalent system during the medieval period. Hindus and Muslims alike practised it. The Emperor Akbar, as already mentioned, tried to abolish the custom, but in vain, and by the eighteenth century it had become more deep-rooted than ever. The growth of the population and the physical degradation of women proceeded side by side. Motherhood at the tender age, with numerous sickly children around her, made the Indian woman the epitome of misery and distress.

Child marriage produced many side evils. In the lowest and most ignorant stratas of society, according to the depth of their economic misery, parents would sell away their child daughters as brides to those who could afford to meet their demands. The bridegrooms, or their guardians, ran into debt in purchasing the brides. There was no concept of a proper match as is understood in modern times. The difference in age between the bride and the bridegroom was of no account.

The greatest evil arising out of child marriage was the growing number of child-widows. Without the economic means by which to sustain themselves, without benevolent treatment from their immediate relations, and being subjected to suspicion, social stigma and superstition, the girl-widows lingered through their unfortunate existences. In the upper stratas of society, some of them escaped misery through the custom of *sati* or self-immolation. But to the vast majority of widows in all stratas and castes, life was one long misery.

POLYGAMY

Polygamy was an old social evil. It pervaded both the Hindu and Muslim societies. But the evil crossed all limits in course of time. It was confined mostly to the richer and higher sections of society. With their affluence and wealth, the rich could afford to become polygamous and licentious. It was neither a matter of shame nor sorrow to maintain a harem and to keep many wives. Rather, it was a matter of personal pride and social prestige if one could afford it.

The worst example of polygamy prevailed in eighteenth century Bengal, and that, too, among the highest classes of Brahmins. As early as the eleventh century, the king of Bengal honoured a few Brahmins for certain excellent qualities of head and heart. Their families ultimately came to be regarded as superior to the rest and became famous as the Kulin families. In course of time, the descendants of the original Kulins had nothing to do with the virtues associated with Kulinism, yet they remained superior in the caste ladder. Out of that superiority complex, a few social evils developed. It was undesirable on the part of a Kulin to marry into inferior Brahmin families. It was equally a strong temptation for inferior Brahmins to give a daughter to a Kulin. To achieve the purpose, the inferior Brahmins offered a large dowry and much money to Kulin bridegrooms. The latter found it difficult to resist such material temptations. Eventually, the Kulins married into Brahmin families of lower rank and thus fell from their original rank. Yet, though fallen and styled as the broken Kulins, they enjoyed a great demand for their hands in the marriage market. The lower Brahmins competed among themselves to offer daughters to Kulins and the latter made marriage a means of livelihood, a business or a profession of profit through many marriages.

By the eighteenth century, such an absurd system of polygamy assumed monstrous proportions. On a single day a Kulin could marry two, three or four wives. In his lifetime he could marry dozens of wives, even a hundred. There were parents who offered all their daughters to a single Kulin. There was no upper age limit for the Kulin; he could be of any age. Similarly, the brides of the same man could be as tender in age as possible.

Still more absurd was the system that the Kulin husband was not required to maintain his numerous wives. The so-called wives remained in the houses of their parents. But now and again the husband would come to collect some money from the unfortunate father-in-law. The result of such a system was dangerous. It encouraged social immorality and vice. Without any sanction of religion, Kulinism developed into a social superstition and ruined the lives of innumerable women while causing degradation to the society as a whole.

Elsewhere, polygamy created various social and domestic complications. The upper class Hindus and Muslims, when polygamous, suffered family unhappiness and economic hardship. Among the Muslims, polygamy made the *purdah* system more stringent. The only happy feature in regard to it was that it did not become a common vice among the general population.

CELIBACY OF WIDOWS

While widow-marriage prevailed among the Hindus in very ancient times, gradually it was abandoned and came to be regarded as a sin. The forced celibacy of widows became a strict social custom which few could dare defy. Society imposed the duties on widows as prescribed in the *Manusamhita*: "Let her emaciate her body by living voluntarily on pure flowers, roots, and fruits, but let her not, when her lord is deceased, even pronounce the name of another man, let her continue till death forgiving all injuries, performing harsh duties, avoiding every sensual pleasure, and cheerfully practising the incomparable rules of virtue which have been followed by such women as were devoted to only one husband." It was one of the most severe codes of conduct which the widow was required to observe in accordance with semi-religious injunctions. Society paid its habitual regard to the widow who remained above suspicion. Her life was adjusted to a formal routine of fasting, devotion, prayer and pious works. Through the centuries, such became the lot of the Hindu widow.

In normal cases, the austere celibacy of the widow was no social evil. But the real trouble arose with the spread of the evil of child-marriage and with the consequent increase in the number of child-widows. Little girls, who while marrying knew nothing of their husbands, became widows on the death of those unknown or even unseen person. For them, the laws of widowhood constituted a code of tyranny. Even in the days of the *Manusamhita*, virgin widows were permitted to marry a second time. But, as time advanced, the practice fell into disrepute and was abandoned. Among the lower castes, widow-marriage was permitted. But in the higher castes, it became impossible. There were widows under the age of five years, not to speak of other age groups, such as five to ten and ten to fifteen.

The treatment of widows varied from place to place, and also according to their age. Old widows had an established place in the Hindu joint family. They commanded respect and played the role of counsellors in domestic matters to their younger relations. It was the younger widows who suffered ill-treatment so frequently. People regarded their persons as inauspicious or even ominous. They deserved neither sympathy nor pity from men since God had shown them no mercy. Extreme ignorance also led people to believe that young widows were responsible for family misfortunes. They were denied many privileges in day-to-day life. They could not take part in many ceremonies and functions. In essence, the life of young widows, especially in places like the Bombay Presidency, was mostly unbearable.'

In 1756, Raja Rajballav of Dacca wanted to give his daughter in remarriage. She became a widow at a very early age. The Raja gathered the opinion of the most learned pandits of Benares, Mithila and of the south to learn if the Hindu *shastras* actually did not sanction widow-marriage. The learned men gave the unanimous opinion that "women are at liberty to marry again if their husbands be not heard of, die, retire from the world, prove to be eunuchs or become outcastes."

Even if the *Shastras* had not closed the doors against widow-marriage, the convention was too firmly established to change. So, against Raja Rajballav there stood Maharaja Krishna Chandra of Nadia with his band of orthodox priests. The time was not ripe in the eighteenth century to bring about a social change of so great an importance. Thus, the non-marriage of the widows continued for yet another century without any formidable body of opinion against it.

SATI

Among many irrational social customs, the most unnatural was the custom of *sati* or the immolation of the Hindu widows on the funeral pyre of her dead husband. The custom appeared revolting to the Europeans who had the occasion to discover it. The Danes at Serampore, the Dutch at Chinsure and the French at Chandernagore did not allow *sati* to be practised within the jurisdiction of their authority. The English East India Company at Bombay, during the period from 1770 to 1780, tried to stop the custom in the territories under their control. Elsewhere, the English rulers in the eighteenth century showed a timid approach towards the rite in fear of general Hindu discontent.

Much before the Europeans, some Muslim rulers in India like Akbar had attempted to abolish sati. Even the Sikh Guru, Amardas, and the Maratha Peshwas tried to stop it in their spheres of influence. But the custom was so much a matter of blind faith among the orthodox that its eradication was only a remote possibility.

The origin of the system remains a mystery. At some unknown time in ancient days it began to take shape through some kind of misinterpretation or misrepresentation of a passage in the Rig Vida. At least that is what Max Mueller believed.* Once the rite gained recognition as a virtuous action of the widow, the priestly class made the best of it for their own advantage. Towards the end of the Hindu period, the custom was fairly well established. Alberuni described it in the eleventh century: "If a wife of a Hindu loses her husband by death, she cannot marry another man. She has only to choose between two things, either to remain a widow as long as she lives or to burn herself; and the latter eventually is considered the preferable, because as a widow she is ill-treated as long as she lives." The purpose of the superstition which inspired the widow to die voluntarily, or prompted her near ones to engineer her death, has been vividly described by the sixteenth century expounder of Hindu Law, Raghunandan. The following are the prescribed words to be recited by the victim herself before entering into

---

* A passage in the Rig Veda referring to widows contained the word *Agre,* while describing her position in the front. But when the word *Agre,* through some mysterious process, became *Agne,* it meant her position in the fire.

the fire: "I, ... desiring to attain the glory of the heavens to be obtained by acting like Aroondhatee, to dwell in the religions of bliss, rejoicing with my husband as many years as there are hairs in the human body, to purify the three families of my mother, father, and father-in-law, to be glorified by the *Apsaras* an long as fourteen Indras last, to enjoy the company of my husband and to purify my husband from sins..., do ascent the flaming funeral pyre of my husband."

It was the hope of attaining heaven which originally led the widows to experience the supreme ordeal. In the same superstitious faith, the society and its leaders did not suffer any revolt of conscience when the custom was celebrated. Superstition blinded the fathers to persuade their little daughters to burn themselves with the dead body of their old husbands. Sons pleaded with their old mothers to sacrifice themselves. Many satis died willingly. But for many others, death in the fire could only have been torture, It was more or less forced on them by society. However, such inhuman performances were mostly confined to the upper classes, including Brahmins, and never became universal among all castes of Hindus.

The campaign against the sati system began in the British occupied territories in the last quarter of the eighteenth century. Christian missionaries began the campaign. Some lone English officers, too, in their remote stations came across the horrid rite and felt moved to rise their voices against it. But the Company's Government was unprepared to offend Hindu sentiment by interfering in their religious customs. So, it continued.

OTHER SUPERSTITIOUS PRACTICES

In eighteenth century India, quite a number of superstitious rites of doubtful antiquity or origin, were practised in different parts of the country. They were neither very common nor even widely known. Mostly they were superstitions of individual preference. The rites represented in certain cases an inner urge of the individuals to give up the best in them and suffer the most. One could sacrifice his own life, or a child, or inflict on himself the most severe physical pain. As far as self-renunciation was concerned it was one thing; but the tragedy of such rites was that they were practised blindly without any rational thinking.

Human sacrifice can be described as first in the series of superstitious practices. Not to speak of the human sacrifice practised by the Khonds in their remote hill fastnesses, it was the upper class Hindus who on very rare occasions resorted to it. It was the legacy of the Sakta cult which prevailed in some form or other. The goddess Kali required human blood or heads and, for the gratification of the *devi,* a human victim was slaughtered. The ceremony was celebrated in the utmost secrecy. Even as late as the second half of the nineteenth century, there were instances when human heads were discovered in some Kali temples of Bengal in sacrificial forms.

In the eighteenth century, self-immolation was yet another form of human sacrifices. Instances are related of a person drowning in the sea or particulary at the confluence of the Ganges with the sea. Instances of such sacrifices were described by Europeans. In some cases, in order to escape disease, one could drown himself in a river. In other cases, life could be taken by way of mortification and penance. The references of the early Europeans to death under the wheels of the chariot of Lord Jagannath (whom they called Juggernaut) came in extremely exaggerated forms and lacked substance.

Among other forms of human sacrifice, there was the sacrifice of one's own child. Parents, under peculiar conditions, used to take a vow to offer their first born child to the river Ganges. In due time, when the child was born, in order to keep that sacred promise, they used to carry the child to the Ganges and throw it into the water. This was a rare custom and was abandoned as soon as people became aware that the government viewed it with great disfavour.

Self-torture was yet another superstitious rite. The familiar form of this was usually observed in the *charak* festivals in the month of *Chaitra.* Quite a number of devotees used to perform the painful practice of piercing their tongues and arms with pointed rods. On the final day of the festival, the still more painful custom of hook-swinging was performed. This was not practised by many but only by those few persons who could endure such pain. The devotees were suspended from a beam fixed on a high pole with hooks piercing the muscles of their backs and they remained swinging in that horrible manner. Such barbarous rites were practised in the belief that good results, either for the individual or the community, followed such self-torture.

Among the women in the eighteenth century, specially in Bengal, the offer of drops of blood from their own bodies to some goddesses was a not uncommon custom. Usually, when a husband or a son developed a serious illness, the woman took a vow to offer her own blood to the goddess Durga or Kali on the recovery of the patient. Such vows were fulfilled in due time. Blood-offering was practised among men on rare occasions. To propitiate the goddess, a man could cut out his own tongue and offer it at her altar.

Irrational as all such practices were, fortunately for the society they could neither be universally adopted nor widely acclaimed. They were bad, nevertheless. No society could have tolerated inhuman customs for the sake of pleasure. It was a wrong faith, followed through ignorance. In an era of mental stagnation, the prevailing abuses continued without affecting the conscience of thinking men. But when the time came, society showed an eagerness to abandon these pernicious systems.

THE STATE OF SOCIAL MORALITY

Socio-religious superstitions and ignorant ways of life no doubt rendered the eighteenth century one of the dark epochs of Indian history, but yet the society was not devoid of social ethics or virtues of a higher order. The traditional ethical standards were habitually maintained by all sections of people, irrespective of the standard of consciousness of enlightenment. People in general followed established codes or moral conduct. They cherished the higher values of life against the background of an ephemeral existence. The most ignorant as well as the highly learned knew in a definite manner what was right and what was wrong, what was virtue and what was vice. Absolute faith in fate, in the doctrine of *karma,* the cycle of birth and rebirth, and in other such religious concepts, kept the people on the right path. Even when one practised a wrong custom, the intention was never bad. Everything passed in the name of religion and virtue. Its merit was that in day-to-day life, one remained pure, pious and virtuous. Its demerit was that in the name of religion one subscribed to what the priests prescribed by way of irrational customs.

The Europeans who criticized Hindu superstitions in vehement terms were greatly prejudiced in their understanding of real conditions. Undoubtedly the society was full of unnatural customs, but yet there was a brighter aspect to the people's character and manners. Some distinguished Europeans who spent a part of their lives in eighteenth century India left a glowing testimony to Hindu character. It is worth our while to take note of their estimates.

While giving evidence before committees of both Houses of Parliament in 1813, Warren Hastings described the national character of the Indian people in the following words: "Great pains have been taken to inculcate into the public mind (in England), an opinion that the native Indians are in a state of complete moral turpitude, and live in the constant and unrestrained commission of every vice and crime that can disgrace human nature. I affirm, by the oath that I have taken, that this description of them is untrue, and wholly unfounded.... In speaking of the people...The Hindoos...are gentle, benevolent, more susceptible of gratitude for kindness shown them than prompted to vengeance for wrongs inflicted.... Gross as the modes of their worship are, the precepts of their religion are wonderfully fitted to promote the best ends of society, its peace and good order; and even from their theology, arguments may be drawn to illustrate and support the most refined mysteries of our own." According to Thomas Munro: "If a good system of agriculture, unrivalled manufacturing skill, a capacity to produce whatever can contribute to either convenience or luxury, schools established in every village for teaching, reading, writing, and arithmetic, the general practice of hospitality and charity amongst each other, and above all, a treatment of the female sex, full of confidence, respect, and delicacy, are among the signs which denote a civilized people—then the Hindoos are not inferior to the nations of Europe, and if civilization is to became an article of trade between the two countries, I am convinced that this country (England) will gain by the import cargo." John Malcolm described the Hindoo character in upper India thus: "They are brave, generous, humane, and their truth is as remarkable as their courage." To Captain Sydenham: "I think the general character of the Hindoo is submissive, docile, sober, inoffensive, as long as his religious prejudices and habits are not violated: capable of great attachment and loyalty, as long as they are well treated by their governors and masters; quick in apprehension, intelligent, active, generally honest, and performing the duties of charity, benevolence, and filial affection with as much sincerity and regularity as any nation with which I am acquainted." With an experience of twenty-five years in distant parts of India, Graeme Mercer described the people as "mild in their dispositions, polished in their general manners; in their domestic relations kind and affectionate".

Such observations of eminent Europeans early in the nineteenth century go a long way to show that in spite of political turmoils and general confusion, the society retained many moral and ethical values as well as the norm of civilized conduct.

IMPACT OF THE WEST

In the eighteenth century, Indian society was rigid within itself, but not closed to external influences. Though the general mental horizon of the people was limited, yet the intellectual horizon was kept open to receive enlightenment. The newness of the West was, therefore, quickly felt when Western contact became definitely established. From the days of Vasco da Gama at the close of the eighteenth century, the European contact began to touch the Indian society at its outer fringe. But by the first half of the eighteenth century, the Europeans had become a definite factor in Indian politics. By way of a historic accident the eighteenth century was an age of enlightenment in the history of Europe and it was during that age of unusual mental and physical activities that Europe came nearer to India. The impact became inevitable. During the second half of the eighteenth century and the early decades of the nineteenth century the effects of that impact became manifest.

European influence operated in three spheres—economic, religious and political. The trade and commerce which the Europeans carried on the different parts of India had no direct bearing on the social life of the people. With the growth of their political domination, the economic impact of the West proved disastrous. As will be discussed later, in her economic relations with Britain India was destinated to suffer badly. Her traditional economic structure in agriculture and industry fell to pieces.

It was through their religious and political activities that the Europeans, of necessity, came very close to the Indian ways of life. Or, more precisely, they broke through the seclusion of the Indian society for the purpose of preaching their own religion as well as of introducing their own political and legal systems. In that process they had to understand India. India, too, had to understand the West. The impact was not merely an imposition. It was also in the nature of an accommodation.

It was the religious activities of the European missionaries which brought Christianity to a direct confrontation with Hinduism. Earlier, the Portuguese authorities, in their various pockets of influence, had combined religious with political activities. They converted their conquered subjects. The Dutch, too, believed in conducting both activities together. It was the French who paid primary attention to politics. The English Company, in its earlier days when they were traders, thought of preaching Christianity. But when they became rulers, it was thought prudent to abandon their Christian zeal in order to avoid rousing popular antipathy against their rule. But if the Company avoided it, Christian missionaries in their private capacity took up the work with zeal. For a time, the Company did not view missionary activities with favour and tried to discourage them. But that did not stop the missionary work. In the last decade of the seventeenth century, men like William Carey, Joshua Marshman and William Ward began their missionary activities from Serampore, which at that time was Danish possession. Their influence spread to Calcutta.

To the missionaries many things in Hinduism appeared abominable. They forgot that Christianity itself was not free from irrational dogmas. Even towards the close of the seventeenth century, "Shrieking Scotch Covenanters were submitted to torture by crushing their knees flat in the boot, women were tied to stakes on the sea-sands and drowned by the slowly advancing tide because they would not attend Episcopal worship, or branded on their cheeks and then shipped to America." Similar fanatical customs elsewhere in Europe were tolerated in the eighteenth century. Even greater barbarities were committed in name of law. In England in the eighteenth century, a man could be hanged for stealing a fish, writing threatening letters, stealing five shillings from a store and pick-pocketing. A Hindu rationalist would have felt shocked to witness many of the customs in eighteenth century Europe, just as European rationalists felt shocked to witness some of the Indian customs.

For India it was a blessing in disguise that the Christian missionaries felt so strongly against some of her socio-religious customs. Practised through ignorance they were required to be exposed by an external agency. The missionaries, in order to convert India, condemned Hinduism in the most vehement manner, affecting every aspect of Hindu belief and practice. From polytheism and idolatry to smaller rituals, nothing missed their observation. Two results emanated from their campaign. Directly, they gained converts to Christianity and created a small but new class inside the existing socio-religious frame of India. Indirectly, the Christian crusade against Hinduism inspired in higher Hindu minds a sense of inwardness to discover in the inner core of their own religion concepts of monotheism, and all other higher philosophies to feel proud of. Thus the impact of Christianity led to external and internal change.

It should not be forgotten that while the precepts of Christianity had had their socio-ethical impact, the conduct and character of the English rulers in the eighteenth century did not prove that the newcomers were the representatives of a higher type of society. They became famous for their violence, rapacity, greed, corruption and licentiousness. A European associate of Sir Thomas Roe, writing in the seventeenth century, described what the Indians thought of the Christians thus: "It is a most sad and horrible thing to consider what scandal there is brought upon the Christian religion by the looseness and remissness, by the exorbitances of many, which come amongst them who profess themselves Christians, of whom I have often heard the natives, who live here near the port where our ships arrive say thus, in broken English, which they have gotten, *Christian religion, devil religion; Christian much drunk; Christian much do wrong, much beat, much abuse others'*. In the eighteenth century, the conduct of the East India Company's servants and merchants was little better. In several among them, their lawless conduct, debauchery, vices, malice, crime and cruelty rendered the name of white men in general disgraceful. Hastings, Francis, Impey and some others, who occupied the highest position among Englishmen in India, were by no means pillars of virtue with the highest ethical standards.

However, it was the freshness of a new religion which counted, not the conduct of its adherents. Moreover, some of the missionaries set a good example in matters of religious sincerity and in devotion to their cause. They began to learn Indian languages for religious propaganda, and at the same time encouraged Indians to learn English. Men like William Carey possessed a wide vision regarding Anglo-Indian relations. In Bengal, he laid the foundation of English education. Bengali literature, too, began to develop under the patronage of the missionaries. In 1801, Carey published his Bengali grammar. Simultaneously, J. C. Marshman wrote a history of India. A printing press was established at Serampore by the missionaries. Though it was meant primarily for printing religious literature, yet its role in spreading knowledge was significant. The press also caused the birth of journalism. While the ground was thus prepared for the spread of the Christian religion and Western ideas, the Company's opposition to missionary activities came to an end. The Charter Act of 1813 granted to the missionaries freedom of action in India.

Christianity spread slowly at first. On account of various factors, Hindus and Muslims did not feel encouraged to abandon their religion and embrace Christianity. For the upper class Hindus, conversion was inconceivable, and on rare occasions only some of them changed religion. The strong bond of caste, Hindu laws regarding right to property, the hold of the joint family, and the natural aversion to abandon their faith on the part of Hindus, were some factors which stood in the way of missionary success. However, it was the spread of Christian ideas rather than the Christian religion which influenced the traditional Indian society to take a fresh look at their own set of values.

The impact of the West was also felt politically. The ladder of the new administration could not, of necessity, have been composed only of Englishmen; its lower rungs had to be filled with Indians. The people, long accustomed to dealing with foreigners in trade, felt attracted to join their administration. There was the necessity for them to learn English. For intelligent young people who wanted jobs in commercial firms or government offices, knowledge of English was a desirable objective. Early in the nineteenth century, Calcutta led the way in the new desire to acquire knowledge of the English language. Surprisingly enough, the demand for the new learning came from leading Hindus. In other parts of India, a similar desire was awakened. At Jhansi, its Maharastrian governor, Hari Damodar, learnt English in order to understand Western science and he actually established a laboratory on the Western model. At Benares, Bombay and Madras, the demand for English education came form leading minds among the Hindus. In their humble way, they began to establish English schools.

Thus as early as 1808, an English school began functioning at Calcutta under an Armenian headmaster. In 1816, Rammohun Roy established another school in the city for English education. In 1817, the famous Hindu College was founded in Calcutta with encouragement from David Here, the Chief Justice, Hyde East, Rammohum Roy and Radhakanta Dev. In 1818, some Christian missionaries, with the help of some influential Indians, established an English school at Benares.

The authorities of the East India Company at first remained indifferent towards English education. In 1824 they established in Calcutta a school for Sanskrit education and another for Arabic and Persian. It still took some time for the Company to officially inaugurate Western education through the English medium. In any case, the greater impact of the West was bound to percolate through education, with far-reaching consequences.

There was yet another platform on which the West-East understanding took shape. At first, to the leaders of Indian thought, Englishmen, either as traders, rulers or missionaries, were enemies of Indian culture, religion and traditions. But such an antagonistic attitude began to subside because of the unique role of some notable Englishmen who dedicated their Indian careers to discovering India. William Jones founded the Asiatic Society of Bengal in 1784. With earnest compatriots like Charles Wilkins and H. T. Colebrooke, he initiated the great movement of discovering India. The history and literature, and many facets of Indian civilization, began to emerge steadily out of the limbo of oblivion. The more western scholarship threw light on India. the greater became the attraction of Indian scholars towards research and learning.

The impact of the West began to operate through perceptible and imperceptible ways. It had its positive and negative aspects. Through actions and reactions, antagonism and assimilation, Western ideas began to penetrate into Indian thought and habits. The orthodox revolted outwardly, but searched inwardly for a change. For the intellectual, there was the need to rationalize the traditional society. To the learned, Hinduism, Islam and Christianity had common grounds on which to meet, the essence of all religions being the same. A wave of unrest swept over the thinking minds during the early years of the nineteenth century. Out of the unrest, the Indian renaissance began to take shape. In the wake of that awakening there also emerged the socio-religious reform movements. The nineteenth century in the history of India possessed the same characteristics which the eighteenth century possessed in the history of Europe. It was an age of enlightenment and awakening, of renaissance and reforms, of rationalism and progress, which all ultimately culminated in a growing consciousness of the need for liberty and unity.

Throughout the nineteenth century there followed phase after phase of various reform movements in India to renovate the society and rationalize religious thoughts. The first in the series was the movement initiated by Raja Rommohun Roy.

RAMMOHUN ROY AND THE BRAHMO MOVEMENT

Rammohun Roy was born in 1774 in the district of Hooghly in Bengal. Those were the days of chaos and confusion flowing Clive's irresponsible government and the great famine. Born in notable Brahmin family in an era of orthodoxy, he grew up amid social evils and religious prejudices. At the age of nine, he had to marry two times, and subsequently once more, because it was impossible for him to escape the privilege of Kulinism. As a grown-up man he saw the burning of his brother's wife a sati, a sight that shocked his conscience.

A prisoner of society and religion, he nevertheless enjoyed certain advantages which even that dark age provided. Rammohun's predecessors had held high offices under the Nawabs of Bengal. Because of the family status, he was sent to Patna to study Persian and Arabic. After acquiring adequate knowledge in those languages, he proceeded to Benares to study Sanskrit. From his knowledge of Persian and Arabic he understood the essence of the Koran and Sufi philosophy; from Sanskrit, the deeper philosophies of the Hindu Upanishads. The inner meaning of Hinduism and Islam drew him to monotheism and created an aversion in him towards idolatry. For reasons not clearly understood, he took to a life of wandering for some time. He saw many parts of India and even, so it is said, visited Tibet. There, instead of finding the inner spirit of Buddhism, he saw endless idolatry and, feeling unhappy, returned.

Finally there began his acquaintance with Christianity. On return to Bengal he was required to spend time at Calcutta where English officials and Christian missionaries abounded in those closing years of the eighteenth and the opening years of the nineteenth century. Rammohun came into close contact with the scholars of Fort William College and next entered the services of the East India Company under John Digby. He learnt English and acquired so much mastery over it that Jeremy Bentham congratulated him, saying: "Your works are made known to me by a book in which I read a style, which, but for the name of a Hindu, I should certainly have ascribed to the pen of a superiorly educated and instructed Englishman." It was not the language, but the ideas which he got from that language which really mattered.

Thus it was that Rammohun grew up to his future role. With profound knowledge of Sanskrit, Arabic, Persian and English, and with a deeper understanding of the philosophies of Hinduism, Islam, Buddhism and Christianity, he became a rare intellectual of his time. He was in search of rationalism and left resentful towards the prevailing socio-religious customs around him. From 1805 to 1814, he was in intimate association with John Digby. The latter left India on leave in 1814, and Rammohun too left the Company's service. Next year he settled in Calcutta to devote his life to the work for which he was mentally preparing.

Rammohun's vision was broad enough to encompass various aspects of Indian life. His movement covered religious, social, economic, educational, political and national issues. A brief reference to his approach to the abovenoted issues will show the nature of his thought and mission.

In religion, Rammohun pointed to a universal inner spiritual synthesis, far from the external forms represented through meaningless practices. A Brahmin himself, he peeped into the inner substance of Brahmanical Hinduism to discover the existence of One Omnipotent Being. The refined ideals of the *Vedanta* were forgotten and lost in ignorance, but they were, the eternal source of Hindu spiritualism. The ideal of monotheism was itself a supreme force in Hinduism, as it was in Islam and Christianity. To turn the mind of India to the truths of *Vedanta* became the prime motive of Rammohun. It meant a crusade against the outer forms of Hinduism, notably, polytheism, worship of images, ritualistic ceremonies, and superstitious rites. "Belief in one Almighty God is the fundamental principle of every religion," he said. And, the union of hearts, with mutual love and affection for all fellow creatures irrespective of colour or creed and religion, was the pure devotion acceptable to God. He established his theories from the *Vedanta,* the Bible and the Koran.

In pursuit of his religious objectives, Rammohun thought of a concerted action by a band of true reformers. In 1815, he formed a society of friends, or the Atmiya Sabha, with a number of distinguished men including Dwarakanath Tagore. The society began to discuss religion and theology, ethics and truth. Reformist propaganda was initiated through books, tracts, articles and translations from the Upanishads. Rammohun declared: "My constant reflections on the inconvenient, or rather injurious rites, introduced by the peculiar practice of Hindu idolatry, which more than any other Pagan worship destroys the texture of society, together with compassion for my countrymen, have compelled me to use every possible effort to awaken them from their dream of error: and by making them acquainted with their scriptures, enable them to contemplate with true devotion the unity and omnipresence of Nature's God."

His crusade against Hindu modes of worship roused in the orthodox a fanatical reaction against the reformer. He was exposed to great risks. But nothing could discourage him. Christian fanaticism was equally directed against him when he ventured to write and publish in 1820 his work entitled. *The Precepts of Jesus, the Guide to Peace and Happiness.* It was a liberal interpretation of Christianity, with emphasis on the spiritual principles of Jesus without the miracles. But the Serampore missionaries, including Marshman, attacked him strongly.

Amid these deep religious controversies Rammohun marched ahead. Finally, on 20 August 1828 he founded the Brahma Sabha which became famous as the Brahmo Samaj in 1830. The samaj stood for the "worship and adoration of the Eternal Unsearchable and Immutable being—who is the Author and Preserver of the Universe but not under or by any other designation or title peculiarly used for, and applied to, any particular Being or Beings by any man or set of men whatsoever." It admitted "no graven image, statue or sculpture, carving, painting, picture, portrait or the likeness of anything'. It further stood for the "promotion of charity, morality, piety, benevolence, virtue and the strengthening of the bonds of union between men of all religious persuasions and creeds."

Thus Rammohun began the first great religious reform movement of the nineteenth century. Since religion was the dominating force in Indian society, reform of religion meant also reform of society. The Brahmo movement was thus a socio-religious reform movement. Rammohun raised his voice against the social abuses which rendered incalculable harm to society. The caste system appeared to him as the greatest obstacle to national unity. It also kept the bulk of the population in degrading conditions. Rammohun proceeded even beyond the frontiers of caste. He adopted a Muslim boy and gave the most daring example of human equality. Besides caste, the Hindu society suffered from other social evils, such as polygamy, degradation of women, and, above all, the horrible sati system. Rammohun's endeavour to rouse opinion against those customs marked the beginning of an era of social change. If ultimately the sati system was abolished, it was as much due to Rammohun as to the Governor-General Bentinck in whose time it was effected.

A pioneer of modernism, Rammohun realized the value of Western education. He established two English schools and showed the way to new and liberal learning. He was not afraid to oppose the orthodox who believed that Sanskrit was the source of all knowledge and wisdom. Instead, he pleaded with the government to give India the benefit of "a more liberal and enlightened system of instruction embracing mathematics, natural philosophy, chemistry, anatomy, with other useful sciences". He negotiated with the missionaries to procure able teachers for Western education. In 1830, he obtained the services of Alexander Duff in the cause of English education.

Though Rammohun's primary concern was socio-religious reform, yet the economic misery of the people touched his conscience deeply. Bengal was passing through two economic evils. A series of revenue experiments culminating in the Permanent Settlement put the peasant at the mercy of the landlord. The second evil was the perpetual drain on the country's economy. The Company's commercial and economic policy, backed by their political power, had brought devastating results. Rammohun raised his voice in support of the poor, though at that time it was a voice in the wilderness.

He also pioneered the political awakening in India. Those were the days when a modern press was emerging as a potential force in public life. A prolific writer on various subjects, Rammohun became a patron of the free press and constructive journalism. His Bengali weekly, *Sambad Kaumudi*, established in 1821, began to discuss political matters, besides religious and moral affairs. Persian weekly, *Mirat-ul-Akhbar*, established next year, discussed national as well as international problems. But then came the Government's Press Ordinance in 1823 to restrict the freedom of the Indian press. In Rommohun's movement against that harmful law there began the modern method of constitutional movement supported by political consciousness. He inspired the intelligentsia to oppose the autocratic measures of the government with a united voice. He also opposed the harmful Juri Act. Before the Company's charter was renewed in 1833, he was busy with his campaign against many of the Company's harmful rights and privileges.

Finally, it was Rammohun's patriotism which made him one of the earliest nationalists in India in a modern sense. He advocated liberal humanitarian nationalism. Emancipation of man from the bondage of ignorance and social tyranny, his freedom of thought and conscience, and his equality with other fellow men were considered as the fundamentals of liberalism. Such free and emancipated individuals, with feeling towards their motherland, could create national unity. The crusade of Rammohun to free the individual from social degradation and to abolish the caste system was for the purpose of building up a nationhood. It was also through a spiritual and mental revival that Rammohun wanted to regenerate the Indian people and unite them into a national fraternity.

In 1830, Rammohun had occasion to proceed to England. He was sent by the titular Mughal Emperor of Delhi, Akbar II, to place his grievances before the British Government. He was also required to give evidence before the Select Committee of the House of Commons on the judicial and revenue systems of India. At the same time he wanted to convince the British Parliament of the validity of the abolition of the sati system. He was the first Indian, the first Brahmin, to cross the oceans and land in Europe, breaking the fantastic Hindu orthodoxy against voyages across the water. Rammohun died at Bristol on 27 September 1833.

History has acknowledged Rammohun Roy as the herald of Modern India and his time as the dawn of Indian renaissance.

The Brahmo movement continued after him. It was not the Brahmo Samaj as an institution which hammered at the root of medievalism, but the original ideas associated with the movement which broke through superstitions and opened avenues for rational thinking.

LATER PHASES OF THE BRAHMO MOVEMENT

The death of Rammohun was no doubt a great tragedy for the Brahmo Samaj since he was the centre of the entire movement. But the mission of the master was taken up by other daring souls. From the beginning, the movement was confined to the intellectually advanced and educationally enlightened minds who believed in reforms. It was not their aim to make it a mass movement, though the purpose was to educate the masses. The Brahmos themselves did not abandon traditional religious ceremonies root and branch. But there was a changed outlook. At least, a challenge had been thrown against formalities and superstitions. The legacies of Rommohun could not die after him as they were in consonance with the requirements of the time. The movement, thus, was destined to grow.

For a time after the death of the founder, the leadership of the Samaj was enjoyed by Dwarakanath Tagore, a close compatriot of Rammohun. In 1843, Devendranath, son of Dwarakanath, took over the leadership. Devendranath was born in 1817, and was educated in the Anglo-Hindu School of Rammohun and in the Hindu College. A product of the new spirit, he believed in reforms. A leaf from the Upanishads revealed to him the grandeur of monotheism. With a profound curiosity to discover and preach truth, he established the *Tattvabodhini Sabha* which played a prominent role in the moral awakening of Bengal. Some notable men of nineteenth century Bengal, like Rajendralal Mitra and Ishwar Chandra Vidyasagar, were members of the sabha. The members turned their energy towards searching for the lost and forgotten values of the culture of the country.

Devendranath introduced into the Brahmo Samaj the famous Brahmic covenant. This included the vows to worship through love the one God, without a second; to worship no created object as the creator; to perform righteous deeds; and to abstain from vicious deeds, etc. He organized a group of preachers to popularize the Brahmo doctrines in the remote countryside of Bengal and established branches of the Samaj at various towns. His *Tattvabodhini Patrika* became the mouthpiece of the movement. Devendranath took up a bold stand on two fronts. Inside Hinduism, his was the reformist movement on the ancient moorings of religion as embodied in the Vedas. Outside, his was the ruthless opposition to the Christian missionaries for their criticism of Hinduism and attempts at conversion. It was in fact a confrontation between Alexander Duff and his band of missionaries on one side and Devendranath and his Brahmo followers on the other. For the time, even orthodox Hindus paid veneration to Devendranath for his faith in the Vedas and opposition to Christian activities.

But before long, a crisis appeared in the core of the Brahmo thought. Were the Vedas infallible? Were they the fountain source of all truth? The more progressive minds among the reformers began to doubt and question the theory of Vedic infallibility. Devendranath himself, after a great deal of mental exercise on the scriptures at Benares, doubted many fundamentals of the Vedas. But the Brahmo movement was based on faith in the Vedas and it was thought unwise to shake that foundation. Amid doubts, Devendranath selected those portions of the Upanishads which advocated monotheism and published them as the Brahmo Dharma. The 'Seed Principles' of Brahmoism were also propounded. Thus the movement was undergoing a philosophical transformation. The rejection of Vedic infallibility made it more radical. The younger members began to advocate more radical social changes. Child-marriage, polygamy, and Kulinism were severely denounced, whereas emancipation of women, and widow-marriage were strongly advocated.

When such were the developments, Keshabchandra Sen joined the Brahmo Samaj in 1858 at the age of twenty. Though born in an orthodox family, he had received an English education and had imbibed Western ideas. His study of the Bible and Christian ethics drew him nearer to a greater understanding of Christianity. After joining the Brahmo Samaj he brought into it a new sense of confidence and purpose. His personal dynamism, vigour, capacity, and, above all, his eloquence proved great assets to Brahmoism. Many intellectuals and young men felt attracted to the Samaj. Keshabchandra established a great hold on the rising generation of progressive intellectuals. Within his close circle, he encouraged free religious discourses and study of Christian literature. It was apparent that he was nearing a new approach.

From its inception, the Brahmo movement was confined mainly to Bengal. But Keshabchandra wanted to make it an all-India concern. In 1864-65, he proceeded on a missionary campaign to Madras and Bombay. Wherever he went, he received encouraging responses from progressive quarters. The Brahmo Samaj was about to assume a much wider dimension.

But, as in the case of many religious movements, a schism confronted the Samaj. Keshabchandra's radical lines of thought and action appeared to the more conservative as too radical. His Society of Theistic Friends became a forum for bolder programmes. Even inter-caste marriage was advocated. To Devendranath Tagore, Keshabchandra's policies appeared aggressive. The culmination came in 1866 when Keshabchandra delivered a lecture on Jesus Christ with the remark: "May the world appreciate him and follow his precepts." It created misgivings among others that he was on his way to embrace Christianity. But Keshab's intention was not to leave Brahmoism but to make it more revolutionary. Whatever was his real intention, the schism between the conservatives and the radicals came in 1866 when Keshabchandra with his followers left the parent body and formed the Brahmo Samaj of India. Thereafter the parent organization came to be known as the original or the Adi Brahmo Samaj.

With the rise of radicalism, the original Brahmo Samaj lost its earlier glamour and began to decline. On the other hand, the new organization of Keshabchandra began to grow for some time with more pronounced zeal. Instead of remaining a mere reformist sect within the Hindu fold, it aimed at assuming a universal character on its religious platform. On the social platform, it rejected the caste system in any and every form.

Keshab introduced devotional elements into Brahmo prayer to stir up religious emotion in men. The *samkirtan,* or the devotional singing of the type of the bhakti religious movement of medieval days, became a feature of the new Brahmoism. The movement appealed to the heart and gained popularity.

But a transformation was going on in Keshabchandra's personality which affected the movement adversely. In their emotional devotionalism, the close disciples of the master regarded him as an incarnation. To his progressive followers, this seemed an excess of human pretensions. Keshab's popularity waned because of it. In 1870, he visited England for a brief period and lectured there on various aspects of his thought. He met Max Mueller, John Stuart Mill and Gladstone. He observed closely the striking aspects of Western culture.

By the last quarter of the nineteenth century, Indian liberalism had progressed. Even Keshabchandra appeared conservative to many of his followers. Moreover, Brahmoism, which stood for religious liberalism, found in Keshab's person elements of authoritarianism as he interpreted his own words as divine will. Thus a second schism in the Brahmo movement became inevitable. And, it came on a relatively small issue. In 1878, Keshabchandra gave his eldest daughter in marriage to a Hindu orthodox family. The bride was less than fourteen and the bridegroom, who was the Maharaja of Cooch-Behar, was just fifteen, both being not strictly of a marriageable age. The occasion was a triumph of Hindu conservatism over the reformer himself. It shocked the conscience of the Brahmos to such an extent that many withdrew from the Samaj of Keshabchandra and formed a new organization named Sadharan Brahmo Samaj.

After the schism of 1878 the Brahmo movement lost much of its earlier novelty and purpose. The consciousness of educated Indians had developed enough to rationalize much of the social and religious thinking. A reform movement to condemn traditional Hinduism was losing ground. Instead, a Hindu revivalism was taking the place of crusades against Hinduism. Revivalism also aimed at rationalism. Thus, within the forces of these new developments the Brahmo movement passively folded itself down within its own orbit. In its doctrinal aspect,

Brahmosim maintained its universal approach and upheld its faith in the synthesis of all faiths. Even after the schism, Keshabchandra announced his new dispensation with the message that "it recognizes in all the prophets and saints a harmony, in all the scriptures a unity and through all dispensations a continuity. His faith in God and Providence became so intense that the latter phase of his life was moulded in the pattern of the true saints of any religion. Meanwhile, the Sadharan Brahmo Samaj was still working for social and educational improvements.

On the whole, the Brahmo movement, from Rammohun to Keshabchandra, covered the greater part of the nineteenth century. In India's mental resource in the modern era, the role of the organization and its pioneers had been outstanding.

RAMAKRISHNA, VIVEKANANDA AND THE HINDU SPIRITUAL AWAKENING

It is a unique phenomenon in the history of Hinduism that there had been spontaneous inner movements for spiritual regeneration within the Hindu world almost at regular intervals. Such movements were based on the true traditions of Indian spirituality and were not directly influenced by external sources. In nineteenth century India such an inward quest for spiritual awakening was represented by Sri Ramakrishna Paramahansa. If the Brahmo movement of Rammohun was an outcome of external influences emanating from the enlightenment and rationalism of the modern West, the movement represented by Ramakrishna and his disciples was the result of an inner resurgence of the Hindu spirit to recover and reassert itself.

Ramakrishna was born in 1836 in the Hooghly district of Bengal. His life, as is ordinarily understood, was as ordinary as that of Kabir or Nanak. But it was a life of extraordinary mystic experiences as in the case of great saints and seers. His message, too, was great. His was a life that defies description in any usual sense.

Ramakrishna was born in a Brahmin family. The religious atmosphere in which the family lived provided the boy with sufficient knowledge in Hindu religious doctrines and the contents of scriptures. From a tander age the boy showed an unusual zeal for devotional practices and at times lost himself in ecstasy. His mystic experiences ultimately opened for him an uncommon life of extreme devotional fervour, a life dedicated to spiritual quests.

At about the age of twenty, Ramakrishna became the priest of the temple of Kali at Dakshineswar near Calcutta. In his intense devotion to the Goddess he saw the Supereme Divine Mother representing that Absolute Force which brought into existence the universe and creation. It was not the Kali of the ordinary mind, associated with superstitions and cruel rites, but the omnipotent and all-pervading divine energy on which rested the world of physical and metaphysical realities. Kali became an avenue for Ramakrishna to attain further realisations. He delved into *Tantric* experiences as well as into Vedantic asceticism. Through yogic disciplines and meditation, through unbounded faith and devotion, through substantive truth of the scriptures as well as by acquired wisdom of experiences, Ramakrishna finally attained the superme realisation.

That realisation can be summed up as follows. Devotion to God was the supreme goal of the mind. The devotion could be expressed through unbounded love. Here he was at one with the medieval saints of the Bhakti school. The God to be attained through love could be very personal, and conceived in any image. Yet, he was beyond any perception, conception, form, quality or character. Thus God could be formless or in forms. It was for man to realise Him in any manner he liked. Such being his conception of God. Ramaksishna conceived the widest sphere for any religion. True religion accommodated any amount of freedom in the true love of God. Religion was just a path towards the supreme goal. It was by genuine liberalism that Ramakrishna aimed to remove all kinds of dogmatism which the orthodox blindly upheld. "Those who believe", he said, "that God is without form attain Him just as well as those who believe He has form. The only two essentials are faith and self-surrender. His views introduced a synthesizing and assimilating force into Hinduism. Dogmas of various sects had no meaning if the truest aspect of Hinduism was taken into account. It was the aim for the Ultimate, the Absolute, the Eternal. The Vedas, the Upanishads, the Sutras and the Shastras, the faiths and doctrines of the worshippers of Siva, Shakti or Vishnu—everything was merely the eternal quest of that Eternal Being. Ramakrishna broke down the barriers which separated various Hindu cults and took them together towards an inward search for the Reality. Hinduism thus received from his teaching a new vigour, and a spirit of unity. It was a trend described at times as neo-Hinduism. Under it, reforms were possible inside Hinduism and there was no need to leave the fold in order to think of reform. Here was the difference between the Brahmos and the disciples of Ramakrishna. If the former partially left the Hindu fold because Hinduism practised idolatry, the liberalism of the latter showed that one could remain a perfect Hindu without worshipping idols. And, those who did not worship idols did not know that in their praise of the qualities of the formless God, they were indirectly subscribing to the faith of the idolators, Ramakrishna pointed out: "God is with form and without form. Images and other symbols are just as valid as your attributes. And these attributes are not different from idolatry, but are merely hard and petrified forms of it." Hinduism stood well defended before the Hindu reformers themselves.

Ramakrishna searched for a universal synthesis of all religions. If diverse faiths in Hinduism had one common meeting ground, the different religions of the world could also be regarded as veritable rivers merging in the ultimate sea. Ramakrishna's study of Islam and Christianity inspired him to appreciate the inner spirit of those religions which was the same as that of Hinduism. The goal of all religions being the realisation of God, paths to the goal varied because of external conditions. Different paths however did not lead to different destinations. Instead, they all culminated at one and the same point. The universality of Truth, oneness of God, and the real values of virtue were the essential fundamentals of all creeds and faiths. Religions ultimately, therefore, possessed the potentiality of uniting all mankind if only men realised and followed the inner meaning of true religion. In nineteenth century India, Ramakrishna's spiritual cosmopolitanism brought to the India mind a new vision of the spiritual unity of mankind.

Many were attracted to Ramkrishna from all ranks and positions. He symbolized all that was godly in man and personified humility and virtue. Among those who became his disciples, the most celebrated was Narendra Nath Dutta, famous in history as Swami Vivekananda. Vikekananda was born in 1863 in Calcutta. Educated, progressive, intellectually gifted and modern in his outlook, his attachment towards Ramakrishna appears paradoxical. But he was the master's choicest disciple. With Ramakrishna's death in 1886, his mantle fell on Vivekananda's shoulders.

The Hindu spiritual concepts were interpreted by Vivekananda in the light of modern rationality and progressivism. Side by side he aimed to associate spiritual attainments with the vigour of mind and body. He was a dynamic personality with boundless physical energy and mental stamina. He became a missionary of spiritual awakening in an era of mental stagnation. In 1888 Vivekananda traversed India with a message of hope. In 1893 he proceeded to America to attend the Parliament of Religions at Chicago were he propounded the true meaning of Hinduism. It was a robust enunciation of the underlying philosophy of the world's most ancient religion. He succeeded in carrying conviction to the minds of many that Hinduism was not really what the Westerners saw in its outward form, but something more vital and more real, the reservoir of inner truths and sound rational conclusions.

While interpreting Hinduism to the outside world, Vivekananda brought to the Indian mind from the materially advanced West the merit of worldly optimism. The physical and metaphysical, the spiritual and the material—all required a balance and a harmony in human life. The East and the West, with their respective traditional achievements in spiritual and material spheres, required an exchange of values for the good of mankind.

One of the most remarkable endeavours of Vivekananda was to bring spirituality from its philosophical and unintelligible scriptural seclusion to the mind and heart of common people toiling in their worldly existence. The message of religion was for the regeneration of man. Spiritual vitality was necessary even in oridinary walks of life. Even in the darkest areas of human thought and action, the spiritual and ethical rays of religion were considered essential. Vivekananda lived at the dawn of the nationalist era. The message of spiritual hope which he gave India proved a powerful force in the course of Indian awakening. He emphasized the upliftment of the individual as well as the collective march of the people towards progress and prosperity. From the individual and national mind he wanted to remove the complexes of inferiority, fear, lethargy and inertia. Doubts regarding man's own capability to achieve higher objectives and the feeling of helplessness in the people as a whole for a purposeful role were the grave defects in Indian national life in those morbid days of poverty and slavery. Vivekananda's tenets were like antidotes to national ills.

In the preachings of Vivekananda one finds a strange but unique combination of modern rationalism and ancient mysticism, of the doctrines of Vedas and Upanishads and the knowledge of the age of science, of the highest spiritual values and hard worldly realities, of religious expositions and secular attainments. He represented the ancient wisdom, the medieval devotion and the modern intellect. Religion was a personal matter, yet universal in character. It was "the manifestation of the Divinity that is already in man". 'Religion,' he said, "is neither in books, nor in intellectual consent, nor in reason. Reason, theories, documents, doctrines, books, religious ceremonies are all helps to religion; religion itself consists in realization.' From scriptures and mysteries, from unattainable heights and impossible concepts, Vivekananda brought to the individual the key to religion. It was far from prejudices but near to the natural instincts of all men of all denominational distinctions. Such an individual realization left no scope for hatred or of denial of others. It breathed a spirit of Catholicism and tolerance. "We reject one, neither theist, nor pantheist, monist, polytheist, agnostic, nor atheist, the only condition of being a disciple is modelling a character at once the broadest and the most intense....We believe that every being is divine, is God."

In the Hindu Vedanta, Vivekananda discovered the most rationalistic and scientific interpretation of God and the universe.

"This universe has not been created by any extra-cosmic God, nor is it the work of any outside genius. It is self-creating, self-dissolving, self-manifesting, One Infinite Existence, the Brahma." Before such Vedantic ideals, the individual man was a part of Nature's great rhythm a realization of God within himself. Vivekananda condemned religious externalities in the most vehement manner.

"Our religion," he sarcastically pointed out, is in the kitchen. Our God is the cooking-pot, and our religion is: "don't touch me, I am holy." Again, "I would rather see everyone of you rank atheists than superstitious fools, for the atheist is alive, and you can make something of him. But if superstition enters, the brain is gone, the brain is softening, degradation has seized upon the life."

Vivekananda was an exponent of an ethical-spiritual internationalism. He declared: "I accept all religions that were in the past and worship them all. I worship God with every one of them, in whatever form they worship Him. I shall go to the mosque of a Mohammedan; I shall enter the Christian's church and kneel before the Crucifix; I shall enter the Buddhistic temple, where I shall take refuge in Buddha and his law. I shall go into the forest and sit down in meditation with the Hindu, who is trying to see the light which enlightens the heart of everyone. Not only shall I do all these, but I shall keep my heart open for all that may come in the future....The Bible, the Vedas, the Koran, and all other sacred books are so many pages, and an infinite number of pages remain yet to be unfolded. I would leave it (my heart) open for all of them."

A spirited missionary, Vivekananda organized the disciples of Ramakrishna into an order and founded the Ramakrishna Mission in 1897. The Mission was given three-fold activities, namely, to spread the meaning of Vedantic spiritualism far and wide, to strive for a synthesis and harmony among various faiths and cults, and to regard the service of mankind as service to God. In 1899, Vivekananda established the Belur Math near Calcutta which became the centre of the Mission's activities.

On a spiritual platform. Vivekananda was a link between India and the modern West. In 1899 he visited the West to preach his message. He travelled extensively over the United States, established Vedanta centres, and collected devoted disciples. From America he came to Europe and in 1900 attended the Congress of the History of Religions in Paris. From there he proceeded to other European countries. His messages left a lasting impression on the minds of men wherever he preached. From the West he brought to India the spirit of a material culture. "From the great dynamo of Europe," he said, "the electric flow of that tremendous power, vivifying the whole world... We want that energy, that love of independence, that spirit of self-reliance, that immovable fortitude, that dexterity in action, that bond of unity of purpose, that thirst for improvement." The hope of Vivekananda was "to make a European society with India's religion."

Vivekananda died in 1902 at the age of 39. He left an enduring mark on his time and a greater impact on the future. In every sense he was the need of his time. He personified the awakened spirit of a new India. He recreated an ethical nationalism, revived the lost spiritualism, and indirectly paved the way to political patriotism. For twentieth century India, he remained a veritable source of inspiration, of courage, confidence and of national pride.

THE PRARTHANA SAMAJ

The reform programmes among the Hindus were not confined to the Brahmo movement alone. Smaller movements in the same direction were also sponsored. A notable organization for reform was the Prarthana Samaj. It was founded in Maharashtra in 1867 with inspiration from Keshabchandra Sen. Mahadev Govinda Ranade was its chief leader. It aimed, like the Brahmo Samaj, at socio-religious reforms. The main difference between the two was that whereas the Brahmos assailed Hinduism by forming an organization more or less outside the Hindu orbit, the members of the Prarthana Samaj remained Hindus and started progressive reforms within Hinduism as Hindus. They were much attracted to the ideals of the modern West, and proceeded to imitate Western methods of education. Rationalization of Hindu socio-religious habits was their main objective. The Samaj initiated a programme of social and educational enterprises to change the existing outlook of an orthodox society and they achieved some success in their mission in Bombay and Maharashtra areas. Ranade's role as a pioneer of Indian political consciousness was remarkable. He was one of the founder-members of the Indian National Congress as well as of the Indian Social Conference. In the wake of the general consciousness among the Hindus, movements as begun by the Prarthana Samaj were useful though they operated silently.

THE ARYA SAMAJ

A more militant type of religious reform movement among the Hindus in the nineteenth century was represented by the Arya Samaj. It did not look to other religions for inspiration. It would not leave the Hindu fold for a separate identity. Instead to wanted to revive Hinduism from within. It aimed to recover the lost values of Aryanism, to re-establish the original Aryan vigour, and to reassert itself against internal and external dangers. Indirectly, it represented a reaction against the rapid invasions of Western ideas and Christianity. Inwardly, therefore, it resembled a Hindu revival. The founder of the Arya movement was Swami Dayananda Saraswati.

Dayananda was born in 1824 in an orthodox Hindu family. His father was Saivite. Young Dayananda studied Sanskrit, learnt the Vedas by heart and became an erudite scholar. While being required to assist his father in the worship of Siva and the practise all kinds of rituals, doubts began to crop up in this mind from an early age if all this really had any meaning. "Is it possible," he asked himself, "that this idol I see bestriding his bull before me, and who according to all accounts, walks about, eats, sleeps, drinks, holds a trident in his hand, beats the drum, and can pronounce curses on men, can be the great deity, the Mahadeva, the Supreme being?" It became difficult for him to accept any idol as the great God of the scriptures and to identify him with an omnipotent living God. At the age of twenty-one, disregarding his father's instruction to marry, he left home, and after pilgrimage to many places in India, became a *sanyasi.*

The more Dayananda assimilated the Vedas, the greater grew his conviction that the Vedas were the fountain source of all truth and of supreme knowledge. All other sacred scriptures of the Hindus of the later ages appeared untrue or mixed with pretensions. The Vedas were the primeval scripture of humanity containing religion in its purest form, the most ancient revelation. There lay the concept of the veritable monotheism, devotion to the one formless God. The Vedic *rishis* had realised the revelation of God in nature, and their religion constituted the real divine knowledge. Like the Vedic religion, Vedic society too was a natural society without the social evils of subsequent ages. The Vedas had advocated only the four-fold natural division of the society in accordance with the character, capability and preference of the individuals for their profession. Thus there was neither the caste system nor untouchability in the Vedic age. Similarly, the status of women in Vedic society was one of honour, privilege, and freedom. Marriage was a sacrament, while the woman was a divine helpmate of man. The later abuses and evils which degraded the position of Hindu woman were unknown to Vedic Aryans. Convinced of the values of the Vedic religion and social conditions, Dayananda raised the cry, "back to the Vedas".

In 1875, Dayananda founded the Arya Samaj at Bombay and, in 1877, at Lahore. The Samaj was required to lay absolute faith in the God and in the Vedas. God, as Dayananda described to his followers, 'is existent, intelligent, and blissful. He is formless, omnipotent, just, merciful, unborn, endless, unchangeable, beginningless, unequalled, the support of all, the master of all, omnipresent, immanent, unaging, immortal, fearless, eternal, and holy, and the maker of all." The Vedas 'are the scripture of true knowledge. It is the first duty of the Aryas to read them, teach them, recite them, and hear them being read." Dayananda defined the duties of the Arya Samaj in much wider terms than as merely religious. Its members were required to devote themselves to the physical, social and spiritual welfare of their fellowmen. Side by side, the spread of proper education and a campaign against ignorance or illusion were regarded as the other objectives of the Samaj.

The movement had a profound effect on the people of western and northern India. Vedic rationalism and ideals had an appeal to progressive intellectuals. Aryan doctrines, too, infused into men's mind a sense of pride and of possessions. The Hindus could look to their own religion for keeping pace with the modern world.

The programme of activities which the Arya Samaj upheld was at once forceful and far-reaching. In an attempt to re-introduce and encourage the ancient Aryan type of education, the Samaj started establishing the *gurukulas* or educational institutions on the Vedic pattern. The most notable of such *gurukulas* was the one at Kangri in the vicinity of Hardwar which developed into a famous centre of Vedic studies. Sanskrit and Hindi became the medium of instruction even at the highest stage, and in those languages the modern subjects of sciences and humanities were taught, besides Vedic studies. The *gurukulas* emphasized character building, and a spirit of service and dedication on the part of youth, side by side with studies. Philanthropic activities were a part of the Arya programme. The Samaj established homes for orphans, widows, destitutes and the distressed.

On a more militant platform, the Arya Samaj condemned the Brahmanic rites and rituals, idol worship and superstitious practices. It strove to bring to the untouchables the status of the Hindus belonging to the upper castes. On the external side, the Samaj threw open the doors of Hindu society to the non-Hindus. Dayananda himself initiated the *Suddhi* movement by which the non-Hindus could be converted to Hinduism. It was a new method in Hinduism which was known to the world as a non-missionary religion. But the Arya Samaj tried to establish that from the dawn of history right through the ancient age, Hinduism embraced various non-Hindu races, such as the Greeks, Scythians, Kushans, Sakas and Hunas who lost their identity in the Hindu society by becoming Hindus. Thus, Hinduism was a missionary religion in its heyday, with an all-absorbing dynamism. It became static and closed its doors in an age of decay. The Arya Samaj aimed at reviving the all-absorbing spirit of Hinduism. Its more specific aim was to bring back to Hindu society all those people who at some time or other had left their original religion and had embraced either Islam or Christianity. It was this attempt at reconversion which alarmed the other religions as well as the British Government.

Dayananda died in 1883. His movement proved successful in the north. But, the extreme reliance on the Vedas, or the motive to ascribe all knowledge and truth to the Vedas, did not make a lasting impression on the mind of the Hindu intelligentsia in general and, as such, the religious aspect of the Arya Samaj did not inspire deeper conviction. But its socio-educational schemes infused newness and vigour into Hindu society.

THE THEOSOPHICAL SOCIETY

In the last decade of the nineteenth century India saw yet another religious movement affecting the Hindus, somewhat different from the rest, but, like the rest, it also led to a good deal of mental ferment for spiritual attainments. It became famous as the Theosophical movement. The word theosophy comes from two Greek words, *theos* and *sophia,* meaning God and wisdom. Thus the meaning of theosophy was the wisdom concerning God. In its Indian equivalence, it meant the knowledge of the Absolute. What the ancient Greeks wanted to ascertain was abundantly available in the Upanishads of the Hindus. Therefore, those who wanted to revive the ancient theosophy had to do so through the Hindu Upanishads. In essence, therefore, the movement aimed at the quest of the Hindu spiritual wisdom through Western enlightenment. Parenthetically, the movement revived and strengthened faith in the ancient doctrines and philosophies of the Hindus. It affected the intelligentsia more than the masses.

It was in the United States of America in 1875 that Madame H.P. Blavatsky, a Russian lady, and Colonel H.S. Olcott, a former army officer of England, laid the foundation of the modern Theosophical Society. In 1879, they came to India and found a more congenial soil for their mission. In 1886, the Theosophical Society of India was founded. Its branches were established at a number of places, such as Bangalore, Bombay, Kumbakonam, Ludhiana and Surat. The headquarters of the society was at Adyar, Madras.

It was Mrs. Annie Besant who later on championed the cause of theosophy in India in a more vigorous manner than the founders of the society. One of its original objectives was to study and preach Aryan philosophy and religion. The

Upanishads revealed the truth of the Absolute, the Universe and Life. The fundamental faiths of the theosophists thus were the neat substance of the Hindu concepts. As Annie Besant explained: "There is one transcendent, self-existent Life, eternal, all-pervading, all-sustaining, whence all worlds derive their several lives, whereby and wherein all things which exist live and move and have their being. For our world, this Life is immanent, and is manifested as the logos, the Word, worshipped under different names, in different religions, but recognised as the one Creator, Preserver, and Regenerator."

The philosophies underlying theosophy were highly intricate concerning the divine, the cosmic process, the Universe, the emanations, the potentialities, the soul, the evolution, the cessation, and all the rest, but they were all there in Hindu philosophies. Similarly, the theories of *karma*, rebirth, *mokshya*, and *nirvana* in which the theosophists believed, were known to Hindu religious men thoroughly well. The novelty of the theosophical movement lay in creating mental conditions for the realisation and appreciation of those ideas. Furthermore, without being a theosophist, one could intellectually assimilate the doctrines of theosophy. Finally, theosophy was cosmopolitan enough to appreciate all forms of religion and all modes of worship. The source of all humanity was the same as the source of all human ideas. Hence all the apparent distinctions were merely several manifestations of the same divinity.

Apart from philosophical and spiritual discourses which the society carried on, its valuable contribution to the Hindu awakening came from its literary and research activities. Hindu scriptures were published and translated. The intellectuals understood the results of the researches which brought to light ancient concepts concerning creation and the Creator. The society also encouraged reforms and framed educational schemes to work them out. In the fitness of things, its role was timely and its impact useful.

MINOR HINDU REFORM MOVEMENTS OF THE 18TH AND 19TH CENTURIES

Through the eighteenth and nineteenth centuries, at different places in India, a number of religious movements arose.

They were not really religious movements, but religious organizations with some distinctive purpose. Their impact on society was neither significant nor deep. Their founders did not propound any noteworthy doctrine. None of the sects made any great spiritual contribution.

Yet, they had some redeeming features. Most of these sects originated among lower caste Hindus, among whom a religious regeneration was very necessary. The tenets of the founders and the faith of the disciples centred around the devotional worship of God. Some were reformist in outlook and discouraged idol worship and polytheism. Almost all the sects breathed a spirit of liberalism and tolerance towards others; some of them opened their doors to all castes and creeds; and surprisingly enough, at the feet of the lower caste gurus even the Brahmins bowed in reverence. A few words on some of the sects will show the nature of their works.

About the time of the Battle of Plassey (1757), a certain Charan Das founded a religious order called the Charan Dasis. It was a devout Vaishnava order with unbounded devotion towards Radha and Krishna. Charan Das was the guru and his disciples paid him the utmost devotion. It was impossible to attain God without the guru and hence the latter was considered almost a divine being. The guru admitted all castes to his order, encouraged human equality, and enjoined that any subsequent guru might come from any caste, Not to lie, not to steal, not to be proud, not to do violence, not to hate and similar injunctions were binding on the disciples. The very existence of strict religious instructions helped improve the moral standard of the members. Delhi was the centre of the Charan Dasi order.

Another sect known as Swami Narayan flourished in Gujarat in the early years of the nineteenth century. Its founder was Swami Sahajananda who was born in Oudh in 1780, but came to Gujarat and stayed there. He became a devoted worshipper of Radha and Krishna. He preached devotionalism and Bhakti. A large number of people became his disciples and considered the guru as a divine being.

Towards the end of the eighteenth and the beginning of the nineteenth century a sect of Rama worshippers became conspicuous in and around Oudh. The founder of the sect was one Paltu Das in whose honour the disciples named their order as Paltu Dasi. They greeted each other with the words 'Satya Rama', that is, Rama is true. Annual fairs were held by the sect of Oudh to celebrate the Rama Navami. A similar group of Rama worshippers came to exist near Oudh named Apapanthi. Munnadas was its founder and they worshipped Rama with great devotion. Munnadas was a goldsmith by caste.

In the first half of the nineteenth century, a man of a very low caste named Balarama founded a sect which came to be known after him as Balarami. Balarama was a man of Nadiya. In spite of his low origin his devotion and religious fervour attracted a large number of disciples who revered him as a sacred person. They even came to worship him as an incarnation of God. While such pretension was monstrous, Balarama and his followers showed rational trends in their thought by discarding idol worship and the caste system. The guru died in 1850.

At the end of the eighteenth century, Jagajibana Das of Oudh established a religious order called the Satnami or the believers in the True Name. The members of the sect came from a much wider area of northern India. The sect was divided into two branches, the householders and the monks. While the former retained their castes, the latter did not. In the Central Provinces in those days another order of Satnamis began to exist among the Chamaras. These Satnamis were highly religious and wanted to worship God in the simplest possible form without the sanction of the priestly class belonging to the higher Hindu order. It was Ghasi Das, early in the nineteenth century, who became the guru of these Satnamis. He was a Chamara himself. He wanted to revive the medieval Satnami cult and preached that there was only the true God manifested in His Name—the Sat Nam. The idols of the Hindus were not true gods. All men were equal in the eyes of God and hence there was no distinction between man and man as prescribed by the castes. Ghasi Das saw among the lower communities common vices such as reckless drinking of liquor and smoking and he wanted to bring about moral reforms by abolishing such vices through religious injunctions. He preached against drinking, smoking and meat eating. Among the Chamaras of Chattisgarh the Satnami movement led to considerable religious and social awakening. By the middle of the nineteenth century, the movement created a good deal of ill-feeling among the orthodox caste Hindus, especially among the priestly classes.

Early in the nineteenth century a religious order named the Karta Bhajas became famous in Bengal. Its inspiration came from Aule Chand who belonged to the previous century and died in Nadiya. His disciples regarded him as a prophet like Chaitanya. He was reputed for the religious miracles he performed and the superhuman powers he possessed. Like Chaitanya, he preached the universality of man and practised catholicism. He accepted Hindus and Muslims as his disciples and preached against the caste system. Aule Chand prescribed a code of ethical conduct to his followers, such as, do not kill, do not steal, do not tell lies. His divinity was so commonly accepted that after his death his soul was thought to have passed to the body of his close disciple, Ram Saran, who became the next guru of the sect. The Karta Bhajas celebrated festivals like Dola and Rasajatra, attended by Hindus and Muslims. Subsequent gurus of the sect, even though they were men of low caste, were venerated by the Brahmins. The sacred places associated with the first guru were considered as places with miraculous attributes.

In Bengal during the early parts of the British rule the influence of Vaishnavism was so deep that quite a number of small Vaishnava sects, each with distinctive features, came into existence. They are at times called the new Vaishnava sects. Notable among them were the Spashtadayaka, the Baul, the Sahaji, and the Sakhibhavaka, The Spashtadayaka sect was founded by Ruparam Kaviraj. The members lives in *maths* or monasteries which were open to both male and female devotees. The latter had to shave their heads. The devotees used to sing and dance in emotional praise of Krishna. They preached the love of God among the householders of Bengal. Inside their group, they had no caste. The Baul sect was constituted of the devotees of the lower castes. They worshipped the child Krishna. They did not shave or cut their hair. The Bauls had an evil reputation of being immoral, which was rather a result of their ignorant faiths. The Sahaji sect was of a similar nature to the Baul. The most peculiar of the sects was the Sakhibhavaka. The devotees dressed in women's apparel and developed feminine habits in order to adore Radha with whom they wanted an imaginary association for attaining Krishna. The devotional emotion apart, such practices were not viewed by others with any admiration or sympathy.

In the middle of the nineteenth century, a certain Uday Chand Karmakar established a sect at Dacca named *Darwesh-Fakir*. The members did not shave their face or cut their hair. They practised various systems of asceticism and showed that they hated nothing. They collected alms to live, practised non-violence to the animal world, and even respected plant life. In Bengal, there existed yet another sect called Haribola. This was a group of devout Vaishanavas who sang the name of Hari for attaining God. In the district of Nadia in Bengal a Muslim named Khusi established a religious order called Khushi Biswasi. This was a Vaishnava sect and the members regarded their guru as an incarnation of Sri Chaitanya himself. Though the membership of the sect was extremely limited, yet its originality lay in the fact that Hindu Vaishnavas could regard a Muslim as their guru. The members of the order did not believe in caste and they ate together. The guru was said to have possessed miraculous power in healing sickness. There was yet another sect in Nadia founded by an ascetic named Sahebdhani and named after him. He did not believe in caste and even took Muslims as his disciples. The members of the order gave up idol worship and practised simple rituals such as placing flowers on a wooden seat, offering cooked food to the invisible God and eating it after worship.

In northern India in the middle of the nineteenth century a blind man named Tulsi Das established a small sect called Kudapanthi. Its members did not worship idols and gave up caste distinctions. They sang devotional songs of the great medieval saints such as Nanak, Kabir and Raidas. There was yet another sect of similar character named Kukas. It was founded about the middle of the nineteenth century by a Sikh of Rawalpindi district named Bolak Singh. The members of the sect offered prayers in a very loud voice. They did not believe in

Brahmanic supremacy and led an austere life in food habits and social manners.

In nineteenth century Orissa, Mahima Goswami founded a movement known as the Mahima movement. His life is shrouded in mystery. He appeared for the first time in 1826 at Puri and died in 1876 at Joranda in the district of Dhenkanal in Orissa. For fifty years Mahima Goswami lived the life of a true saint by practising *yoga* and penances. Gradually, devoted followers gathered round him, and one of them, Bhima Bhoi, received the blessings of the master to compose a large number of philosophical treatises. The followers of the Mahima cult believed in the adoration of 'Alekh Param Brahma'. The *sanyasis* of the cult were required to travel continuously, to beg not more than one meal from any householder, and not to stay more than one night in any village. They took only one principal meal in the day time and took nothing in the night. The followers of the cult believed in the praise of "the Eternal, Unsearchable and Immutable Being who the Author and Preserver of the Universe". He is 'Alekh' (without description), 'Anakar' (without shape), and 'Anadi' (without beginning). Self-surrender to the 'Param Brahma' or the 'Sunya Purusha' was the highest goal of the believer. The Mahima cult laid sufficient stress on disciplined habits to control the body and the mind. It did not recognize caste, creed, colour or any narrowness that divided human beings. In course of time, the Mahima cult spread in Andhra, Bengal and as far north-east as Assam.

The Ramsanehi order, which was founded by Ramcharan in the eighteenth century at Shahpur, continued to exist in the nineteenth century. The members of the discipline were required to follow a number of regulations. Specially, the monks of the sect lived a life of celibacy; they did not smoke and take liquor and did not eat fish or meat. The sect was open to all castes. It did not believe in idol worship. God was worshipped in the name of Rama. At a number of places in Rajputana, such as Jodhpur, Udaipur, Jaipur and Chittor, the Ramsanehis constructed their places of worship called Ramadvara. Another small sect called Ramaballavi existed in nineteenth century Bengal. Its founder was Ramballav, a disciple of Aule Chand.

The peculiarity of the sect was that its members believed in the Hindu, Muslim and Christian scriptures which they recited during their annual religious ceremony. They did not believe in caste, ate together and respected the food habits of all communities.

Last in the list of minor religious movements of the nineteenth century was the Deva Samaj. It was founded in 1887 by Sivanarayan Agnihotri. He was born in 1850, studied at Rurki College and became a teacher in the Government College in Lahore. He was member of the Sadharan Brahmo Samaj. But ultimately he founded a Samaj of his own and began to preach monotheism. He assumed for himself the position of a prophet and his disciples venerated him as the Deva Guru. The Deva Samaj believed in social reforms and exerted itself in that direction. Lahore was the headquarters of the sect with branch offices at Rawalpindi, Hoshiarpur, Patna and Rurki. But theoretical assertions apart, the organization did not attract any noteworthy following.

The rise of all such orders or sects did not affect the general Hindu society to any considerable degree. Within their limited spheres, however, they exercised influence on their respective groups by way of religious and moral upliftment.

19TH CENTURY RELIGIOUS AND REFORM MOVEMENTS AMONG THE MUSLIMS

Among the Muslims, the need for socio-religious reform movements was very much less. Yet there were some movements to liberalize the medieval rigidity in religious outlook. Before a reference is made to them, it is necessary to recollect the formidable politico-religious ferment which passed under the name of the Wahabi Movement. To many ardent Muslims, it was *Jihad* or holy war; its objective being to convert the Dar-ul-Harb into Dar-ul-Islam.

The movement was the work of Syed Ahmad of Rae Bareli in present-day Uttar Pradesh. It began during the opening decades of the nineteenth century. He believed himself to be the distant descendant of the Prophet and felt inspired to devote himself to the cause of Islam. After acquiring sufficient knowledge of religious laws, he developed certain convictions regarding the causes of Islam's decline in India and fall from political power. He searched for remedies as well and for the strength for revival. By absolute devotion to the cause of God and by resorting to holy war, he wanted to attain the latter objectives. For some time Syed Ahmad worked as a soldier in the army of Amir Khan of Tonk and learnt military techniques. Thereafter, he moved through Uttar Pradesh to preach his gospel and attracted a large number of followers everywhere. The core of his disciples formed themselves into a militant band of fighters. The master next needed further inspiration before actual action, and, with that in view, proceeded on a pilgrimage to Mecca and Medina in 1822. There in that holy land he came under the spell of the Wahabi cult, propounded by Abdul Wahab of Arabia. It was the cult of *Jihad* against those who had displaced the Muslims from power and had thereby disgraced them.

Syed Ahmad returned to India in 1824 to play the role of a sworn enemy of the British. His religious enthusiasm became an example to many Muslims who prepared to organize themselves under the banner of their leader to fight a war unto the last. The campaign was to be conducted from the lands of the frontier tribes on the north-west. Syed Ahmad, with about six hundred followers, reached Peshawar in November 1826. He was proclaimed on the frontiers as Imam Mahdi and Khalifa.

The *Jihad* began in right earnest. But before Syed Ahmad could proceed to liberate British occupied territories, he had to face the Sikh power on the north-west. In 1831, in a battle with the Sikhs at Balakot, Syed Ahmad with many of his followers died. The loss of the leader was a terrible blow to his cause. Yet the Wahabi influence remained in many places of India for many years to come. Patna was the centre of Wahabi activities. For long the British suffered from the spirit of revolt among the Wahabis, till the movement was destroyed by force and diplomacy.

The real reform movement among the Muslims in the nineteenth century was the Ahmadiya movement which began in 1889. Its founder was Mirza Ghulam Ahmad. The aim was to liberalize the tenets of the religion in the context of modern enlightenment. Mankind was divided into many religions, but yet, the real spirit of a true religion could be nothing but universal. Ghulam Ahmad became a believer in the new spirit of the time and the rationalism as represented by the modern West. The liberal trends in India which aimed at emancipating the minds of men also had their influence on him. He was intensely hostile to the medieval concepts of religious crusades or *Jihad* which destroyed the basic philosophy of true religions, namely, human brotherhood. On social issues, the Ahmadiya movement stood for Western systems of education. The Muslims were hostile to the English language and kept away from government schools. The Ahmadiya movement broke down that exclusive tendency and opened institutions for new learning at many places.

The Aligarh movement of Sir Saiyad Ahmed Khan also stood for social reforms among the Indian Muslims. It emphasized the utility of Western education for the material prosperity of the Muslims. The Muhammedan Anglo-Oriental College was established at Aligarh in 1875, which became a University in 1890. The movement began well with the task of liberalizing Muslim society. It aimed at emancipating women from various evils including polygamy. But before much was done, Aligarh became the centre of political awakening among the Muslims, and the leaders of the Aligarh movement thought more of political goals than socio-cultural reforms.

REFORM MOVEMENTS AMONG THE SIKHS

Sikhism, being the latest of the world's major religions and having its origin in reformist and synthesizing ideals, was not old enough by the nineteenth century to need any radical change. But by the period under review, two unhealthy tendencies were noticeable, which required timely remedy. First, the Sikh aristocracy was turning away from the religious austerity of the earlier days, and many aspects of religion were losing their meaning through negligence. Secondly, the inevitable Hindu influence was silently operating to revive among the Sikhs a desire for traditional festivities and ceremonies. Amid such perceptible trends, some reformers thought of restoring the puritan simplicity of the creed.

A Hindu by birth, Dyal Das was the pioneer of the Sikh reform movement. He was born at Peshawar in 1783. The practice of Hindu ceremonies by the Sikhs shocked his religious feelings and he began to preach on behalf of the Sikhs against such unholy tendencies. He was a bold denouncer of idol worship. Gradually, the Sikhs felt attracted to his preaching and became his disciples. They were called the Nirankaris. The Nirankari movement became conspicuous in the Punjab and the North-West Frontier Province. Dyal Das issued the *Hukam Nama* or the Book of Ordinances. So great was his impact on his disciples that they worshipped the Book together with the Granth Sahib. Dyal Das died in 1858, He enjoyed the status of a guru in his lifetime, and his successors, too, were obeyed as gurus. The movement retained its vigour till the middle of the twentieth century.

The next band of reformers belonged to the Namdharis movement. Its leader, Ram Singh, was born in 1815. He preached extreme puritanism, His disciples were required to give up meat and fish-eating. They were asked to dress themselves in pure white clothes. Greater emphasis was laid on devotional prayer. The Namdharis used to pray for long periods and became noted for it. In course of time, Ram Singh assumed enough temporal power and finally quarrelled with the British. Consequently, he was deported to Rangoon where he died in 1885. The succeeding gurus, therefore, confined their activities purely to religion.

In the eighteen seventies, the Sikh reformers formed yet another organization named the Singh Sabha. The objective of the movement was two-fold. It wanted to bring to the Sikh community the benefits of Western enlightenment through new learning and education. And, it worked to counteract the activities of Christian missionaries as well as Hindu revivalists among the backward and ignorant Sikhs. The movement was successful in its mission. A number of modern educational institutions were founded, the most notable being the Khalsa College at Amritsar, established in 1892.

LEGISLATIVE MEASURES AGAINST SOCIAL EVILS IN THE 19TH CENTURY

During their first forty years of rule in Bengal which constituted the last four decades of the eighteenth century, the

British authorities came to understand the nature of the social evils prevailing in those days, but possessed neither the intention nor the courage to initiate legislative measures against them. The missionaries, in their campaign against Hinduism, exposed the religious irrationalities of the Hindus in vehement terms. They even magnified many social features to rouse the conscience of Englishmen in India. But they failed to awaken the government of the East India Company to a sense of its duty. Any interference in the religion of the ruled might lead to grave discontent against the rulers and hence the Government thought it prudent to allow the people to continue with their customs.

But times began to change. In the early decades of the nineteenth century there began internal movements within Hindu society against its own customs and practices. In the light of the changing consciousness among the people, the Government too changed its policies. It was a coincidence that the British initiated social legislation when the Indian reformers created an opinion in their favour.

The first notable social measures was effected at the begnning of the nineteenth century. Lord Wellesley was the Governor-General and Carey, the noted missionary of Serampore, drew the former's attention to the custom of throwing children into the water at the confluence of the Ganges and the sea. In August 1802, the Government prohibited the practice by law.

The East India Company proceeded very hesitantly and cautiously against the abolition of the custom of sati till Rammohun Roy represented the view of rational Indians against the evil. The attention of the Government had been drawn to it right from the beginning. In 1789, the Collector of Shahabad, M.H. Brooke, while refusing his assent to the burning of a widow, wrote to the Governor-General, Lord Cornwallis: "The rites and superstitions of the Hindu religion should be allowed with the most qualified tolerance, but a practice at which human nature shudders I cannot permit without particular instructions. I beg, therefore, My Lord, to be informed whether my conduct in this instance meets with your approbation." The Government informed him not to exercise official powers to prevent the practice, but to use dissuasion. Similar requests from other district magistrates came to the Government over a number of years. At length Lord Wellesley was moved to pay attention to the matter and in 1805 he called upon the judges of the *Nizamat Adalat* to ascertain how far the sati system was related to Hindu religion. The judges consulted the Hindu pandits and reported that girls of the four higher castes might burn themselves except under certain circumstances, and advised that, "while the custom could not be abolished generally without greatly offending religious prejudices, it might be abolished immediately in some districts, where it had almost fallen into disuse, and checked or prevented in others on lines indicated by the replies of the pandits." Wellesley, however, did nothing. The subsequent Governors-General remained passive. For example, Lord Minto's Government declared in 1812 that the practice of sati "must be allowed in those cases in which it was countenanced by religion, and prevented wherever it was not." Such orders were vague and therefore ineffective. Certain circular orders against indiscriminate sati were introduced in 1812, 1815, and 1817. These orders aimed at stopping the use of force in making a woman commit sati, to stop pregnant women or girls under puberty or mothers with infants at the breast being made satis. However laudable were the orders, without the sanctity and strength of law behind them, did not prove successful.

There were ardent officers and judges who advocated 'entire and immediate abolition' of the practice. But the Governor-General, Lord Hastings, felt in 1821 that with the growth of education, the Indians themselves would abandon it. For his part, he decided to wait. Yet another Governor-General, Lord Amherst, felt that official steps in the matter might lead to discontent in the Bengal army. He too decided to leave the matter to Indians themselves and as late as 1828 wrote: "I cannot believe that the burning or burying alive of widows will long survive the advancement which every year brings with it of useful and rational learning...."

While the supreme authorities thus hesitated, the Indian reformers began to create opinion against it. Rammohun had himself seen in 1812 the burning of his brother's widow. From 1818 he boldly raised his voice against the orthodox leaders who criticized the government circular orders. He pointed out to the authorities that there were cases when women were induced by persuasion to burn themselves, that they were forced upon the pyre and bound down with ropes and pressed with green bamboos until consumed with flames, and that some, after fleeing from the flames, were carried back by their relatives and burnt to death. To Rammohun, all such instances were "murders according to every Shastra as well as to the common sense of all nations". He published brochures, wrote articles in his journal *Sambad Kaumudi,* and made passionate appeals to the government to abolish the rite. There was considerable risk to his life from fanatical quarters, but he showed unusual courage in his crusade for the cause.

Thus, the grounds were ready for the abolition of sati by legislation when Lord William Bentinck came as Governor-General in the middle of 1828. Bentinck was a true representative of the era of reforms in his country and his coming here was a happy coincidence. Moreover, himself kind and humane, he was a friend of the Indian people and a bold administrator for reforms.

Bentinck proceeded prudently. He confidentially gathered opinion from the army officers, judges and the executive, and felt satisfied that the abolition of sati would neither create any discontent in the army nor any disturbance in the country. He consulted Rammohun Roy about the step he wanted to take. It is surprising that Bentinck's boldness even alarmed Rammohun who advised the Governor-General that the "practice might be suppressed quietly and unobservedly by increasing the difficulties and by the indirect agency of the police", rather than by any immediate, direct and prompt suppression through government measures which might lead to popular agitation. Rammohun pleaded cautiousness as he did not like, as an Indian, the possible government coercion of his countrymen on a social issue. The famous Orientalist, Horace Hayman Wilson, also advised against government legislation to end sati. But Bentinck was determined. On 8 November 1829 he put before the Council his minute for the abolition of sati. The Council gave its consent saying: "We are decidedly in favour of an open, avowed and general prohibition, resting altogether upon the goodness of the act and our power to enforce it." So, on 4 December 1829, by Regulation XVII of the Government, the custom of sati was declared "illegal and punishable by the Criminal courts". It said: 'The practice of Suttee, or of burning or burying alive the widows of Hindoos, is revolting to the feelings of human nature; it is nowhere enjoined by the religion of the Hindoos as an imperative duty; on the contrary, a life of purity and retirement on the part of the widow is more especially and preferably inculcated, and by a vast majority of the people throughout India the practice is not kept nor observed; in some extensive districts it does not exist; in those in which it has been most frequent it is notorious that in many instances acts of atrocity have been perpetrated which have been shocking to the Hindoos themselves, and in their eyes unlawful and wicked." The courts were empowered to pass death sentence on persons held responsible for the rite.

The champions of Hindu orthodoxy submitted a petition to the Governor-General against the regulation that the custom was sanctioned by the laws of religion. Bentinck met their leaders like Raja Radhakanta Dev, Maharaja Kalikrishna Bahadur, Bhavani Charan Bandopadhyay and others to say that no attack on Hindu religion was committed or intended. If they disputed his interpretation of Hindu or British laws, they might appeal to the King-in-Council." Against the move of the orthodox party, Rammohun Roy and other progressive people submitted a petition congratulating Bentinck on his measure. The orthodox party sent its petition to the King-in-Council. Rammohun, too, prepared a counter-petition and proceeded to England to present it to the British Parliament. Finally, in July 1832, the Privy Council rejected the appeal against the abolition of sati. That put an end to the orthodox agitation.

A less significant social measure than the abolition of sati was the introduction of widow marriage. Opinion in its favour developed very slowly though no widespread interest was noticed. The abolition of sati indirectly brought into prominence the problem of the fate and future of the young widows who were saved from destruction but thrown into a pitiable state of existence. In a sporadic manner, views in support of widow marriage were expressed in some journals in the nineteen thirties and forties. Some rare individuals like Maharaja Shrischandra of Nadia actually tried to initiate the measure, but failed. The orthodox pandits, at their most liberal consideration, would countenance widow marriage in case of Sudra girls only, but never of higher caste Hindus.

In the middle of the nineteenth century, Ishwarchandra Vidyasagar began a campaign for widow marriage. His profound learning and scholarship made him a leader of the Bengali elite. The Hindu Shastras, in his opinion, did not prohibit widow marriage, rather they permitted it. Supported by other enlightened Hindus and hopeful of government support, Vidyasagar at last came forward to start a constitutional demand for it. In 1854, in a booklet on widow marriage, he explained the need for the measure. Orthodox Hindus campaigned against the proposal. Vidyasagar published his reply to the criticisms. In 1856, his ideas were brought out in the form of an English book entitled *Marriage of Hindu Widows*

Such justifications had no meaning unless law came to the help of the widows for their marriage and subsequent legal status. Vidyasagar, therefore, presented a petition to the government on behalf of about one thousand prominent persons. Some notable landlords like Maharaja Mahatab Chand of Burdwan and Maharaja Shrischandra of Nadia also submitted petitions in support of the measure. Finally the government felt convinced that there would be no great conservative agitation if widow marriage was legalized. Accordingly, on 26 July 1856, the Act XV was passed legalizing widow marriage and giving the status of legitimacy to the children of the married widows. The Act declared: "No marriage contracted between Hindus shall be invalid and the issue of no such marriage contracted between Hindus shall be invalid and the issue of no such marriage shall be illegitimate by the reason of the woman having been previously married or betrothed to another person, who was dead at the time of such marriage, any custom and any interpretation of Hindoo law to the contrary notwithstanding."

The Act provoked the orthodox Hindus to such an extent that thirty thousand men signed a petition against it and submitted it to the government. But in vain. The tragedy of this social legislation lay, however, in the fact that except for rare instances it was never widely practised. Hindu conservatism did not encourage marriage of widows and even more than a century after the legislation, the old habits and inertia continued.

After the Widow Marriage Act, the Bengal reformers became desirous of abolishing polygamy by legislation. For quite some time they had been creating opinion against the vices of Kulinism with zeal and determination. Vidyasagar was the mastermind behind this move as well. In June-July 1856, petitions signed by fifty thousand men and women were submitted to the government to abolish polygamy. The petitioners prayed "for the immediate interference of the legislature for the suppression of polygamy which was practised on a very large scale and in a manner most offensive to morality and decency". Some were equally conscious of the evils associated with child marriage. Had the Government come forward to abolish polygamy and Kulinism by law, the next move of the progressive party would have been to appeal for legal sanction against early marriages.

But there came a sudden turn in the social policy of the British in India. The Rising of 1857 swept over the country and prolonged discussions were held in England on the possible causes of Indian discontent. Rightly or wrongly, one of the causes was supposed to be British interference with the socio-religious habits of the people. The Indian empire was saved with much difficulty and the British regarded it as the reconquest of India. But with the victory, the rule of the East India Company was brought to an end and the Crown's rule established. The new administration wrongly decided not to interfere in the social affairs of the Indian people. Thus polygamy and child marriage were left untouched. In a sense, the government of the East India Company was more progressive in its socio-religious policies than the succeeding government of the British Crown.

MEASURES AGAINST HUMAN SACRIFICE AND INFANTICIDE

Before the transfer of power, the government of the East India Company had to their credit two more meritorious works, namely, the suppression of human sacrifice among the Khonds of the Orissa-Madras hill tracts, and the abolition of infanticide among the Rajputs and Bedis in the north and north-west.

The practice of human sacrifice in the hill tracts of Orissa, Madras and the then Central Provinces was discovered by the British authorities in 1836. It was in that year that the Hindu Raja of Ghumusar revolted against the British and in the course of the military operation against him, the British troops made their first acquaintance with the Khonds and their country. "It was then discovered that these people had been in the immemorial habit of performing annual sacrifices of human victims, the victims being usually purchased or stolen in the plains below, and sold to the Khonds, by persons who made a trade of such dealings." On the report of G.E. Russell the Madras Government decided to take measures against it. But the task was extremely difficult. It was felt that any law denouncing the rite and providing for punishment would prove abortive. Partial measures were recommended, such as the rescue of *meriahs* or the victims kept for sacrifice. In 1841, Lord Elphinstone, the Governor of Madras, suggested to the Central Government to institute an agency to rescue the *meriahs,* and it was sanctioned in 1845.

From 1848 the matter received the serious attention of Lord Dalhousie. During the course of operations, a large number of *meriahs,* men, women, and children, were rescued by a young officer named Campbell. He reported in March 1849 that the total number of *meriahs* rescued that year was 307 making aggregate of 547 in the two past seasons. Vast areas never before traversed by Europeans were surveyed that season in the Khond country. By 1853 the total number of victims rescued was 1260. Of these, two hundred children were sent to missionary schools for education.

By 1854, the *meriah* practice was almost at an end. Before this, the Khonds had been not only oblivious to all sense of their crime and confident that it was directly sanctioned by the deity, but they also lived in strongholds, which it was scarcely possible to invade. Legislation was useless among a people who were beyond the pale of law. Threats were absurd when they could not be enforced even by a campaign. Bribery was fruitless when the people believed a crime to be their greatest earthly gain. Among such a people Campbell worked, and when his work ended "an entire people has been induced to forgo a crime sanctioned alike by antiquity and by superstition". The Khonds substituted in every place animal for human sacrifices. For some time the government kept vigilance over the entire area. Credit goes to the British officers for having persuaded a tribal people to give up a primitive custom within so short a time. Dalhousie declared in 1856 that the *meriah* sacrifice was at an end.

It was also during the rule of Dalhousie that the custom of female infanticide was abolished in the then North-West Provinces and the Punjab. Charles Raikes, the magistrate of Mainpuri, deserves credit for starting a campaign against it by the middle of the nineteenth century. His examples were followed in the Punjab. At Mainpuri, Raikes issued a few regulations. In the villages of the Chauhan Rajputs and the Pathak Ahirs who practised infanticide, watchmen were employed to give information at the police station of the birth of a female child. After one month the health of the child was to be reported, and if any illness attacked her, a superior police officer was at once to see her and report to the magistrate. In suspicious cases, the body of the child was to be submitted to the civil surgeon. It may be noted here that one of the methods of killing the baby daughter was to willfully neglect her and leave her to die, and to say that the death was natural.

The Court of Directors in England appreciated the activities of Raikes and directed the Indian Government to pay to the subject 'most careful attention'. But James Thomason, the Lieutenant-Governor of the North-West Provinces, did not approve of any system of prevention through police or watchmen. To him "the best method of suppressing the crime was to direct one's efforts to the correction of the social institutions and customs which prompt its".

One of the main causes of infanticide among the Rajputs was the heavy expenses of marriage, The government decided to strike at the root. Accordingly, W.H. Tyler, the Commissioner of Agra Division, arranged a meeting of the chief Rajputs of Etawah, Farrukkabad, Agra, Patiali, Badaon and Mainpuri in

December 1851. An agreement was reached to reduce marriage expenses and 360 signatures of the chiefs and headmen were attached to it. Every chief took a solemn pledge to assist the government in its noble object.

In the Punjab, the British authorities came to know in 1846, after the acquisition of the trans-Sutlej territories, that there were many hundreds of families throughout the Punjab among whom not a single female child for generations had been allowed to live, and there were thousands of families among whom the practice of female infanticide was a social custom. The Bedis of Punjab were known as the 'Koreemor' or 'daughter slayers'. It was after the final annexation of the Punjab that the question of suppression was taken up seriously. In 1852, Charles Raikes was transferred to the Punjab as the Commissioner of Lahore and, thereupon, the matter received fresh attention. John Lawrence, the Chief Commissioner, suggested a rather mild policy. But Lord Dalhousie advocated a strong policy. In August 1853, he issued a minute saying: "There are two causes alleged for female infanticide; the one is a religious one, founded upon peculiar tenets or considerations of caste; the other is a pecuniary one, arising out of the habitual expenditure of large sums upon marriage ceremonies. The government can bring its authority to bear upon both causes by proclaiming that the destruction of female children is murder, whatever may be the moving cause of the crime, and that it shall in case of conviction be implacably visited with the punishment justly due to every murderer."

The Punjab authorities arranged a grand meeting at Amritsar on the last three days of October 1853. It was said that so large a body of civil officers, the representatives of the British Government, were never perhaps before assembled together in India. Among those assembled were also the members of the late Sikh darbar, the representatives of all the leading families among the Sikhs, the chieftains of the Kangra hills, the Bedis of Dera Baba Nanak, the commercial heads of every city of note within two hundred miles of Amritsar, and the delegates from every district representing agricultural and trading interests. There was "not a single expression of disapproval, disappointment or displeasure". The meeting opened with an announcement of the Governor-General's determination to punish all who might be thereafter convicted of female infanticide, as for murder. It ended with an *Ikrarnamah* or agreement signed by the people which said: 'The crime of infanticide being so hateful to God, and execrable in the eyes of government, and of all pious and good men, we will, at once, cause the apprehension of any person of our tribe who may perpetrate the crime in our *illaquahs* or villges, and bring the same to the notice of the authorities; and we will expel from caste any person who may refuse or show reluctance to join in the endeavours to accomplish the above object."

The grand meeting of Amritsar gave a death blow to the custom of female infanticide. A silent change was taking place among the people themselves which made government intervention easy. To Dalhousie, the Amritsar affairs marked "the commencement of a new social era among a people of the countries beyond the Jumna". Within a few years the custom disappeared like sati and became "a thing to be wondered at in recollection".

MAIN SOCIAL LEGISLATIONS IN THE TWENTIETH CENTURY

In the twentieth century, policies regarding social change mainly resulted from Indian opinion rather than from British interests. The progress of Western education and the growth of political consciousness created a new atmosphere in the country affecting various socio-economic problems. The press played a useful role in giving appropriate prominence to these issues. The legislatures, which Indians entered, became the forum for the discussion of popular needs. Finally, with independence, social problems were viewed entirely in a new perspective. In the context of such developments during the century, a number of social legislations were brought about. Many acts were passed by the provincial or state legislatures to meet the needs of their respective areas. Some laws, coming from the Central Legislature, covered the whole country. A brief reference is made below to a few of the significant social laws which affected the whole of India.

The Child Marriage Restraint Act XIX of 1929 was a long awaited social measure in favour of which opinion had been growing for many years. It came into force on 1 April 1930. "No marriage to which a child, i.e., a male under 18 years of age or a female under 15 years of age, is a party may be solemnized." The intention was to restrain the marriage of children. The Act provided that any person performing, conducting, or directing any child marriage, was punishable with imprisonment for a period of three months and fined. The parent of a child who promoted or even failed to prevent the marriage of his child was liable to three months' imprisonment and a fine. The Act required that a complaint should be filed whenever a child marriage took place. But in actuality, complaints were rare even though performances were many. As was natural, neighbours or villagers did not want to carry the matter to the court if somebody performed a child marriage. But the act was a great check on the prevailing custom and in the course of subsequent decades child marriage became an abandoned practice to a large extent. Yet among the poorer people it still holds ground because of economic reasons.

The Hindu Women's Right to Property Act XVIII of 1937 aimed to restore to women, in certain cases, an economic status. Under its provisions, at places where the *Dayabhaga* system of inheritance prevailed, the widow of a person dying intestate was entitled to the same share of property as that of a son. Where a Hindu died with an interest in a joint family property, his widow was given the right to inherit that interest.

With the independence of India, a great social evil of many centuries, namely, untouchability was taken up for immediate eradication. Article 17 of the Constitution of India declared that 'untouchability' is abolished and its practice in any form is forbidden. The enforcement of any disability arising out of 'untouchability' shall be an offence punishable in accordance with law. Article 15 (2) provides that no citizen shall, an grounds of religion, race, caste, sex or place of birth, be subject to any disability, liability, restriction or condition with regard to *(a)* access to shops, public restaurants, hotels and places of public entertainment; or *(b)* the use of wells, tanks, bathing ghats, roads and places of public resort maintained wholly or partly out of State funds or dedicated to the use of the general public. Thus, a great step was taken to reorient Hindu society in progressive directions through constitutional provisions. The Caste

Disabilities Removel Act XXI, 1950, provided that no forfeiture of property or right of inheritance shall follow upon the deprivation of caste, and no court shall enforce any custom prescribing such forfeiture. The Untouchability Offences Act XXII of 1955 was passed to make the constitutional provisions regarding abolition of untouchability a social reality rather than mere theoretical intentions. The scheduled castes suffered many disabilities in society. The law declared the enforcement of any such disability illegal. Moreover, the institutions which were open to Hindus in general were now thrown open to members of the scheduled castes. Any attempt at obstruction of the exercise of the rights under Article 17 was made an offence. One of the greatest obstacles in the way of Hindu equality was the restriction of entry into temples for the lower caste people. The Act made it free for every person to enter any place of public worship open to other persons of the same religion. Finally, any encouragement of the practice of untouchability was made an offence, punishable with imprisonment or fine or both.

The success of social legislation depends on the nature of cooperation rendered by the society at large. The extent of such co-operation depends on the extent of the mental and educational development of the people as a whole. In the latter part of the twentieth century, social liberalization has been rapidly accelerated. In spite of the existence of outer semblances of age-old systems and customs, the inner social consciousness has gone far enough to render these vestiges valueless.

SPIRITUAL QUESTS IN THE TWENTIETH CENTURY

To the evolution of spiritual ideas in India, the twentieth century presents the messages of Sri Aurobindo as the most distinct contribution. Aurobindo arranged in their proper places the multiple spiritual endeavours and experiences spread over the ages and made a synthesis of them. He tried to cover all the Indian ways of realisation.

"An eternal perfection is moulding us into its own image", said Aurobindo. In his vision, man, as he is, is not the final result of the process of evolution. With unexplored potency in his consciousness, he is capable of growing into a radically new being. In fact, the process of such a growth is perpetually at work, through his conscious or unconscious aspiration towards perfection, his thirst for greater knowledge, his urge for greater mastery, his craving for greater freedom. To Aurobindo, Life evolved out of Matter and Mind out of Life. Matter had Life hidden in it; Life had Mind hidden in to. So also Mind hides in it a higher principle, the spirit. "If a spiritual unfolding on earth is the hidden truth of our birth into Matter, if it is fundamentally an evolution of consciousness that has been taking place in Nature, then man as he is cannot be the last term of that evolution: he is too imperfect an expression of the Spirit, mind itself a too limited form and instrumentation; mind is only a middle term of consciousness, the mental being can only be a transitional being. If, then, man is incapable of exceeding mentality, he must be surpassed, and supermind and superman must manifest and take the lead of the creation. But if his mind is capable of opening to what exceeds it, than there is no reason why man himself should not arrive at supermind and supermanhood or at least lend his mentality, life and body to an evolution of that greater term of the Spirit manifesting in Nature."

Aurobindo traces the divine reality in both Spirit and Matter, thereby bringing together two conventionally warring schools of philosophy. He says: "The affirmation of a divine life upon earth and an immortal sense in mortal existence can have no base unless we recognize not only eternal spirit as the habitant of the bodily mansion, the wearer of this mutable robe, but accept Matter of which it is made as a fit and noble material out of which He weaves constantly His garbs, builds recurrently the unending series of His mansions."

Aurobindo explained the Indian idea that man is a spirit veiled in the works of energy, moving to self-discovery, capable of Godhead. He is a soul that is growing through Nature to conscious self-hood; even, he is in his uttermost reality identical with the Transcendence from which he came and greater than the godheads whom he worships. The natural half-animal creature that for a while he seems to be is not at all his whole being and is not in any way his real being. Man has the spiritual capacity to pass to a supreme and extraordinary pitch of manhood.

The supreme spiritual quest of Aurobindo was to realize a transforming force which will, as he believed, eventually take humanity out of the present crisis which is an evolutionary crisis. He terms this Force as the Supermind. The realisation and manifestation of this sublime state of consciousness of course will depend on the aspiration of man, his sincerity in surrendering to Truth and his rejection of falsehood. In his seer-vision, the victory of the Supermind is certain, although:

> A few shall see what none yet understands;
> God shall grow up while wise men talk and sleep;
> For man shall not know the coming till its hour;
> And belief shall be not till the work is done.

20

The Nineteenth Century

1. BIBLIOGRAPHIES

The best bibliography on social reform movements that I have seen so far is *Heimsath, op. cit.*, pp. 357-71. K. K. Datta's *A Survey of Recent Studies on Modern Indian History* (2nd edition, Firma K. L. Mukhopadhyay, Calcutta, 1963) contains a chapter (Section VII) on social and cultural history; many of the thesis subjects listed here, however, seem to have been modified in course of later work and relatively few have been published so far. For movements within Islam, there is the excellent bibliographical introduction by Muir Ud-Din Ahmad Khan, already cited. The works listed below vary widely as regards the extent and value of their bibliographical appendices, as I have tried to indicate wherever this was felt to be necessary.

2. GENERAL WORKS

In sharp contrast to the previous period, social reform has been universally acknowledged to be an important component of Indian history from the beginning of the nineteenth century onwards. Practically every general work or textbook on India since Rammohun, therefore, contains a section or sections on social reform. There seems little point in noting all such references, even if anything like a complete list had been feasible, which it is obviously not. We many take as a good illustration of this kind of material *British Paramountcy and Indian Renaissance.* Part II (ed., R. C. Majumdar, Bharatiya Vidya Bhavan, Bombay, 1965), Chapter VII (also written by R. C. Majumdar), which provides a fairly adequate introduction to the subject, and includes a brief but useful bibliography. Mention should be made also of Tara Chand, *History of the Freedom Movement in India*, Volume II (Publications Division, Government of India, New Delhi, 1967), Chapter VI of which is on social reform, with references particularly to Bengal, Bombay and Gujarat.

Three major attempts have been made in recent years to present a general survey of social reform movements in India since the beginning of the nineteenth century. S. Natarajan's *A Century of Social Reform in India* (Asia, 1959) is sketchy on Bengal, but contains much useful information about Bombay, Madras, and the all-India reform movement in the last years of the century centred around the Indian Social Conference. The author has made good use of the files of the *Indian Social Reformer* which has father had edited from 1890 to 1940. The book is marred, however, by bad arrangement, occasional startling inaccuracies (e.g., the statement on p. 27 that Rammohun "founded the first English school in India"), and numerous incomplete references, and there is little attempt to go beyond a mere chronological description. A more scholarly work, covering more or less the same ground, is V.A. Narain. *Social History of India—The Nineteenth Century* (Meenakshi Prakashan, Meerut, 1972). This is well-annotated, and contains a good bibliography.

At quite another level of sophistication and analysis, however, is Charles H. Heimsath's work, which has been referred to several times already. Heimsath begins with a careful definition of social reform and an attempt to distinguish between "traditional" and "modern" reform movements. His main theme is the interaction between religious, social, and political reform movements, representing "the primary areas of creative intellectual endeavour for most educated Indians" (p. 6) in the nineteenth century. Chapters IV, X, and XI describe provincial reform movements; the relatively well-known developments in Bengal are deliberately treated rather briefly (though there is a good account of Sasipada Banerji, pp. 269-72), but a lot of information is given about the movements in Bombay, Madras and Northern India. The detailed account of Dayananda and the Arya Samaj (Chapter V) is partly based on an unpublished Yale thesis by J. Reid Graham, and along with the section on the Age of Consent Bill agitation (Chapter VII) and the controversies within the National Social Conference (Ranade and Telang vs Bhandarkar, Chandavarkar and Natarajan—Chapter VIII), comprise the best parts of the book. More controversial, however, is Heimsath's theoretical schema (pp. 6-8), distinguishing between three phases in the history of social reform: an alleged preoccupation with *individual* revolt and reform, together with strong religious links, from Rammohun to the early 1880s; the elevation of the movement to a national plane, combined with a more secular approach (Malabari, and the National Social Conference); and a rather vaguely-defined third stage "in which social reform began to mean a regeneration of the traditional spirit of the nation" (p.8), associated with "the reconstruction of Indian nationalism" by the extremists.

A. R. Desai's *Social Background of Indian Nationalism* (4th edition, Popular Prakashan, Bombay, 1966; first published, 1948) contains four chapters (XIII-XVII) on social reform movements directed against caste, untouchability, and the subordinate status of women. An attempt is made by this Marxist scholar to relate such movements to "the rise of new social classes in India" (Chapter XI), but the discussion remains usually on too general a level. Another pioneer Marxist attempt to analyse Indian society was Dhurjatiprasad Mukherji's *Modern Indian Culture—A Sociological Study* (2nd edition, Hind Kitab Ltd., Bombay, 1948; first published, 1942). K. C. Vyas' *The Social Renaissance in India* (Vora and Company, Bombay, 1957) is a rather elementary survey based on well-known secondary material. The more ambitious work of D.S. Sharma (*Studies in the Renaissance of Hinduism in the Nineteenth and Twentieth Centuries*, Benaras Hindu University, 1944) concentrates on four movements: Brahmoism, the Arya Samaj, the Theosophical Society, and the Ramakrishna movement; the emphasis throughout is on the reinterpretations of Hindu religion and philosophy, and there are only stray references to social reform. Religion—though missionary-Christian rather than revivalist-Hindu—constituted the basic interest also of two earlier surveys: J. N. Farquhar's *Modern Religious Movements in India* (New York, 1924) and C. F.

Andrews' *The Renaissance in India—Its Missionary Aspects* (Church Missionary Society, London, 1912). An early general account is P. N. Bose's *A History of Hindu Civilization during British Rule* (4 volumes, Calcutta, 1894-96), with a sketch of the history of Brahmoism in the first volume (Chapter V), and a description of the movements against sati, child-marriage, polygamy and in favour of widow-remarriage and an end to the taboo on sea-voyages in the second (Chapter II-IV).

The improvement of the status of women constituted the central theme in the social reform movements of the nineteenth century. For the period prior to 1857, the major work here is Kalikinkar Dutta's *Education and Social Amelioration of Women in Pre-Mutiny India* (Patna Law Press, Patna, 1936) which brought together a mass of information about women's education, sati and the campaign against it, and the beginnings of the widow-remarriage movement (Chapters I-III). The book was based on a careful study of contemporary British records, English and Bengali pamphlets, journals, and biographies. Incidentally, there is some information here also about the eighteenth century, including an account of the effort made by Raja Rajballabh in 1756 to get the consent of pundits to the remarriage of his widowed daughter. A more recent work on the same subject is Neera Desai's *Women in Modern India* (Vora and Company, Bombay, 1957), with two chapters (IV and V) on the "social reform movement with special reference to women". The book is based partly on the reports of institutions connected with women's welfare (like the Gujarat Vernacular Society or the Deccan Education Society), and of particular value is the bibliography, which provides a glimpse of the wealth of vernacular sources by listing some twenty tracts in Gujarati and Hindi. Reference may be made also to Usha Chakrabarti's *Condition of Bengali Women around the 2nd Half of the 19th Century* (Calcutta, 1963).

For reform movements in nineteenth century Indian Islam, the best available general account is Aziz Ahmad's *Islamic Modernism in India and Pakistan,* 1857-1964 (Oxford University Press, 1967). There is an excellent analysis here of the ideas and activities of Sir Sayyid Ahmad Khan (Chapter II). W. Cantwell

Smith's *Modern Islam in India* (London, 1946) is also useful, though perhaps somewhat over-schematic. Professor M. Mujeeb's Evelyn Hersey Memorial Lecture (*Social Reform among Indian Muslims,* Delhi School of Social Work, Delhi University, 1968) is much too brief, but it does make one important point: the evils attacked by reformers have little to do with the Shariat, as Indian Islam is a society "where the official representatives of orthodoxy are more official then orthodox, and where the mass of the people are in a process of conversion" (p-5). Some incidental information is contained also in Ram Gopal, *The Indian Muslims—A Political History, 1858-1947* (London, 1959).

It has been noted in the introduction that works on British administrative policies have generally been left out of this survey, but an exception seems necessary in the case of social evils like slavery, female infanticide, and thuggee which were banned or suppressed almost entirely at the initiative of the foreign rulers without very much evidence of indigenous pressures behind such decisions. For slavery, the relevant works include W. Adam, *Law and Custom of Slavery in British India* (London, 1840), J. Peggs, *Slavery in India* (London, 1840), H.A. Stark, *Calcutta in Slavery Days* (Calcutta, 1917), R. Coupland, *The British Anti Slavery Movement* (London, 1933) and D.R Banerji, *Slavery in British India* (Bombay, 1933). For thuggee, see E. Thornton, *Illustrations of the History and Practices of the Thugs* (London, 1837), and Meadows-Taylor, *Confessions of a Thug* (London, 1839). M.N. Das' *Studies in the Economic and Social Development of Modern India: 1848-56* (Firma K.L. Mukhopadhyay, Calcutta, 1959), Chapter IX, surveys the efforts made to abolish infanticide by Charles Raikes in the North-West Provinces, M.R. Gubbins in Agra, and John Lawrence in Punjab. The earlier anti-slavery and anti-infanticide attempts made by officials in Bengal Presidency have been described in Amitabha Mukherji, *Reform and Regeneration in Bengal, 1774-1823* (Rabindra Bharati University, Calcutta, 1968), Chapter IV. For female infanticide, see also C.R. Mody, *Female Infanticide* (Bombay, 1849), J. Wilson, *History of the Suppression of Infanticide in Western India* (n.a. 1855), and W. R. Moore, *Female Infanticide in the Benaras Division* (Calcutta, 1868).

The role of Christian missionaries in exposing abuses and stimulating social reform movements and legislation is well-known, and has been the subject of numerous recent works. Kenneth Ingham's *Reforms in India, 1793-1833: An Account of the Work of the Christian Missionaries on behalf of Social Reform* (Cambridge University Press, 1956) is based on a careful study of the papers of missionary societies, and includes chapters on missionary attitudes towards caste, "idolatrous festivals" and sati, education, and the status of women (Chapters II-V). The Serampore missionaries have been studied in detail by Daniel E. Potts, *British Baptist Missionaries in India, 1793-1837* (Cambridge University Press, 1967), Chapter VII of which is on social reform. Indian work in this field includes R.C. Majumdar, *Christian Missionaries and the Renaissance in Bengal (Bengal Past and Present,* Jubilee Number, Calcutta, 1967), S.B. Chaudhuri, *Christian Missionaries in Bengal* (N.K. Sinha, ed., *The History of Bengal 1757-1905,* University of Calcutta, 1967) and K.P. Sengupta, *Christian Missionaries in Bengal 1793-1833* (Calcutta, 1971). Also worth mentioning in this context is Muhammad Mohar Ali's *The Bengali Reaction to Christian Missionary Activities, 1833-1857* (Chittagong, 1965). The missionaries, themselves, of course, were prolific writers and of the innumerable nineteenth century accounts left by themselves, special mention may be made of Alexander Duff's highly provocative *India and Indian Missions* (Edinburgh 1840), Reverend James Long's *Handbook of Bengal Missions* (London, 1848), Weitbrecht's *Missionary Sketches in North India* (London, 1858), J.C. Marshman's *The Life and Times of Carey, Marshman and Ward* (2 volumes, London, 1859), George Smith's *The Life of Alexander Duff* (2 volumes, London, 1879), M.A. Sherring's *The History of Protestant Missions in India* (London, 1884), and the *History of Christianity in India* (compiled from Sherring, Smith and Bradley, Madras, 1895). Among the numerous missionary tracts dealing with social abuses and demanding reforms, mention should be made of Reverend James Peggs, *India's Cries to British Humanity, Relative to the Suttee, Infanticide, British Connexion with Idolatry, Ghaut Murders, Slavery and Colonization in India to which is added humane hints for the Amelioration of the State of Society in British India* (Seely and Son, London, 2nd Edition, 1830), and Reverend H. Bower's prize *Essay on Hindu Caste* (Calcutta Christian Tract and Book Society, Calcutta, 1851). In the National Library (Calcutta), the latter pamphlet is bound together with a number of other tracts, of which the most interesting for the present-day reader is Krishnamohan Banerji's essay on caste.

The missionaries, of course, were not the only people in England concerned about Indian social reform, though they were by far the most organised and vociferous. The more secular approach to reform, often associated with utilitarianism in the first half of the nineteenth century and positivism in the second, was typified in the 1820s, for instance, by the *Calcutta Journal* edited by James Silk Buckingham, extracts from which have been published recently (Satyajit Das, edited, *Selections From the Indian Journals, Volume I, Calcutta Journal* 1818-19; Firma K.L. Mukhopadhyay, Calcutta, 1963). Of interest in this connexion also is I. J.Prichard, *The Inaugural Lecture of the London Association in Aid of Social Progress in India,* delivered at the Society of Arts'room, Adelphi, 8 June 1871 (W.H. Allen and Co., London, 1872), which emphasized the need for women's education, technical schools, and jail reform, and deplored the missionary near-monopoly of the social reform field. The National Library also has an *Annual Report of the National Indian Association in Aid of Social Progress and Education in India for the Year 1890* (Dodd, Eyton and Company, London, 1891), containing information about the working of an Indian Female Education Fund, the main beneficiary of which seems to have been Sasipada Banerji's Widows' Home at Baranagore. No full-length study exists, however, of the role—and the limitations—of such nineteenth century "Indophile" Englishmen unconnected with missionaries; a critical study of this theme might contribute greatly to the understanding of the specific style, content, and techniques of our own social reform movements.

3. BENGAL

Social reform movements in nineteenth century Bengal have generally been studied as an integral part of the so-called "Bengal Renaissance", about which there exists a vast and growing literature. Amit Sen (Susobhan Sarkar's) *Notes on the Bengal Renaissance* (Bombay, 1946; recently reprinted as part of

relevant for our purpose—an interesting study, entitled *Old Elites and New Horizons* (Chapter VIII), of the "liberal" or "new Brahmins". Useful biographical sketches are given here of Gopal Hari Deshmukh, Vishwanath Narayan Mandlik, Ganesh Vasudev Joshi, Vishnu Shastri Chiplunkar, and, of course, Mahadev Govind Ranade. Chapter IX contains accounts of Jyotiba Phule's anti-Brahmin movement, the conservative resistance to the social reformers typified by Bhima Shastri Zhalkikar and Pandit Gattulalji Sharma, and the orthodox revival among the "new Brahmins" themselves beginning with Chiplunkar and reaching its climax with Tilak.

Ellen E. McDonald's article, *English Education and Social Reform in Late 19th Century Bombay—A Case-Study in the Transmission of a Cultural Ideal (Journal of Asian Studies,* Volume XXV 3, May 1966) attempts an analysis of the precise character of Western intellectual influences on Bombay social reformers through a study of the curriculum of Bombay University. The emphasis on changes in individual behaviour characteristic of Ranade's generation is related to the influence of Butler's *Analogy of Religion,* a prescribed English text from 1862 to 1885, while a certain shift of interest towards institutional changes in explained in terms of the growing impact of J.S. Mill and Spencer. The currently much more fashionable "Namierite" approach, stressing material "connections" in place of ideology, has found expression in two recent articles in Leach and Mukherji (ed.), *Elites in South Asia* (Cambridge, 1970). Though neither article is specifically about social reformers, Christine Dobbin's *Competing Elites in Bombay city Politics in the Mid-Nineteenth Century* (1852-83) throws much new light on the social origins of the intelligentsia and their conflicts with the dominant "shetia" families of Bombay city. Gordon Johnson's *Chitpavan Brahmins and Politics in Western India in the late Nineteenth and Early Twentieth Centuries* is similar in methodology but nowhere near as striking or original in its conclusions.

In his address to the Bombay Provincial Social Conference of 1901, N.G. Chandavarkar attempted a brief general review of the social reform movement in Maharashtra. This has been reprinted in *The Speeches and Writings of Sir Narayan*

G. *Chandavarkar* (edited by L.V. Kaikini, with an introduction by K. Natarajan, Bombay, 1911). Among other early general surveys, mention should be made of Uttamlal K. Trivedi, *Social Reform in Gujarat: A Retrospect (Indian Review*, Volume VI, n. 12, December 1905), and Manohar Lal Zutshi's seris entitled *Hindu Protestantism* in the *Hindustan Review* of 1906-1907. A some-what critical, Christian missionary account of the Bombay reformers, specially the Prarthana Samaj, is contained in J. Murdoch's *Papers on Indian Religious Reform* (Madras, 1890).

More first-hand sources on the social reform question include certain published official records, like *Repression of Female Infanticide in the Bombay Presidency* (Government of Bombay, Selections from the Records, CXLVII, New Series, Bombay 1875). Some information is obtainable also from *Source Material for a History of the Freedom Movement in India* (collected from Bombay Government Records), Volumes I (1818-1885) and II (1885-1920) (Bombay, 1957, 1958), but even more valuable apparently, judging from the use Ravinder Kumar has made of them, is the unpublished material still lying with the Bombay State Committee for the History of the Freedom Movement in India. The latter include an article entitled *Pioneers of the Reform Movement in Maharashtra* giving details about the career of Gopal Hari Deshmukh, a *Note on the Life and Work of G.V. Joshi*, and a biography of Jyotiba Phule. As always, contemporary newspapers constitute a vitally important primary source, but unlike Bengal, no attempt seems to have been made so far to publish extracts from these. The journals important in the history of social reform include the *Bombay Darpan* of Bal Gangadhar Shastri Jambhekar in the 1830s and '40s (the first to espouse social reform in Western India); the *Prabhakar*, which published Gopal Hari Deshmukh's famous *Shatapatre* series during 1848-50; *Rast Goftar*, founded by a syndicate which included Dadabhai Naoroji, Kharsedji Nasarwanji Cama (who was the financial patron), S. S. Bengalee, and Karsondas Mulji, and edited later on by K. N. Kabraji: Karsondas Mulji's *Satya Prakash*; the *Indu Prakash* and the *Quarterly Journal of the Poona Sarvajanik Sabha*, associated with Ranade; the *Indian Spectator* of *Behramji Malabari*: the *Mahratta* and the *Kesari* of Tilak; and the *Sudharak* of Agarkar and Gokhale.

The major part of the information currently available about Western Indian social reform, however, lies scattered amidst the biographies and actual writings of a series of prominent personalities. For the early, mid-century period, marked by the activities of Elphinstone College products (the secret Paramhans Mandali of 1840, and the Student's Literary and Scientific Society of 1848 with its Gujerati and Marathi branches) and the writings of Jambhekar and Gopal Hari Deshmukh, the main sources are James Kellock's *Mahadev Govind Ranade* (Calcutta, 1926); R.P. Masani's *Dodabhai Naoroji—The Grand Old Man of India* (Allen and Unwin, London, 1939), Chapters IV and VI; the four-volume *Memoirs and Writings of Acharya Bal Shastri Jambhekar* (ed., Ganesh G. Jambhekar, Poona, 1950), and two contemporary tracts used by Heimsath, Lakshmana Ganapati's *Essay on the Promotion of Domestic Reform among the Natives of India* (Bombay, 1843), and *The Student's Miscellany; containing a Selection of the Essays Read at the Students Literary and Scientific Society*, No. 1 (Bombay, 1850). The latter collection is evidently the counterpart of the Society for Acquisition of General Knowledge proceedings in Calcutta, and a comparative study should prove extremely rewarding.

The small but very influential Parsi community of Bombay, as is well known, proved more receptive to Western influences than practically any other group in India. A brief introduction to the subject of Parsi reform is provided by Dr. J. F. Bulsara's fifty-page booklet, *Social Reform among the Parsis* (Evelyn Hersey Memorial Lecture, Delhi School of Social Work, Delhi University, 1968). The treatment is inevitably somewhat too general, but there is also a short two-page "bibliography on the Parsis". For information about the community in general, the standard source is still Dosabhai Franji Karaka's two-volume *History of the Parsis* (Macmillans, London, 1884). Chapters III, IV and VI of the first volume describe the traditional manners, customs, and educational standards of the Parsis. The accent in the second volume is on economic and religious activities, but the account of distinguished Parsis of Gujarat and Bombay (Chapters I and II) has some relevance for our subject, and even more useful is Appendix B, which gives a detailed history of the Parsi Marriage and Divorce Act of 1865 (Act XV of 1865), the first legislation on the subject in India. The Natesan publication, *Famous Parsis—Biographical and Critical Sketches of Patriots, Philanthropists, Politicians, Reformers, Scholars, and Captains of Industry* (Madras, 1930) contains fourteen biographies, among which particularly relevant for us are the accounts of Framji Cowasji Banaji, a pioneer of English education within his community; Naoroji Ferdoonji and K. R. Cama, close associates of Dababhai; Dababhai Naoroji himself; Sorabji Shapurji Bengali, fighter for women's rights and philanthropist interested in labour welfare, the counterpart of Bengal's Sasipada Banerji; and Behramji N. Malabari. Ṛ. P. Masani's biography of Naoroji has been cited already, and the considerable literature on Malabari will be discussed in connection with the all-India reform movement of which he may be considered the pioneer.

The early social reform movement in Gujarat produced personalities like Mehtaji Durgaram Mancharam, Naramada Shankar, Dalpatram, and Mahipatram Rupram, and organizations like the Gujarat Vernacular Society of Ahmedabad (1848) and the Buddhi-Vardhak Hindu Sabha of Bombay (1851). Apart from the already-mentioned article by Uttamlal K. Trivedi, Neera Desai's *Women in Modern India* (Bombay, 1957) contains much information about Gujarati reform, and it includes material from an unpublished history of the Gujarat Vernacular Society by H. T. Parekh. But the most outstanding reform figure produced by Gujarat was undoubtedly Karsondas Mulji, whose exposure of the immoral practices of the priests of the Vallabhacharya sect led to the famous Maharaja Libel Case of 1861-62, and who was also one of the pioneers of widow-remarriage in Western India. Heimsath's account of Karsonadas (pp. 103-104) is brief and incomplete, but a more detailed picture is given in Natarajan (pp. 53-60). The standard biography is B.N. Motivala, *Karsondas Mulji, A Biographical Study* (Karsondas Mulji Centenary Celebration Committee, Bombay, 1935), apparently based in part on a Gujarati life by Mahipatram Rupram which I have been unable to trace. Motivala emphasizes as the three main achievements of Karsondas the exposure of the Maharajas through his paper *Satyaprakash,* the rejection of "prayaschitta" rules after his visit to England, and the arranging of the Madhavdas Raghunathdas widow remarriage in May

1871. The third chapter also presents in a systematic manner Karsonadas' views on caste, foreign travel, status of women, and other reform issues, while the fourth describes his contributions to the *Satya Prakash* and *the Rast Goftar* as well as his published books; *The Sect of the Maharajas* in English and *Niti-Vachan, Sansar-Sukh,* and *Kutumb-Mitra* in Gujarati.

The central position in the Western Indian reform scene, however, came to be occupied increasingly by Maharashtrians. Maharashtrian reform was marked by a rich diversity, including such different figures and movements as Vishnu Shastri Pandit, who tranlasted Vidyasagar into Marathi and founded the Bombay Widow Marriage Association in 1866; Visvanath Narayan Mandlik, advocate of slow internal change who became increasingly conservative with age; the Telang-Ranade School, with its tendency to move along the "line of least resistance"; the more militant reformers, led by R. G. Bhandarkar and then by N. C. Chandavarkar; G. G. Agarkar, friend and later bitter rival of Tilak; the revivalist trend, beginning with Chiplunkar had developed by Tilak; and the "kunbi" Protest against Brahmin domination, started by Jyotiba Phule.

For Mandlik, the basic source is the *Writings and Speeches of the Late Honourable Rao Saheb Vishvanath Narayan Mandlik, CSI* (ed., N.V. Mandlik, Native Opinion Press, Bombay, 1896). This includes a 30-page sketch of Mandlik's life by Damodar Ganesh Padhye which emphasises the change in Mandlik's attitudes towards social reform, from a moderate advocacy to increasing conservatism. It is the later near-orthodox Mandlik who is represented by the three papers on social reform issues included in this collection. The memorandum to the 1882 Education Commission still supports female education while strongly objecting to mixed schools; the April 1885 letter to the Bombay Government on *State Interference in the Matter of Social Reform amongst Hindus* is virtually a point-by-point rejoinder to Malabari's pleas against enforced widowhood and infant marriages; and orthodoxy reaches its climax in the December 1887 memorandum, *On the Proposal for the Abolition of Imprisonment in Execution of Decrees for Restitution of Conjugal Rights* concerning the case of Dadaji Vs Rakhmabai. A critical assessment of Mandlik's views on social reform is N.G. Chandavarkar's 1893 speech. *The Mandlik School and Reform from Within,* included in *The Speeches and Writings of Sir Narayan G. Chandavarkar* (ed. L.V. Kaikini, Bombay, 1911).

Chandavarkar's collection also contains an analysis of the standpoint of K.T. Telang *(The Telang School and "The Line of Least Resistance"),* founder-member of the Prarthana Samaj and prominent leader of the National Social Conference who yet advocated a middle-of-the-road position on many social reform questions, a cautious moderation which Ranade too identified himself in his 1895 address. *The Telang School of Thought* (included in Ranade's *Religious and Social Reform,* Bombay, 1902). On Telang, the available material includes the Telang Centenary Number (1951) of the *Social Reform Annual* published by the Bombay Presidency Social Reform Association, as well as his own writings: *Notes on the Age of Consent Bill* (n.d. or pub.) critical of R.C. Mitter and Sasadhar Tarkachudamani, yet trying at the same time to tone down Malabari's extremism; and *Selected Writings and Speeches* (with an introduction by Dinshaw Wacha; Bombay, 1916), The latter contains five papers on the social reform question: review of Malabari's note on infant marriage and enforced widowhood, two discussions on the relationship between social and political reform and speeches at the second and the third Social Conferences, 1888-89.

Literature on Mahadev Govind Ranade, the most outstanding figure in the history of the Western India reform movement, is naturally abundant. Good general accounts are available in Heimsath (Chapter VIII), Natarajan (Chapters IV and VI), and Ravinder Kumar (Chapter VIII). Among the numerous biographies, the early life by James Kellock *(Mahadev Govind Ranade,* Calcutta, 1926) is still frequently used by historians. T.V. Parvate's *Mahadev Govind Ranade—A Biography* (Asia, Bombay, 1963) is a more recent study, containing chapters on "Bombay's Formative Influences" (Chapter III), Prarthana Samaj activities (Chapter IV), Ranade as "Protagonist of Social Reform" (Chapter IX), as well as of course studies of Ranade's economic, political, and historical ideas (Chapters X-XI). D. G. Karve's *Ranade, the Prophet of Liberated India* (Poona, 1942) attempted a somewhat more theoretical analysis of Ranade's ideas; the relevant section here is Chapter III, entitled "Social Reform". Another "search for the theories behind Ranade's writings" is P. J. Jagirdar's *Studies in the Social Thought of M. G. Ranade* (Asia, Bombay, 1963), containing a bibliography which lists several Marathi works on the subject, and an interesting analysis (in Part II, Appendix) of "Western Elements in the Social Thought of Ranade".

But the major source on Ranade naturally remains his own writing: the thirteen essays and speeches collected in his *Religious and Social Reform* (compiled by M.B. Kolaskar, Gopal Narayan and Company, Bombay, 1902), and the *Miscellaneous Writings of the late Hon'ble Mr. Justice M.G. Ranade, with an Introduction by Mr. D.E. Wacha* (published by Mrs. Ramabai Ranade, Poona, 1915), which contain most of his Social Conference addresses. Ranade could not always live up to his ideals in practice, yet in sheer intellectural power he remains perhaps the most impressive of our nineteenth-century social reformers. Most striking of all is his breadth of vision: while mainly concerned like all contemporary reformers with infant marriage and widow remarriage, Ranade's speech on *Revival and Reform (Religious and Social Reform*, Chapter VI) dealt with virtually all the issues raised by the reform movement (female education, foreign travel, inter-caste marriages, the "purity movement" comprising the anti-nautch and temperance agitations, re-entry into Hindu society of ex-converts, reduction in marriage expenses, etc.), and his *Heslop College Address* (Nagpur, 1891—included in *Miscellaneous Writings)* offered a brilliant analysis of the four methods of social reform—reinterpretation of texts, appeals to conscience or public opinion, imposition of penalties by caste tribunals or through state action, and the formation of new re-formed sects. His speeches at the eighth and the ninth National Social Conference (1894-95—*Miscellaneous Writings)* gave an excellent account of the *Past History of Social Reform.* Another noteworthy feature is Ranade's determined efforts to link modern social reform with the traditions of the country, as shown both by his meticulous analysis of the shastras in *The Age of Hidnu Marriage* and *Vedic Authorities of Widow Marriage (Religious and Social Reform*, Chapters II-III), and by his interesting, if historically rather controversial, account of *The Saints and Prophets of Maharashtra* as Protestant rebels in *Rise of the Maratha Power* (Bombay, 1901).

Late nineteenth-century Maharashtra produced a second out-standing scholar-reformer in R. G. Bhandarkar, whose ideas (particularly on caste) were often much more radical than those of Ranade. For Bhandarkar, the basic source is the four-volume *Collected Works* (Bhandarkar Oriental Research Institute, Poona, 1927-1933), of which the second volume contains the major writings on religious and social subjects. The essays combine deep scholarship with militant commitment to social reform, and particularly remarkable are the critiques of the caste system: *The Indian Caste System* and the *Presidential Address at the Poona National Social Conference,* 1895 (Volume II, sections 2-3). The former article contains interesting information about the secret Paramhans Mandali; the latter led to the first National Social Conference resolution of the untouchability question.

After Ranade's death, the leadership of the National Social Conference passed into the hands of N. G. Chandavarkar, ably backed by K. Natarajan and the *Indian Social Reformer,* and together they developed the line already put forward by Bhandarkar, rejecting the Telang-Ranade approach. On Chandavarkar, there is a Marathi biography by D.G. Vaidya published in 1937, as well as Ganesh L. Chandavarkar, *A Wrestling Soul, Story of the Life of Sir Narayan Chandavarkar,* with a Foreword by D.K. Karve and an Introduction by P.B. Gajendragadkar (Popular Book Depot, Bombay 1956). This is based on Chandavarkar's private papers, as well as on published writings and Vaidya's Marathi biography, and three chapters are particularly relevant for social reform history: III *(The Indu Prakash),* VII *(The Reformers' Faith),* and VIII *(The Reformer).* The *Speeches and Writings of Sir Narayan G. Chandavarkar* (edited by L.V. Kaikini, with an introduction by K. Natarajan. Manoranjak Grantha Prasarak Mandali, Girgaon-Bombay, 1911) contain, besides the critiques of the Mandlik and the Telang schools already mentioned, numerous speechs at National Social Conferences and other platforms. These tend to be popular rather than scholary in tone, with one notable exception: the paper entitled *The British Government and Hindu*

Religious Customs, which represents quite an impressive historical study.

Telang, Ranade, Bhandarkar, and Chandavarkar comprised the central axis of the Maharashtrian reform movement, and they were the principal managers also of the National Social Conference. But late-nineteenth-century Maharashtrian reform also includes two other strands. The anti-Brahmin kunbi or rich peasant movement was started by Jyotiba Phule in the 1870s with his Satya Shodak Samaj (1873) and polemical tracts like the *Gulamgiri.* A translation of the latter is available in the material lying unpublished with the Bombay State Committee on the History of the Freedom Movement, and on Phule himself there are two biographical studies: A.K. Ghorpade's *Mahatma Phule* (in Marathi, 2nd edition, Poona, 1959), and D. Keer, *Mahatma Jyotiba Phooley: Father of Our Social Revolution* (Bombay, 1964). A second current, mainly Chitpavan Brahmin in composition like the Ranade connection and unlike Phule. but differing from both in its links from the beginning with rising Extremist sentiment, began with Vishnu Shastri Chiplunkar and found expression in the Deccan Education Society founded by Agarkar and Tilak in the 1880s. For this, an important source is P.M. Limaye's *the History of the Deccan Education Society* (Poona, 1935), which contains an account of the split between Tilak on the one hand and Agarkar and Gokhale on the other, a quarrel with momentous consequences for the history of both social reform and nationalism in our country. No detailed English biography of Gopal Ganesh Agarkar is as yet available, which is a pity, since Agarkar seems to have been one of the few who were able to combine political militancy with social radicalism. His works are available, however, in Marathi: *Sampurna Agarkar,* 3 volumes (Poona, 1940). Among the numerous works on Tilak, N.C. Kelkar's *Life and Times of Lokamanya Tilak* (Madras, 1928) contains much information about social reform; see also G.P. Pradhan and A.K. Bhagwat, *Lokamanya Tilak* (Bombay, 1985), Chapters II-IV, and T. V. Parvate, *Bal Gangadhar Tilak* (Navajivan Publishing House, Ahmedabad. 1958), Chapter V (on the Tilak-Agarkar split). S.A. Wolpert's *Tilak and Gokhale* (California, 1962) is an excellent and very well-documented comparative study. On Gokhale, see R.P. Paranjpe. *Gopal Krishna Gokhale* (Poona, 1915);

J.S. Hoyland, *Gopal Krishna Gokhale* (Poona, 1915); J. S. Hoyland, *Gopal Krishna Gokhale: His Life and Speeches* (Calcutta, 1933); Tejumal K. Shahani, *Gopal Krishna Gokhale: A Historical Biography* (Bombay, 1929) and, yet another work by the indefatigable biographer, T.V. Parvate's *Gopal Krishna Gokhale* (Ahmedabad, 1959). The later activities of both Tilak and Gokhale, however, fall outside chronological limits, and the same applies to the Bombay Presidency Social Reform Association (1903), the Servants of India Society (1905), the Social Service League of 1911, and the major part of the distinguished reform career of Maharshi D.K. Karve. About Karve, the main sources are his own *Looking Back (An Autobiography)*, Poona, 1942, *Professor D.K. Karve: A Sketch of His Life and Life-Work* (from a work by Professor Paranjpye), Madras, 1918, and G.L. Chandavarkar, *Maharshi Karve* (Bombay, 1958). Another Poona figure who became prominent from the 1890s was Pandita Ramabai, about whom see Mary Lucia Bierce, *The Triumph of An Indian Widow: The Life of Pandita Ramabai* (Philadelphia, n.d.). Finally, our account of the sources on the Western Indian reform movements may be rounded off by a brief mention of Sind, which produced the first formally incorporated social reform society. Dayaram Gidumal is the outstanding figure here, close ally of Malabari and founder of the Hindu Social Reform Association of Sind (1886), and information about the latter is to be found mainly from his *The Status of Women in India*, or *A Handbook for Hindu Social Reformers* (Bombay, 1889), which will be mentioned again in connection with the all-India Age of Consent Bill agitation.

5. NORTHERN INDIA—THE NORTH-WEST PROVINCES AND PUNJAB

Social reform ideas of the "modern" or more precisely nineteenth century type first reached Narthern India via the English-educated expatriate Bengalis who had followed the British flag into these regions, and some of whom had come under the influence of Brahmoism. Largely confined within a small and never particularly popular linguistic group, however, Brahmoism was soon swamped by the rise of Dayanand Saraswati's Arya Samaj, that peculiar amalgam of revivalist "purificatory" movement and reform, insisting on the infallibility of the Vedas, militantly anti-Christian and anti-Muslim, yet advocating marriage reforms, widow-remarriages, foreign travel, and a drastic simplification of the case system. Though founded initially at Rajkot in Saurashtra by a man hailing from Kathiawar, the Arya Samaj became (and remains) a formidable force in the Northern Indian Hindi-speaking belt. Echoes of the Brahmo-Arya quarrel, incidentally, have been preserved in a pamphlet by an unnamed "Punjabi Brahmo" entitled *The Arya Samaj and a Refutation of Its Tenets* (Lahore, 1883), as well as in a letter of Rajnarayan Basu to Sadharan Brahmo Samaj Secretary Sibchandra Deb reprinted in the *Tettvabodhini Patrika* of Aswin 1801 SE (1879) admitting that very few Hindustanis had joined the Brahmo Samaj in the North-West Provinces, and that "the Arya Samajes bid fair to outstrip the Brahmo Samajes as has been the case at Monghyr and elsewhere" (Benoy Ghosh, ed., *Samayikpatre Banglar Samajchitra,* Volume II, Calcutta 1963, p. 338).

Sections on Dayanand and the Arya Samaj are to be found in most general works on nineteenth century social reform, but the space accorded varies sharply with the author's views regarding the reform status of this undoubtedly very controversial movement. Thus S. Natarajan tackles the subject in less than three pages (Chapter V, pp. 71-73); D. S. Sharma devotes a big chapter to it (Chapter IV); both the concluding section and the very title of B.B. Majumdar bear witness to that historian's very high estimate of Dayanand as a reformer; while Heimsath's sections (Chapters V and XI) have some claim to be considered the best in the entire book. The strength of Heimsath's detailed and well-written account comes in part from the use it has made of an unpublished Yale thesis by J. Reid Graham, entitled *The Arya Samaj as a Reformation in Hinduism with Special Reference to Caste* (2 volumes, 1942).

The first-hand sources on Dayanand include, of course, the *Satyarth Prakash* (Beneras, 1875; English translation by Chiranjiva Bharadwaja, 2nd edition, Allahabad, 1915) and *Autobiography of Pandit Dayanand Sarasvati,* written by him expressly for the *Theosophist* edited by A. P. Blavatsky (The Theosophical Publishing House, Adyar, Madras, 1952). The 37-page autobiography, however, contains little about social reform activities. *The Dayanand Commemoration Volume, a Homage to Maharshi*

Dayanand Saraswati from India and the World in celebration of the Dayanand Nirvana Ardha Shatabdi (edited by Har Bilas Sarda, Vedic Yantralaya, Qaisargung, Ajmer, 1933) is a huge collection of 122 articles in English, Hindi and Urdu which contains some interesting reminiscences and personal impressions about the founder and about the early days of the Arya Samaj, but is generally too adulatory to be of much historical use. A large number of the articles, as is to be expected, consist of little more than bricf formal tributes. Among the numerous biographies of Dayanand, mention may be made of Bawa Chhajju Singh, *The Life and Teaching of Swami Dayanand Saraswati* (Lahore, 1903); Har Bilas Sarda, *Life of Dayanand Saraswati* (Ajmer, 1946); and Suraj Bhan, *Dayanand, His Life and Work* (Jullunder, 1954), the last presenting a brief but succinct account based largely on Dayanand's letters and statements.

For the history of the Arya Samaj, there is a two-volume account in Hindi, Indra Vidyavachaspati's *Aryasamaj ka Itihas* (Delhi, 1957), and Diwan Chand's *The Arya Samaj, What It is and What It Stands for* (Lahore, 1942). Prakash Tandon's *Punjabi Century*, 1857-1947 (New York, 1961) also contains some relevant information. But the best account perhaps still remains Lala Lajpat Rai's *The Arya Samaj, An Account of Its Origin, Doctrines and Activities, with a Biographical Sketch of the Founder* (Longmans, London, 1915: revised edition, entitled *A History of the Arya Samaj*, ed. Sri Ram Sharma, Orient Longman's *India, 1967.* Impressive in its documentation and accuracy, the work contains a good biography of Dayanand (Part I) and an analysis of the religious, social, political, organizational, educational, and philanthropic tenets and activities of the Arya Samaj (Parts II-III). There is also a brief bibliography. Lajpat Rai's *Autobiographical Writings* (ed. V.C. Joshi, New Delhi, 1965) contains a translation of the Urdu *Story of My Life*, written in 1914; this is particularly valuable as a first-hand account of the Arya Samaj split of 1893. The first volume of Lala Lajpat Rai's *Writings and Speeches*, 1888-1919 (University Publishers, Delhi-Jullundur, 1966), also edited by V.C. Joshi, may be consulted in connection with the Arya Samaj reform activities. For Hans Raj, there is the biography by Sri Ram Sharma, *Mahatma Hansraj*,

Maker of the Modern Punjab (Lahore, 1941), while copious information about a later Arya Samaj Social Reform enthusiast is to be found in the 188 articles of the 555-page *Har Bilas Sarda Commemoration Volume, presented on the occasion of his completing seventy years* (edited by P. Seshadri, Ajmer, 1937). Finally, a fascinating and very original attempt has been made recently to explore the links between the Arya Samaj and other revivalist movements in Upper India and certain urban commercial groups in C.A. Bayly's paper, *Patrons and Politics in Northern India* (Gallagher, Johnson, and Seal, ed., *Locality, Province and Nation—Essays on Indian Politics*, 1870-1940, Cambridge University Press, 1973). Based in large part on the private papers of Mahajan families, the article represents Namierism at its best.

Caste associations played an important, though obviously often rather controversial, part in the social Reform history of Northern India, specially perhaps in the North West Provinces. Heimsath, Chapter XI, contains a good account of these activities, focusing particularly on the Kayastha Conference with its pro- and anti-social reform tensions. The *Hindustan Review* of Allahabad is a major source for this caste association. The Vaishya community produced a very notable social reform enthusiast in the Allahabad lawyer Lala Baijnath whose writings include *Social Reform for the North-West Provinces* (Bombay, 1886), *Some Problems of Social Reform* (Aligarh, 1891), and *Suggestions for Religious Education and other Reforms in Hindu Society, with selections from the opinions of leading European and Indian thinkers on questions of religious and social Reform* (office of the Vaishya Hitkari, Meerut, 1909), the latter based on replies to a questionnaire drawn up by the author and containing 71 items.

Historians of social reform seldom remember the Sikhs, though the evolution of this reformed breakaway from Hinduism under British rule and influences can hardly be considered entirely irrelevant. The material may be searched for in the pages and copious bibliographical references of Khushawant Singh's *A History of the Sikhs*, Volume I (Princeton, 1963), while some first-hand sources on Sikh social history have been made easily available in Ganda Singh (ed.) *Early European Accounts of the Sikhs* (Indian Studies: Past and Present, Calcutta, 1962).

6. SOUTH INDIA

Material on social reform movements in nineteenth-century South India seems scantier than for any other part of the country, a paucity in part due perhaps to the relatively undeveloped state of historical research, but connected basically with the weakness of such movements themselves. Heimsath, who has discussed the South Indian movements in Chapters IV and X of his book, attributes this weakness to the well-known lag in higher English education in the southern Presidency, plus the fact that "social innovation by Madras Brahmins...could mean the extinction of the privileges which separated them...from the benighted lower orders" (pp. 111-112). The time-limit adopted for the present survey further reduces the material at our disposal, since both the backward castes movement and Annie Besant's spectacular conversion to social reform (as publicised in her *Wake Up, India: A Plea for social Reform* (Theosophical Publishing House, Adyar, Madras, 1913) were essentially twentieth-century phenomena.

Reform ideas reached the South initially through the missionary activities from Bengal and Bombay of the Brahmo and the Prarthana Samajes, about which some information has been collected in Manilal Parekh's *Brahmo Samaj* (Rajkot, 1929) and J. Murdoch's *Papers on Indian Religious Reform* (Madras 1890). Sibnath Sastri's tour of the South is described in detail in his *Atmacharit* (Signet edition, Calcutta, 1952). About Viresalingam Pantulu, Prathana Samajist, widow remarriage enthusiast, founder of the Rajahmundry Social Reform Association (1878) and pioneer of modern Telugu literature, there is a very brief sketch by V. R. Narla recently published by the Sahitya Akademi of New Delhi, Venkateswara Rao's *Viresalingam* (New Delhi, 1968), and the much more substantial earlier account by J. Gurundadhan, entitled *Viresalingam: The Founder of Telugu Life* (Rajahmundry, 1911). The second major southern reform figure was Sibnath Sastri's convert, R. Venkata Ratnam, the crusader for temperance and against temple prostitution, and one of the few upper-caste leaders to strive sincerely for the upliftment of the depressed classes. There is an English biography, K. Suryanarayana's *Sir R. Venkata Ratnam* (Rajahumundry, 1952), while his major writings have been edited by V. Ramakrishna

Rao, *The Message and Ministrations of Dewan Bahadur R. Venkata Ratnam*, 3 volumes (Madras, 1922-1924).

In the 1890s a group of young social reform enthusiasts emerged in Madras, connected with the Indian *Social Reformer* and the Madras Hindu Social Reform Association founded in 1892 and sharply critical of Annie Besant during her revivalist phase and also at first of Vivekananda. This group soon became extremely important in the National Social Conference, and helped Chandavarker to overcome the tradition of the Ranade-Telang "line of least resistance" school, but as sometimes happened in nationalist politics also, involvement and importance at the all-India level reflected weakness in local position. Cartainly Kamakshi Natarajan's *Indian Social Reformer,* which in any case soon shifted to Bombay, deserves to be remembered far more as the mouthpiece for all-India reform than as a journal of southern reformers. The ideas of one member of this group can be studied in K. Srinivasa Raw's *Papers on Social Reform: Being the Speeches and Writings of K. Srinivasa Row* (Madras, 1906), while some information is available also in K. Subba Rao's reminiscences, entitled *Revived Memories* (Madras, 1933).

A more active and successful phase of southern reform was inaugurated by Annie Besant after her conversion with the Hindu Association of 1904, decicated to "reform along national lines" and opposed therefore, to Western-style rationalistic movements like the National Social Conference or the *Indian Social Reformer* group. Though in strict chronology this is going beyond our period, a reference seems due here to N. Subbarao Pantulu's collection, *Hindu Social Progress* (G.A. Natesan's, Madras, 1904), which includes the proceedings of the inaugural meeting of the 1904 association, and numerous articles of M. Rangachariar and others putting forward this new style of social reform.

Reforms in the Nayar community of Kerala have been described in M. S. A. Rao's *Social Change in Malabar* (Bombay, 1957). For developments in Kerala, there is also E.M.S. Namboodripad's *The National Question in Kerala* (Bombay, 1952) one of the few really outstanding Marxist studies of modern Indian history.

7. THE ALL-INDIA REFORM MOVEMENT

Though Vidyasagar's widow-remarriage call met with some response from other parts of the country (the Bombay Widow Remarriage Association of 1866, Viresalingam's activities in Andhra), the real pioneer organizer of an all-India reform movement was Behramji Malabari with his sustained campaign in the 1880s for legislation to regulate child-marriages in Hindu society. Heimsath, Chapter VIII, gives a detailed and excellent account of Malabari and the Age of Consent Bill agitation. The text of Malabari's *Notes on Infant Marriage in India and Enforced Widowhood* (1884), from which Heimsath dates "the beginning of the all-India social reform movement" (p. 151), were reprinted in the Government of India, Home Department, *Selections from Records No. 3, Papers Relating to Infant Marriage and Enforced Widowhood in India* (Calcutta, 1886). The *Notes* elicited a massive response, both positive and negative, and much of this material was carefully collected and published by Dayaram Gidumal in his invaluable *The Status of Women in India: Or A Handbook for Hindu Social Reformers* (Bombay, 1889). This contains a mass of information about the facts, causes, legal position, and possible remedies concerning infant marriage and enforced widowhood. Dayaram Gidumal was also the author of *The Life and Lifework of Behramji M. Malabari/Being a biographical sketch, with selections from his writings and speeches on infant marriage and enforced widowhood, and also his Rambles of Pilgrim Reformer* (Bombay, 1888). This contains a biographical sketch, plus no less than 132 articles by Malabari extracted from his *Indian Spectator of 1884-1887.* The biography was revised and extended a few years later in Dayaram Gidumal's *Behramji M. Malabari, A Biographical Sketch,* with intoroduction by Florence Nightingale (J. Fisher Unwin, London, 1892). For Malabari, see also R.P. Karkaria, *Forty Years of Progress and Reform, Being a Sketch of the Life and Times of Behramji M. Malabari* (London, 1896).

The central organ of the all-India reform movement was, of course, the annual National Social Conference, from 1887 onwards. The first-hand source here is obviously the Social Conference Reports, published from Poona from 1889 onwards, and very good use of these have been made by Heimsath. Also very useful is C.Y. Chintamani's collection, *Indian Social Reform* the same author's *Bengal Renaissance and Other Essays,* People's Publishing House, New Delhi, 1970) has provided a handy introduction to the subject for a whole generation of students, despite the author's own description of his book as a mere "sketch of the narrative of events on the surface", Written "to supply background material to political workers on the Left" (pp. 3-4). Nemai Sadhan Bose's *The Indian Awakening and Bengal* (2nd Edition, Firma K.L. Mukhopadhyay, Calcutta, 1969) provides a more recent textbook summary. Chapter VIII of this book is specifically about social reform, and describes the anti-sati movement, the reform ideas of Rammohun and of Young Bengal, and, above all, Vidyasagar and the campaign for widow-remarriage. Another useful general survey is the collection of essays commemorating the centenary of Bipinchandra Pal, entitled *Studies in the Bengal Renaissance* (ed., Atulchandra Gupta, National Council of Education, Jadavpur, 1958). The relevant articles here include those on Rammohun (Prabhatchandra Ganguli), Derozio and Young Bengal (Susobhan Sarkar), Debendranath (Dilip Kumar Biswas), Vidyasagar (Benoy Ghosh), Keshabchandra Sen (Amiyacharan Banerji), and the Brahmo Samaj (Jogananda Das). *The History of Bengal 1757-1905* (ed., N.K. Sinha, Calcutta University, 1967) contains a chapter on social changes by Pradip Sinha, and the sections on Bengali literature (Amales Tripathi) and religion (Nisithranjan Roy, Dilip Kumar Biswas, Jagadishnarayan Sarkar, and Sashibhusan Chaudhuri) also contain some relevant information. Pradip Sinha's *Nineteenth Century Bengal—Aspects of Social History* (Firma K.L. Mukhopahdyay, Calcutta, 1965) is refreshingly, if at times controversially, different from the general run of descriptions of by now fairly well-known facts, and the section on the men he has called the "Bengal Victorians" (Chapter VI) is particularly interesting. Way back in 1934, Bimanbihari Majumdar broke new ground through the use of rare contemporary newspapers in his *History of Political Thought from Rammohun to Dayananda* (Calcutta, 1934); the revised and enlarged edition of this work (*History of Indian Social and Political Ideas from Rammohun to Dayananda,* Bookland, Calcutta, 1967) remains invaluable for its impressive collection of data, if not for its analytical strength. This contains a preliminary section (Chapter I) on "The Problem of Social Reform", while the chapters on "Philiosophical Radicals", "Liberal School of Political Thought", "Critics of Liberal Thought", and "Social Thinkers and Reformers of the Pre-Congress Era" (Chapters III, V-VI, VIII) are also extremely informative.

Among the very large number of general works in Bengali, mention may be made of Kazi Abdul Wadud, *Banglar Jagoran* (Viswabharati, Calcutta, 1956,) Asit Kumar Bandopadhyay, *Unabingsa Satabdir Bengali O Bangala Sahitya* (Calcutta, 1956), Sushil Kumar Gupta, *Unabingsa Satabdite Banglar Nabajagoran* (Calcutta, 1959), and the every useful collection of essays based on much first-hand material of Jogeshchandra Bagal, *Unabingsa Satabdir Bangla* (2nd edition, Calcutta, 1963). The biographical gallery of Bengal's literary worthies, *Sahitya-Sadhak-Charit-mala* (Brojendranath Bandopadhyay, Sajanikanta Das, and Jogeshchandra Bagal, Bangiya Sahitya Parishad, Calcutta, Volumes I-IX, 1939-1952), often provides information about social reform activities, since literature and reform were closely associated in the lives of so many. But the truly classic work on the subject in the vernacular is Sibnath Shastri's *Ramtanu Lahiri O Tatkalin Bangasamaj* (Calcutta, 1903, 1909; New Age edition, Calcutta, 1955), an impressive near-contemporary historical reconstruction, of which the one major criticism has to be that its very excellence and readability has led many latter historians to depend a little too much upon it.

Contemporary journals and newspapers obviously provide a major source of information about social reform activities, and though many of these have been lost, a part of this rich material has become readily available in course of the last thirty years through the labours of two scholars. Brojendranath Bandopadhyay's *Sambadpatre Sekaler Katha*, 2 volumes, 1818-30, 1830-40 (3rd Edition, Calcutta 1949, 1950) brought together extracts from the missionary newspaper *Samachar Darpan*. The latter was in the habit of copiously quoting from its contemporaries, and the extracts from the Derozian *Jnananvesana*. for instance, provide one of the few really first-hand sources of information about Young Bengal. The more recent volumes of Benoy Ghosh, *Samayikpatre Banglar Samajchitra*, Volumes I-IV

(Pathabhavan, Calcutta, 1962-66), have presented scholars with an enormous mass of data from no less than seven journals: *Sangbad Prabhakar* (Volume I), *Tattavabodhini Patrika* (Volume II) *Bengal Spectator, Sangbad Bhaskar, Sarbashubhakari Patrika, Vidyadarshan* (volume III), and *Somprakash* (Volume IV). The use Benoy Ghosh himself has made of this material, in his introductions to these volumes and his *Banglar Samajik Itihaser Dhara* (Pathabhavan, Calcutta, 1968), is of course a rather more controversial matter.

Turning to specific periods, there is naturally a considerable amount of literature on Rammohun Roy and his times. The standard biography still remains that of Sophia Dobson Collet, *The Life and Letters of Raja Rammohun Roy* (London, 1900; 3rd Edition, ed. Dilip Kumar Biswas and Prabhatchandra Ganguli, Sadharan Brahmo Samaj, Calcutta, 1962), Chapter VII of which provides abundant information about sati and the campaign against it. The Biswas-Ganguli edition also includes a valuable and up-to-date bibliography of works on Rammohun. The earlier Bengali biography, by Nagendranath Chattopadhyay, *(Mahatma Raja Rammohan Rayer Jibancharit,* Calcutta, 1881; 5th Edition, Allahabad, 1928; reprinted, Calcutta, 1972) still remains useful; the section of social reform is Chapter VII. Among recent works on the period dominated by Rammohun, Amitabha Mukherji's *Reform and Regeneration in Bengal, 1774-1823* (Rabindra Bharati University, Calcutta, 1968) has a chapter (IV) on Early Social Reforms (the campaigns against infanticide, slavery, and , of course, sati), based mainly on fairly well-known sources. A.F. Salahuddin Ahmad of Bangladesh made good use of the Bentinck Papers and of newspaper files preserved only at the India Office Library in his *Social Ideas and Social Change in Bengal,*1818-1835 (Leiden, 1965). Much more controversial is David Kopf's *British Orientalism and the Bengal Renaissance* (California, 1969), based in large part on Fort William College papers, which emphasizes the positive contributions not only of Orientalists and Serampore missionaries but also of the much-abused "conservative" critics of Rammohun like Radhakanta Deb and Bhabanicharan Bandopadhyay. And finally, of course, there are the writings of Rammohun himself: the *English Works* In six parts (ed. Kalidas Nag and Debajyoti Burman, Sadharan

Brahmo Samaj, Calcutta, 1945-51), of which the third part contains the classic tracts against sati; and the Bengali works, recently published in a single Volume (*Rammohun Rachanabali*, ed. Ajit Kumar Ghosh, Haraf Prakashani, Calcutta, 1973). Very useful also is J. K. Majumdar (ed.), *Raja Rammohun Roy and Progressive Movements in India, 1775-1845* (Calcutta, 1941), with its extracts from contemporary newspapers, tracts and other sources.

The dominant interpretation of Rammohun, his social reform activities, and the "renaissance" supposed to have been inaugurated by him has tended to remain heavily eulogistic. Even the occasional dissidents (like Brojendranath Bandopadhyay in the 1930s and Rameshchandra Majumdar more recently) have focused mainly upon personal trivialities (e.g., the alleged Muslim mistress) or at best questioned Rammohun's priority in matters like English education or the beginnings of Bengali prose. Recently, however, a more critical tendency seems to be gaining ground, reflected, for instance, in the papers presented by Ashok Sen, Barun De, Sumit Sarkar, and Pradyumna Bhattacharyya to a seminar on Rammohun organized by the Nehru Memorial Museum and Liberary (New Delhi, October, 1972) and being published shortly by the Museum. The emphasis here has been upon the colonial context of our "renaissance" and the ways in which it is held to have distorted the efforts of even our greatest "modernizing" intellectuals. A second line of interpretation, put forward, for instance, by S. N. Mukherji, *Class, Caste and Politics in Calcutta,* 1815-38 (in Leach and Mukherji, *(Elites in South Asia,* Cambridge University Press, 1970) has tried to relate conflicts like that between the Dharma Sabha and the Brahmo Sabha, previously explained entirely in terms of ideology, to factional conflicts in upper-class Calcutta society. In his analysis of this 'daladali' S.N. Mukherji has drawn heavily on contemporary works like Bhabanicharan Bandopadhyay's *Kalikata Kamalaloy* (Calcutta, 1823; edited by Brojendranath Bandopadhyay, Calcutta, 1936).

Recent accounts of the Derozians include the already cited works of Jogeshchandra Bāgal (*Unabingsha Satabdir Bangla*, 1963, Chapter IV, VI-IX), Bimanbehari Majumdar (*History of Indian*

Social and Political Ideas, 1967, Chapters III-IV) and Susobhan Sarkar (*Bengal Renaissance and Other Essays,* 1970—*Notes on the Bengal Renaissance,* Chapter III, and Part II, Chapters 3-4), as well as Benoy Ghosh, *Bidrohi Derozio* (Calcutta, 1961) and Arabinda Poddar, *Renaissance in Bengal—Quests and Confrontations, 1800-1860,* Chapter V (Indian Institute of Advanced Studies, Simla, 1970). The *Sahitya-Sadhak-Charitmala* series contain biographies of Krishnamohan Banerji (Volume VI, n. 72, 1948) and Pearychand Mitra (Volume II, n, 21, 1948). All later writers on Young Bengal have been greatly indebted to the biographical literature produced in the late 19th and early 20th centuries: Pearychand Mitra, *Biographical Sketch of David Hare* (Calcutta, 1877); Thomas Edwards, *Henry Derozio, the Eurasian Poet, Teacher and Journalist* (Calcutta, 1884), supplemented by E. W. Madge, *Henry Derozio, the Eurasian Poet and Reformer* (Calcutta, 1905; New Edition, ed. Subir Ray Chaudhuri, Metropolitan Book Agency, Calcutta, 1967); Sibnath Sastri's *Ramtanu Lahiri* (Chapter III); and Monmothanath Ghosh, *Raja Dakshinaranjan Mukhopadhyay* (Calcutta, 1917) and *Karmabir Kishorichand* (Calcutta, 1926). To this list might be added certain articles in old journals; biographical sketches of Tarachand Chakrabarti and Krishnamohan Banerji in the *Indian Reivew* of March 1840 and October 1842; and account of Radhanath Sikdar, based on an autobiography (never published and now apparently lost), in the *Aryadarshan* of Aswin-Kartik-Magh 1291 (1884-85); and H. Das, *The Reverend Krishna Mohan Benerji—Brahmin Christian, Scholar and Patriot 1813-1885 (Bengal Past and Present,* Volumes 37-38, January-June, June-December, 1929).

Of the extant writings of the Derozians themselves, the *Public Speeches of the Late Babu Ramgopal Ghosh* (Calcutta, 187[illegible]) are entirely on political themes. Krishnamohan Banerji's *The Persecuted, or Dramatic Scenes Illustrative of the Present State of Hindu Society in Calcutta* (Calcutta, 1831) vividly reflects the rebellious mood of the early 1830s, while the same author's *A Prize Essay on Native Female Education* (Bishop's College Press, Calcutta, 1841) and *Hindu Caste* (Calcutta, 1851) are important tracts on social reform, analysing the evils produced by the ignorance of women following from their seclusion and by the caste system, particularly in its modern degenerate forms.

A considerable part of the proceedings of the Derozian Society for Acquisition of General Knowledge (1838-1843) has been made readily available recently by Gautam Chattopadhyay (ed.), *Awakening in Bengal in the Early Nineteenth Century* (Progressive Publishers, Calcutta, 1965). Of the twenty-four papers reprinted here, three deal specifically with social reform: Krishnamohan Banerji's *Reform, Civil and Social;* Maheshchandra Deb's *A Sketch of the Condition of the Hindoo Women;* and Pearychand Mitra's *A Few Desultory Remarks on... Reverend K.M. Banerjee's Prize Essay on Native Female Education,* Brojendranath Bandopadhyay's *Sangbadpatre Sekaler Katha,* Volume II (1841) contain numerous extracts from the *Jnananesvana* on the themes of women's education and emancipation and widow-remarriage, and the case for the latter is cogently argued, a full decade before Vidyasagar, in the *Bengal Spectator* extracts reprinted in Benoy Ghosh's *Samayikpatre Banglar Samajchitra,* Volume III (Calcutta, 1964). Much information may still be obtained from the files of the *India Gazettee* and *Bengal Hurkaru* preserved in the National Liberary (Calcutta), while a group of young scholars in Calcutta have recently discovered seven issues of the *Hindu Pioneer* (1835-1836) and reprinted some of the articles, along with a full contents list, in *Nineteenth Century Studies,* Volume I, No. 4 (Calcutta, October 1973).

For obvious reasons, opinions about the Derozians have been much more divided than about Rammohun, but here, too, the somewhat iconoclastic trend which has emerged very recently perhaps represents something new, for it criticises Young Bengal not for its alleged wildness and excessive radicalism, but for its dependence on not-entirely disinterested " Indophile" Englishman and on the ideology of free-trader liberalism. Barun De offered a very new and provocative reinterpretation in his *Role of David Hare in Colonial 'Acculturation'* during *the Bengal 'renaissance'* (a paper, as yet unpublished, presented to the Asiatic Society, Calcutta, in September 1972), and perhaps a reference may be permitted also to Sumit Sarkar, *The Complexities of Young Bengal (Nineteenth Century Studies,* October 1973). As with the papers on Rammohun cited above, social reform is not the central issue in these revaluations, but what is being questioned at least by implication is the entire context within which social reform operated with such fanfare in the nineteenth century, the choice of priorities and the problematic of an intelligentsia working under the hegemony of colonialism.

Literature in English is still surprisingly scantly about Ishwarchandra Vidyasagar, certainly the most impressive figure in the social reform world of nineteenth century Bengal. Heimsath's account (*op. cit.*, Chapter IV) is consequently based mainly on Vidyasagar's one translated work, *Marriage of Hindu Widows (Calcutta, 1856)*, together with Pandit Narayan Keshab Vaidya (ed.), *A Collection Containing the Proceedings which led to the Passing of Act XV of 1856, an Act to remove all legal obstacles to the Marriage of Widows* (Bombay, 1885). The only other existing account in English seems to be S. C. Mitra's *Isvar Chandra Vidyasagar: A Story of His Life and Work* (Calcutta, 1902). A full-scale English biography was commissioned, however, on the 150th anniversary of Vidyasagar's birth, and is being written by Amales Tripathi of Calcutta University, under the title *Vidyasagar, the Traditionalist Modernizer.* Vaidya's book is an useful compilation on the widow remarriage controversy, including the text of Vidyasagar's petition of October 1855, the rejoinders it provoked from othodox pundits and from men like Radhakanta Deb, and the relevant legislative council proceedings of 1855-56. In Bengali, the principle source is obviously Vidyasagar's own works, recently published in three volumes *Vidyasagar Rachanasangraha,* Volumes I-III, Vidyasagar Smarak Jatiya Samiti, (Calcutta, 1972), the second of which contains his famous tracts on widow-remarriage, child-marriage, and Kulin polygamy. The most detailed biography is Benoy Ghosh, *Vidyasagar O Bengali Samaj,* Volumes I-III (Calcutta, 1957-1959), while other accounts include Sambhuchandra Vidyaratna, *Vidyasagar Jiban-charit* (n.d.), Biharilal Sarkar, *Vidyasagar* (Calcutta, 1895), Chandicharan Bandopadhyay, *Vidyasagar* (3rd edition, Allahabad, 1909), Brojendranath Bandopadhyay's article in the *Sahitya-Sadhak Charitmala* series (Volume II, n. 18, Calcutta, 1948), and Jogeshchandra Bagal's *Vidyasagar Parichay* (Calcutta, 1960).

Turning now to the social reform activities of the Brahmos, the first general survey made of Brahmo history was that of G.S. Leonard, *A History of the Brahma Samaj, from its Rise to the*

Present Day (Newman and Co., Calcutta, 1879; 2nd edition, Adi Brahmo Samaj Press, Calcutta, 1935). This offered a summary of Brahmo history under Rammohun, Debendranath, and Keshabchandra Sen. I have not been able to see two other early accounts, C.H. A. Dall's *The Brahmo Samaj of India, Led by Baboo Keshub Chundar Sen* (Calcutta, 1874) and Ramchandra Basu's *Brahmoism or History of Reformed Hinduism* (New York, 1884). The best available general account is still probably Sibnath Sastri's two-volume *History of the Brahmo Samaj* (Cherry Press, Calcutta, 1911-12), the first dealing with Rammohun, the Adi Samaj and Keshabchandra's Brahmo Samaj of India, and the second with the Nababidhan and the Sadharan Samaj. There is no systematic separate study of social reform activities, but a lot of relevant information is naturally present—the anti-sati campaign, for instance, in Part I, pp. 46-58, the marriage reform issue in I 3, pp. 244-251, and social welfare activities in II 5, Sibnath Sastri inevitably writes as a Sadharan Brahmo, though considering everything he remains remarkably fair and objective towards Keshabchandra Sen; for the alternative, Nababidhan, interpretation of Brahmo history and standard work is P. K. Sen, *Biography of a New Faith,* 2v (Calcutta, new edition 1950). For later general surveys, see Upendranath Bal, *A Century of Service: A Survey of the Services Rendered by the Brahma Samaj in First Hundred Years 1828-1928* (Lahore, 1928); Manilal C. Parekh, *The Brahmo Samaj—A Short History* (Rajkot, 1929), dealing mainly with the religious aspect; the highly eulogistic article by Jogananda Das in the *Studies in the Bengal Renaissance,* and the more scholarly, but very brief, treatment by Dilip Kumar Biswas in the *History of Bengal 1757-1905* (both works already cited).

The nineteenth century Brahmos seem to have had a fairly well-developed historical sense, and biographies, memoirs, and other contemporary accounts are here available in some abundance, though overwhelmingly in the vernacular. For the Tattvabodhini Sabha phase (1839-59), dominated by Debendranath and Akshoykumar Dutta and marked by important developments in Brahmo theology and theoretical assertions of the need for social reforms rather than specific Brahmo-led reform campaigns, there is the Maharshi's own autobiography *(Atmajibani,* Calcutta, 1898; ed. Satischandra

Chakrabarti, 1927; 4th edition, Viswabharati, Calcutta, 1962; English translation by Satyendranath Tagore and Indira Debi, London, 1914), the excellent biography by Ajitkumar Chakrabarti (*Muharshi Debendranath Tagore,* Allahabad, 1916; Jignasa, Calcutta, 1971), and biographies of Akshoykumar Dutta by Mahendranath Roy Vidyanidhi (*Srijukta Babu Akshoykumar Datter Jiban-brittanta,* Calcutta, 1885), Nakurchandra Biswas (*Akshay Charit,* Calcutta, 1887), and Brojendranath Bandopadhyay (*Sahitya-Sadhak-Charitmala,* Volume I, No. 12 Calcutta, 1941). There is a brief sketch of Debendranath also in James W. Furrell's *The Tagore Family: A Memoir* (2nd Ed., Thacker Spink and Co., Calcutta, 1892), though the main value of this book comes from its detailed account of the life and writings of a Tagore of an earlier generation: Prasannakumar (pp. 82-152). A first-hand source has become readily available through Benoy Ghosh's copious extracts from the *Tattvabodhini Patrika (Samavikpatre Banglar Samajchitra,* Volume II, Calcutta, 1963). These include Akshoykumar Dutta's plea for widow-remarriage on rationalist grounds alone (Chaitra, 1776 S. E./1855); attacks on polygamy (Chaitra, 1777/1856, Bhadra, 1778/1856, Baisakh, 1788/1866); two sketches of Brahmo history (Aswin. 1769/1847, Falgun, 1782/1860), the second of them by Rajnarayan Bose; and interesting evidence concerning the growing caution in Adi Samaj circles about social reform following the split with Keshabchandra, accompanied by an increasing emphasis on patriotic values (e.g., Kartik. 1789/1867, also two, sharply contrasting, articles on the Durga Puja. Aswin 1784/1862, Aswin 1798/1876). A vivid picture of the age is conveyed also by Rajnarayan Bose's *Atmacharit* (Calcutta, 1909), as well as by his other writings: *Hindu-dharmer Sreshthata* (Calcutta, 1873); *Sekal O Ekal* (Calcutta, 1874); *Hindu athaba Presidency Colleger Itibritta* (Calcutta, 1876); and *Vividha-Prabandha* (Calcutta, 1882—consisting of reprints from the *Tattvabodhini Patrika* which include an essay on caste and three articles on social reforms). The cautious, centrist, position of many Brahmos of the pre-Keshabchandra generation on questions of social reform is reflected in Nareshchandra Sengupta's *Selections from the Writings of Hurrish Chunder Mookerji, compiled from the Hindu Patriot* (The Cherry Press, Calcutta, 1910), Section IX, where pleas for ending "divisions" within Hindu society are balanced by a defence of caste as "merely the embodiment... of the natural inequality between men" against Duff *(Caste, Its Attributes and History, Hindu Patriot,* 11 June, 1857.

Brahmoism, despite bitter internal squabbles, attained its point of maximum dynamism and influence in the 1860s and '70s. A magnificent picture of this age can be obtained from Sibnath Sastri's *Atmacharit* (Signet Edition, Calcutta, 1952), with its vivid description of the widow-remarriage activities of the young Brahmos (Chapter V) and detailed first-hand account of the 1878 split (Chapters VI-XII). Another excellent vernacular account is Ajitkumar Chakrabarti, *op. cit,* the first five chapters of the second part offers a careful and critical analysis of the split between Debendranath and Keshabchandra in the early 1860s, while Chapter VIII is about the marriage act controversy (which is discussed in detail also in Rajnarayan Bose's autobiography, *op.cit.*). On Keshabchandra Sen there is Jogeshchandra Bagal's biography in the *Sahitya-Sadhak-Charitmala* series (Volume IX, n. 97, 1958), as well as a considerable Nababidhan hagiographical literature: P. C. Mozoomdar's *Life and Teachings of Keshabchandra Sen* (Calcutta, 1887, 1931); P.K. Sen's *Keshub Chunder Sen* (Keshabchandra Sen Centenary Committee, Calcutta, 1938); Premsundar Basu, *Brahmananda Keshav—Life and Works,* Part I, 1838-1866 (Harisundar Memorial Series, Calcutta, 1937); *Keshab Chandra Sen—Testimonies in Memoriam,* compiled by G.C. Banerji, 2 volumes (Allahabad, 1934, 1937); G. C. Banerji (ed.). *Keshab As Seen by His Opponents—A Series of Confessions* (Allahabad, 1930); and also by G.C. Banerji, Keshabchandra and Ramkrishna (Allahabad, 1931). There are also, of course, Keshabchandra's own speeches: *Lectures in India,* 2v (Cassell and Co., London, 1901, 1904). Particularly notable here is the March 1872 speech at the Bengal Social Science Association *(The Reconstruction of Native Society),* as well as *Religion and Social Reformation.* Both lectures illustrate Keshabchandra's demand for total and simultaneous reforms, as well as his insistence; "If you wish to regenerate this country, make religion the basis of all your reform movements." Extracts from the *Sulabh Samachar,* Keshabchandra's pioneer effort at low-priced journalism have been collected in Jogendranath Gupta (ed.), *Keshabchandra O Sekaler Samaj* (Calcutta, 1949). The Nababidhan viewpoint is put forward in Protap Chunder Mozoomdar's *Faith and Progress of the Brahmo Samaj* (Calcutta, 1882), as well as in his *Lectures in America and Other Papers* (Navavidhan Publication Committee, Calcutta, 1955), while the doctrines of this "New Dispensation" are also discussed in Romain Rolland's *Life of Ramakrishna* (Almora, 3rd edition, 1944, p. 113f. and Appendix II), Hemchandra Sarkar's *A Life of Ananda Mohan Bose* (A.C. Sarkar, Calcutta, 1910) is an excellent biography of a Sadharan Brahmo Samaj stalwart, based on private letters and an unpublished diary. Early Sadharan Brahmo radicalism on social reform issues is well reflected in Sibnath Shastri's *Jati-bhed* (Calcutta, 1884; ed. Dilip Biswas, Sadharan Brahmo Samaj, Calcutta, 1963), while another useful first-hand account is Bijoykrishna Goswami, *Brahmo Samajer Vartaman Abastha ebang Amar Jivane Brahom Samajar Parikshita Vishay* (Calcutta, 1872, 1886). Details of Brahmo organizations and activities are preserved in Sophia Dobson Collect's *Brahmo Year-Book* series, published in London from 1879 onwards, of which the National Library in Calcutta has the 1881-82 volume. Among Brahmo-run journals, the National Library has the *Indian Mirror*, connected with Keshabchandra, from 1883 onwards, and the Sadharan Brahmo Samaj mouthpiece, *Brahmo Public Opinion*, of 1878-1880.

A Brahmo not entirely indentified with any of the conflicting sects who won a very special position in the social reform world of Bengal was Sasipada Banerji, promoter of normal schools to train women teachers, organizer of the Baranagore Widow's Home (1887-1901) and of no less than 35 widow-remarriages, and pioneer in the field of working-class upliftment through night schools, a Workingmen's Club, temperance societies, and a monthly pice magazine, the *Bharat Sramajibi*. Heimsath includes a good summary of Sasipada's activities (Chapter X, pp. 269-272), and there are three more detailed accounts: *Sasipada Banerji's Life and Lifework* (author unnamed; Natesan's, Madras, 1918); B. N. Motivala, *The Romance of a Great Indian Social Servant, or The Life and Career of Mr. Sasipada Banerji* (Bombay, 1915), and Sitanath Tattvabhushan, *Social Reform in Bengal—A Side-Sketch* (Calcutta, 1904).

Tattvabhushan's book, consisting of reprints from the *New India* and the *Indian Mirror,* also contains general soctions on women's education and widow-remarriage, but is mainly about Sasipada's manifold activities. Very recently, a young research scholar (Kanailal Chattopadhyay) has unearthed a year's copies of the *Bharat Sramajibi* from a Bangladesh collection.

Despite the undoubted importance of the Brahmos in the 1860s and 1870s, it would be a serious (and, unfortunately, a not uncommon) mistake to ignore the presence of numerous other individuals and groups connected with, or concerned about, social reform in one way or another. Benoy Ghosh (*Samayikpatre Banglar Samajchitra,* Volume IV, Calcutta, 1966) has presented us with nearly seven hundred pages of extracts from *Somprakash,* the very influential journal edited by Dwarkanath Vidyabhushan, a close friend of Vidyasagar who supported moderate reforms without ever becoming a Brahmo. A good proporation of these pages deal with social reform issues. Platforms for non-sectarian discussions of contemporary issues, including social reform, were provided by the Bethune Society, most active between 1851 and 1869, and the Bengal Social Science Association, founded in 1867 and patronized by Mary Carpenter and Florence Nightingale. *The Proceedings and Transactions of the Bethune Society, Number 1859-April 1869* (Calcutta, 1870), give an idea of the activities of the first, while many of the Social Science Association papers have been reprinted recently by Bela Dutta Gupta in her *Sociology in India* (Calcutta, 1972).

For a section of the Bengali intelligentsia, the positivism of Comte became a major influence, serving as a justification for a kind of centrist position which advocated slow and cautious social changes but occasionally tended to slide over into neo-conservatism. This is the group analysed by Pradip Sinha, *op. cit.,* in his chapter on the "Bengal Victorians". The centrist attitude is well typified by Girishchandra Ghosh, about whom we happen to be exceptionally well-informed, thanks to the labours of his grandson, Manmathanath Ghosh, the editor of *The Life of Girish Chunder Ghosh, the founder and first editor of the "Hindoo Patriot" and the "Bengalee", by one who knew him*

(R. Cambray and Co., Calcutta, 1911), as well as of *Selections from the Writings of Girish Chunder Ghosh* (Indian Daily News Press, Calcutta, 1912). The 680-page *Selections* include two articles on the condition of women in India, as well as essays on temperance, female education and female labour, The works of Bankimchandra (*Rachanabali*, Volume II, Sahitya Sansad, Calcutta, 1969) and Bhudeb Mukhopadhyay (*Paribarik Prabandha*, Calcutta, 1882; *Samajik Prabandha*, Calcutta, 1892; *Vividha Prabandha*, volumes I and II, Calcutta, 1895, 1905) are also vitally important in this context, and a critical account of Bankimchandra's social thought has been attempted by Asitkumar Bhattacharya, *Banglar Nabayug O Bankimchandrer Chintadhara* (Calcutta, 1964). Bipinbihari Gupta's *Puratan Prasanga* (Calcutta, 1913, 1923; Vidyabharati Edition, Calcutta, 1966), based mainly on interviews with the Comte enthusiast Krishnakamal Bhattacharji, provides an illuminating picture of the age.

In the 1880s and 1890s social reformers in Bengal were increasingly swamped by the flood-tide of Hindu revivalism, which was later to link up with the reaction against moderate political "mendicancy" to constitute the characteristic Extremist mood. The reminiscences of Bipinchandra Pal, *Memories of My Life and Times* (2 volumes, Calcutta, 1932, 1951) convey very well the atmosphere of this new period, and Pal also made a notable attempt to analyse the causes of the shift away from social reform in his Bethune Society lecture, *The Present Social Reaction—What Does It Mean?* (Calcutta, 1889). Another description of the times is provided in Shib Chunder Bose's *The Hindoos As They Are, A Description of the Manners, Customs and Inner Life of Hindoo Society in Bengal. With a Preparatory Note by the Rev. W. Hastie* (Newman and Co., Calcutta 1881; 2nd Edition, Thacker Spink and Co., Calcutta, 1883); a comparison of this with an earlier description, S. C. Mitter's *A Discourse on the Domestic Life and Condition of the Bengali Society* (Calcutta, 1856), should prove quite rewarding for the social historian. From the 1880s onwards, Rabindranath was a powerful and prolific, though not always unambiguous, commentator on matters connected with social reform, and an attempt to extract a chronological pattern of development from his writings has been made by Susobhan

Sarkar (*Rabindranath Tagore and the Ranaissance in Bengal, Enquiry, No.* 5, 1961; reprinted in *Bengal Renaissance and Other Eassys*, pp. 148-183).

The one major social reform issue on which progress was being made in the Bengal of the 1890s was the so-called sea-voyage movement for readmission of overseas travellers to their castes. *The Hindu Sea-Voyage Movement in Bengal* (published by the Standing Committee on the Hindu Sea-Voyage Question, Calcutta, 1894) brought together numerous "Vyavasthas" of pandits, as well as the opinions of "men of light and learning", in a bid to prove that trips abroad were not forbidden by the shastras. The new mood of Bengal was well revealed, however, by the isolation of the Brahmos in 1892 as virtually sole supporters of the Age of Consent Bill promoted by Malabari. The collection of lectures brought together in the pamphlet *Hindu Marriage Customs* (Calcutta, 1886 or 1887) almost unanimously took a stand against social reform: the evils of child marriage and enforced widowhood were said to have been grossly exaggerated, and free choice of partners was ruled out as incompatible with Hindu society. The speakers at this meeting (organized by the Debs of Sobhabazar) had included Gurudas Banerji, Chandranath Bose, Akshoychandra Sarkar, Haraprasad Shastri, and Jogendrachandra Ghosh.

The precise position of the Ramakrishna-Vivekananda movement in the history of social reform in Bengal remains a matter of much controversy. Heimsath has subsumed Ramakrishna under the category of "traditional reform"—"of practial measures for social amelioration he apparently had nothing to recommend". Vivekananda's thought, in sharp contrast, to him marks "the culmination of the 19th century social revolt"—an estimate somewhat difficult to reconcile with the general picture of "the failing social reform movement in Bengal" in the late 19th century, presented elsewhere in the book (pp. 263-274). The obvious rejoinder—that Vivekananda in rightly condemning existing social reform groups as alienated and upper class in character was pointing the way towards a genuine wholesale transformation of Hindu society—still leaves some doubts regarding the specific content of the Swami's programme of social change (as distinct from social service activities), quite apart from the very open question as to the extent to which has ideals have been maintained or implemented by his followers. There is much scope for research on these matters, though this might prove a rather delicate business. For Ramakrishna, the available literature in English includes Max Mueller's *Rammohun to Ramakrishna His Life and Sayings* (New York, 1899) and *Rammohun to Ramakrishna* (Calcutta, 1952); Romain Rolland's *The Life of Ramakrishna* (3rd edition, Almora, 1944), and the *Life of Ramakrishna, Compiled from Various Authentic sources* (Calcutta, 1955). A very useful Bengali collection of contemporary views on the saint of Dakshineswar is Brojendranath Banerji and Sajanikanta Das, *Sri Ramakrishna Paramhansa—Samasamayak Dristite* (Calcutta, 1952). For Vivekananda, the primary material is contained in the eight-volume *Complete Works* (Birth Centenary edition, Calcutta, 1963). along with Marie Louise Burke, *Swami Vivekananda in America: New Discoveries* (Calcutta, 1958). Out of the mass of secondary literature might be mentioned Bhupendranath Dutta, *Swami Vivekananda, Patriot-Prophet* (Calcutta, 1954), Sister Nivedita, *The Master as I Aaw Him* (Calcutta, 1910), R. C. Majumdar, ed., *Swami Vivekananda Centenary Volume* (Calcutta, 1963), Girijasankar Raychaudhuri's *Swami Vivekananda O Banglar Unabinghsha Satabdi* (Calcutta, 1927), Bimanbihari Majumdar, *Militant Nationalism in India and Its Socio-Religious Background,* Chapter III (Calcutta, 1966), and Amales Tripathi, *The Exteremist Challenge,* Chapter I (Orient Longmans, Bombay, 1967).

4. WESTERN INDIA

Social reform movements in other parts of nineteenth century India have on the whole received much less publicity and historical attention than what has been liberally bestowed on "renaissance" Bengal, yet as least in the case of the Bombay Presidency this neglect in no way reflects intrinsic relative significance. Passing through Bombay in 1881, Bipinchandra Pal admitted with some regret that "Bombay was socially far ahead of Bengal....Female education and the freedom of social intercourse and movement of respectable Mahratta ladies was a new and inspiring experience which I had in Bombay"

(*Memories of My Life and Times,* Volume I, p. 392—quoted in Heimsath, pp. 267-268). If religious reform in the western Presidency had been less influential and much less militant, that had only helped the cause of social reform. As W. M. Kolhathar pointed out in 1897, in a Social Reform Conference presidential address reprinted in C. Y. Chintamani's valuable collection, *Indian Social Reform,* in Bengal the Brahmos had virtually developed into a kind of new (and numerically insignificant) caste, "while in Bombay the refusal of the reformers to claim a separate caste for themselves has set the whole society in a ferment" (quoted in Heimsath, p. 99). Yet the available literature remains somewhat scanty, at least so far as English-language sources are concerned, and it will be obvious that the present author's ignorance of Gujarati and Marathi has been here a severe handicap.

Among the general works already cited, Heimsath, Chapters IV and X, and Natarajan, Chapters III and IV provide good introductions to the subject of Parsi, Gujarati, and Maharashtrian social reform. D. S. Sharma, Chapter III, and Manilal Parekh, Chapter XI, describe the activities of the Prarthana Samaj, while B.B. Majumdar's *History of Indian Social and Political Ideas from Rammohun to Dayananda* is a notable and worthy exception to the general tendency among most Bengali historians to take too literally Gokhale's notorious and very dubious compliment.

Kenneth Ballhatchet's *Social Policy and Social Change in Western India,* 1817-1830 (Oxford University Press, London, 1957), despite its ambitious title, is mainly about the administrative attitudes and policies of Elphinstone, but there is some relevant material, particularly concerning the sati issue, in Chapter X *(Education and Religion).* Much more impressive and important is Ravinder Kumar's *Western India in the Nineteenth Century—A Study in the Social History of Maharashtra* (London/Toronto, 1968). This includes a somewhat novel interpretation of the medieval bhakti saints, as essentially disseminators of Brahminical "advaita" values among the masses, and not Protestant rebels as Ranade had imagined them to be (Chapter I); a detailed analysis of British revenue and educational policies; and—most

(Madras, 1901), which includes "original papers" by Bhandarkar, Gidumal, Lala Baij Nath, Mudholkar, Mahendralal Sircar, Chandavarkar and other prominent reformers, Ranade's Social Conference speeches, and Social Conference presidential addresses from 1889 to 1899. Finally, there are the files of K. Natarajan's weekly, *Indian Social Reformer*, which are available at the National Library (Calcutta) from 1895 onwards.

8. ISLAMIC REFORM

Down to the third quarter of the nineteenth century, the predominant cultural and political force in the world of Indian Islam was that usually described, perhaps somewhat inaccurately, as the Wahabi movement. Though diametrically opposed to modernistic or westernised reform, Wahabi fundamentalism did bring about crucial changes in the social life of its numerous adherents in an Islamicising movement which in some ways seems to parallel the purificatory drive of the Arya Samaj in Hindu society. Early Western accounts of Wahabism and related movements include the articles in the *Calcutta Review*, Volumes XL (1864) and LI (1870) on Sayyid Ahmad, Shah Ismail, Titu Mir, Shariat Allah and Dudu Miyan, as well as of course the very influential but controversial analysis by W. W. Hunter, *Our Indian Musalmans: Are They Bound in Conscience to Rebel Against the Queen?* (London, 1871). The most up-to-date history of the Wahabis is Qeyamuddin Ahmad, *the Wahabi Movement in India* (Firma K. L. Mukhopadhyay, Calcutta, 1966), which includes a detailed bibliography and an appendix listing a large number of Wahabi pamphlets. A mass of information has been made easily available also by Muin-ud-Din Ahmad Khan's *Selections from Bengal Government Records on Wahhabi Trials*, 1863-1870 (Asiatic Society of Pakistan, Dacca, 1961). Muin-ud-Din Ahmad Khan is also the author of a detailed *History of the Fara'idi Movement in Bengal*, 1818-1906 (Pakistan Historical Society, Karachi, 1965), which contains an introductory section, on "Socio-Religious Conditions of the Muslims in Bengal". An unpublished doctoral thesis used by Khan is Muhammad Abdul Bari, "A Comparative Study of the Early Waḥhabi Doctrines and Contemporary Reform Movements in Indian Islam" (unpublished Ph.D. thesis, Queen's College, Oxford University, 1953). Also relevant in this context is Muin-ud-Din Ahmad Khan's article,

"Research on the Islamic Revivalism of the Nineteenth Century and Its Effect on the Muslim Society of Bengal", included in Pierre Bessaignet (ed.), *Social Research in East Pakistan* (Asiatic Society of Pakistan Publications No. 6, Dacca, 1960). A general study of the initial British impact on Bengali Muslims is Azizur Rahman Mallick's *British Policy and the Muslims in Bengal*, 1757-1856, *A Study of the Development of Muslims in Bengal with Special Reference to their Education* (Dacca, 1961). The post-Wahabi continuation of orthodox ulama hostility to British rule has been analysed in Ziya-Ul-Hasan Faruqi, *The Demand School and the Demand for Pakistan* (Bombay, 1963).

The more positive Islamic response to the West is the main subject of Aziz Ahmad's *Islamic Modernism in India and Pakistan*,1857-1964 (Oxford University Press, 1967). The introduction deals with the little-known early accounts of Europe by Itisam al-Dain and Mirza Abu Talib Khan (about whom see also Humayun Kabirs' *Mirza Abu Talib Khan*, Patna, 1961), as well as with the very interesting early-nineteenth century Oudh culture and the transitional figure of Karamat Ali Jaunpuri. Chapter II is a good account of Sayyid Ahmad Khan and the Aligarh movement, and Chapters III and IV deal with the "speculative modernism" of Chiragh Ali, Muhsin al-Mulk, and Mumtaz Ali (a critic of the purdah and of child marriages, and an advocate of equal rights for women), as well as with the distinctive approaches to Islamic history of Shibli Numani, Hali, and Amir Ali. The last days of the old imperial culture have been sympathetically described in Percival Spear's *Twilight of the Mughals* (Cambridge, 1951).

The published English works of Sayyid Ahmad Khan himself include *Loyal Muhammedans of India* (1860-61) and *Lectures* (Ed., Munshi Siraj al-Din, Sadhora, 1892). The earliest biography was by C. F. I Graham, *The Life and Work of Syed Ahmad Khan* (Backwood, Edinburgh and London, 1885). Among later accounts, mention should be made of J. N. S. Baljon, *The Reforms and Religious Ideals of Sir Sayyid Ahmad Khan* (Brill, Leiden, 1949) and B. A. Dar, *Religious Thought of Sayyid Ahmad Khan* (Institute of Islamic Culture, Lahore, 1957). Much interesting information is available also in W. S. Blunt's contemporary descriptions: *The Future of Islam* (London, 1882) and *India Under Ripon* (London, 1909), as well as in C.F. Andrews' *Zaka Ullah of Delhi* (Cambridge, 1929). For Nawab Abd Al-Latif, the two main sources are his own *A Short Account of My Public Life* (Calcutta, 1885) and *Nawab Bahadur Abdul Latif, C.I.E.—A Memorial Volume* (Calcutta, 1915).

Bibliography

Ali, Amir, *The Spirit of Islam*, London, 1949.

Ali, M., *The Founder of the Ahmadiya Movement*, Lahore.

Banerji, Surendranath, *A Nation in Making*, London, 1925.

Bell, W.M., *Rammohan Roy*, Calcutta, 1933.

Besant, Annie, *Wake Up, India: A Plea for Social Reforms*, Madras, 1913.

Besant, Annie, *Birth of New India*, Madras, 1917.

Candwell, Christopher, *Studies in a Dying Culture*, London, 1938.

Chintamani, C.Y. (ed.), *Indian Social Reforms*, Madras, 1892.

Dayananda Nirvana Ardha Shatabdi Sabha, *Dayanand Commemoration Volume*, ed. by Har Bilas Sarda, Ajmer, 1933.

Dayananda Saraswati, *Autobiography*, ed. By H.P. Blavatsky, Madras, 1952.

Desai, A.R., *Social Background of Indian Nationalism*, Bombay 1959.

Diwan Chand, *The Arya Samaj: What it is and what it stands for*, 1942.

Farquhar, J.N., *Modern Religious Movement in India*, New York, 1913.

Griffiths, Sir P., *The British Impact on India*, London, 1952.

Gwyer, M. and A. Appadorai, *Speeches and Documents on Indian Constitution, 1921-47*, London, 1957.

Habib, Irfan M., *The Political Role of Sheikh Ahmad Sirhindi and Shah Waliualla, Enquiry No. 5*, New Delhi, 1962.

Hunter, W.W., *The Indian Mussalmans*, London, 1884.

Iqbal Mohammad, *The Reconstruction of Religious Thought in Islam*, Lahore, 1944.

Iqbal Singh, *Rammohan Roy: A Biographical Inquiry into the Making of Modern India*, Vol. 1, Bombay, 1958.

Khan, Sir Syed Ahmed, *The Present State of Politics* (Speeches), Allahabad, 1888.

Khan, Sir Syed Ahmed, *The Review of Dr. Hunter's Indian Mussalmans*, London, 1872.

Macauliffe, Max Arthur, *The Sikh Religion. Its Gurus, Sacred Writings and Authors*, 6 Vols., Oxford, 1909.

Mazoomdar, P.C., *The Life and Teachings of Keshub Chander Sen*, 1887.

Mehta, Ashok and Achyut Patwardhan, *The Communal Triangle in India*, Allahabad, 1942.

Morrison, John, *New Ideas in India during the Nineteenth Century*, 1907.

Mukherji, D.P., *Diversities*, New Delhi, 1958.

Mukherji, D.P., *Modern Indian Culture*, Bombay, 1948.

Munshi Ram, Ram Deva, *The Arya Samaj and its Detractors*, Dayanandabad, 1919.

Natarajan, S., *A Century of Social Reforms in India*, London, 1959.

Pal, Bipin Chnadra, *Swadeshi and Swaraj*, Calcutta, 1954.

Pal, Bipin Chnadra, *Story of My Life and Times*, Calcutta, 1932.

Pal, Bipin Chnadra, *Memories of My Life and Times in the Days of My Youth*, Calcutta, 1932.

Rai, Lajpat, *The Arya Samaj*, London, 1915.

Rai, Lajpat, *Young India*, New York, 1961.

Rao, Raja and Iqbal Singh, *Changing India (Speeches and Writings of Indian Leaders)*, London, 1934.

Rolland, Romain, *Prophets of New India*, London, 1930.

Roy, Rammohan, *The English Works of Raja Rammohan Roy (Social and Educational)*, Calcutta, 1935.

Roy, Raja Rammohan, *His Life, Writings and Speeches*, Madras, 1952.

Roy, Rammohan, *Rammohan Roy Centenary Commemoration Volume—The Father of Modern India*, Calcutta, 1935.

Saraswati, Dayananda, *Satyartha Prakash*, Allahabad.

Sarda, Har Bilas, *Life of Dayananda Saraswati*, Ajmer, 1946.

Smith, W.C., *Modern Islam in India*, London, 1946.

Stater, T.E., *Keshab Chandra Sen and the Brahmo Samaj*, Madras, 1884.

Tara Chand, *History of the Freedom Movement in India*, Vols. I and II, Delhi 1961.

Vivekananda, Swami, *Selections from Swami Vivekananda*, Almora, 1944.

Vivekananda, Swami, *The Complete Works of Swami Vivekananda*, 7 Vols., 1924-32.

William, Theodore De Bary and Others, *Sources of Indian Tradition*, New York, 1958.

Zacharias, H.C.E., *Renascent India, from Rammohan Roy to Mohandas Gandhi*, London, 1933.